Black Charlie

Admiral Sir Charles Napier
from a painting by W. W. Simpson

Black Charlie

A LIFE OF

ADMIRAL SIR CHARLES NAPIER KCB

1787-1860

PRISCILLA NAPIER

MICHAEL RUSSELL

© Priscilla Napier 1995

The right of Priscilla Napier to be
identified as author of this work has been asserted
by her in accordance with the
Copyright, Design and Patents Act, 1988

First published in Great Britain 1995
by Michael Russell (Publishing) Ltd
Wilby Hall, Wilby, Norwich, NR16 2JP

Typeset in Sabon by The Typesetting Bureau
Allen House, East Borough, Wimborne, Dorset
Printed and bound in Great Britain
by Biddles Ltd, Guildford and King's Lynn

To my grandson
Lennox Edward Charles Napier

Contents

Acknowledgements

My grateful thanks to Henry Johnstone for permission to quote from the letters and journals of his great-great-great-grandfather, Captain Henry Napier, RN; to the British Library Add. Mss, collection of Napier letters, and to the Bodleian at Oxford, collection of General Sir William Napier's letters; and to Philip Ziegler for permission to quote from his biography of William IV.

Maps

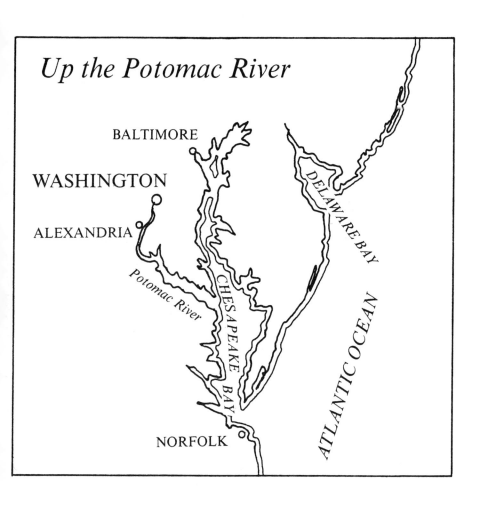

Up the Potomac River

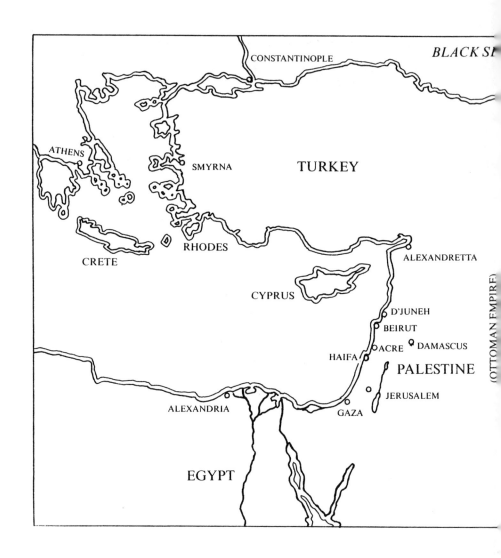

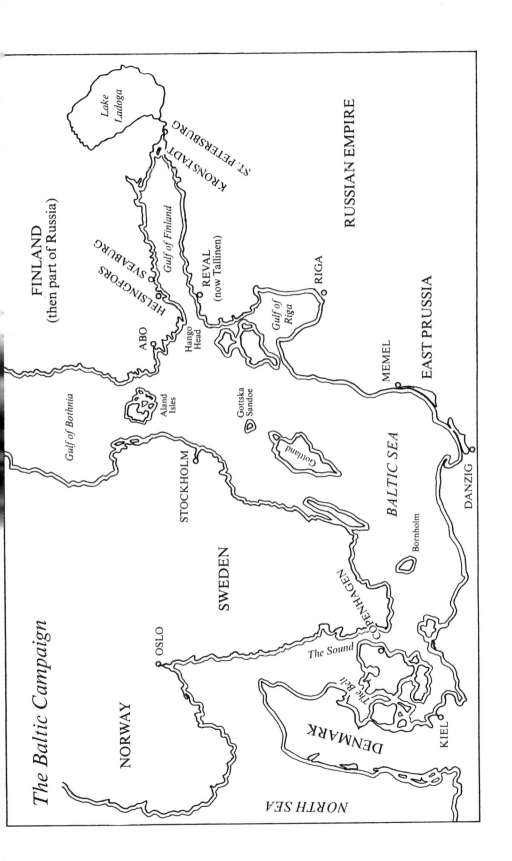

The Baltic Campaign

NORTH SEA

NORWAY

OSLO

SWEDEN

STOCKHOLM

Gulf of Bothnia

Aland Isles

DENMARK

The Belt

The Sound

KIEL

COPENHAGEN

Bornholm

Gottska Sandoe

Gotland

BALTIC SEA

DANZIG

EAST PRUSSIA

MEMEL

RIGA

Gulf of Riga

REVAL (now Tallinen)

Gulf of Finland

Hango Head

ABO

HELSINGFORS

SVEABURG

FINLAND (then part of Russia)

KRONSTADT

ST. PETERSBURG

Lake Ladoga

RUSSIAN EMPIRE

I

Recruit

Flying in the face of all parental wishes and advice, Charlie Napier went to sea in the year 1800 at the age of twelve – a tough little black-haired fighting Edinburgh boy. Born at Merchiston Hall, near Falkirk, on 6 March 1787, he was the son of another Charles Napier, fifth son of the sixth Lord Napier. Black Charlie, so-called for his jet-black hair and unusually swarthy skin, was schooled for six years at Edinburgh High School, leading in his spare time a happy gang-leader life in and around George Square, or making tracks to Leith harbour to see all he could of the many ships that frequented its waters. At home he was tutored by the Revd William McCall, 'full of fun and good humour', who combined his other duties with that of factor to Black Charlie's mother, who inherited Westburn in Lanarkshire from her father, Gabriel Hamilton. Though Charlie was besotted by ships, forever watching real ones or sailing toy boats of his own construction, his father was implacably opposed to his seagoing desires, and forbade his entering the Navy. It was no, and again no, and *finally* no.

Captain the Hon. Charles Napier was himself a retired naval officer, whose career had not been crowned by glittering success. Influence, so vitally needful, had proved unequal to his expectations. There was, he considered, altogether too much jobbery in the Navy, too much jiggery-pokery and unfair influence and God knew what. He had, besides, a strong Scots suspicion of what went on amongst officials in London. Unless a young man were really well power-based in the Navy, he had better stay ashore, where there were plenty of opportunities for a bright boy with all the right relations. His eldest son, Francis, was to join the East India Company, and Tom was going for a soldier. Why could not Charlie be something sensible and static like a writer to the signet?

Furthermore, the Napiers had not had much luck at sea. A hundred and thirty years back, in 1672, John Napier, second son of the second Lord Napier, had been killed in his early twenties in a sea-fight at Solebay against the Dutch. In the early 1700s this young man's nephew, another John, Master of Napier and dearly loved only surviving son of his parents, had sweated away in a fever off the Guinea Coast, as a lieutenant on board HMS *Deptford*.

Then, Charles senior pointed out, warming to his argument, there were his own younger brothers (he was one of ten sons). Patrick Napier, although a skilled and popular captain, had, in the words of his sister-in-law, Sarah Napier, 'nearly moped himself to death' for lack of a ship at the time of the Glorious First of June when the French ships were making their way home to Brest across the Atlantic and the British Navy had failed to sink more than eight of them. Another brother, John, had been killed fighting the French, as a lieutenant in the *Fox* frigate. It was true that William John, later ninth Lord Napier, was doing well enough at sea (and would shortly be serving on board *Defence* at Trafalgar) but *his* younger brother, Francis, had very recently been lost at sea in the *Hussar* frigate.

One way and another it was a gloomy record of early death and any parent who faced facts and cared for his children could hardly fail to take account of it. And, unless she was by nature a Roman matron, what was life like for a mother with *all* her sons away?

Words of warning flowed over Charlie's head like so many ocean waves, leaving him gasping but determined. Uncle Napier was called in, to shake his head at Charlie, and Cousin Hopetoun (Charlie's grandmother had been Lady Henrietta Hope). Charlie was undeterred. In 1799, aged eleven, he gathered his gang about him and, in desperation, led them to his father's library in George Square to press the point in unison. One of them was called Ainslie, and recounted the experience when he grew up:

> Captain Napier looked with most stern surprise at the liberty we had taken in thus invading his sanctum. Charlie . . . reiterated his wish and we took courage and urged in tremulous voices in support of his petition. But it was all in vain, and we were dismissed in no very courteous tones by the gallant veteran, who declared in decided language 'that Charlie should never enter the Navy'.

Once again, the bosses had won. This was, as Ainslie said, 'a tyrannical stretch of parental authority'; Charlie knew it, the boys knew it and so, upon reflection, did Captain Napier, disappointed sailor though he was. Confronted by this infant sit-in, by all those fair and freckled faces, reproachful above their frilled shirts and cutaway coats, taking a trembling stand in their knee-breeches and buckled shoes, he had no intention of giving in at once.

A few weeks later the Captain agreed that Black Charlie at eleven should decide his own destiny. Flown with triumph, Charlie raced round the square with whoops of joy to inform his colleagues that the management had collapsed.

Charlie was entered on the books of the sloop *Martin*, commanded by Captain the Hon. Michael Sinclair, a friend of his father, and early revealed that he had the essential quality for a naval officer – luck. The *Martin* lay in Leith Roads, due to sail in a week; Charlie's sea-chest was packed, his blue tail-coat with a stand-up collar and plain, raised gilt buttons was ready, his round hat and gold lace loop with cockade, his white duck trousers. Two days before he was due on board Charlie began to feel exceedingly ill, ill past the stage where concealment was possible. Next morning his swimming eyes and riotous rash revealed the dreadful truth. Measles! The ignominy of it – a would-be dashing sea-officer thus laid low! Whilst Charlie turned restlessly in his darkened room, HM Sloop *Martin* sailed out of Leith Roads without him, dwindling down the Firth of Forth into the North Sea; and was never seen or heard of again. Somewhere there, or in the Atlantic, she was lost with all hands, and never so much as a spar or a floating body to signal where or how.

At the end of the year Charlie set forth in the coach for London, then a considerable journey from Edinburgh, on the way to Portsmouth to join HMS *Renown*, a new 74-gun ship of the line. The uncle, General Mark Napier, who met him in London, took him to the Tower to see the lions. 'This one', the keeper told them proudly, 'is so very tame that you might put your hand in his mouth.' Though small for his age, Charlie was just able to reach his arm far enough through the bars for the experiment. His luck held; the lion was either too surprised, or too sleepy, to take steps. The General, Charlie's uncle, was not.

Mildly chastened, Charlie arrived next day at Portsmouth. The *Renown*, Captain Eyles, and wearing the flag of Rear-Admiral Sir John Borlase Warren, lay at Spithead. Charlie would have had some acquaintance in the ill-fated *Martin*, but had never laid eyes on a single soul on board of *Renown*. He clambered up the side and in the full impact of her tremendousness.

Hundreds of oaks had been felled to build her, dozens of skilled craftsmen involved in her construction. With pride Charlie strode her newly scrubbed decks and gazed aloft into her intricate rigging. How wonderful a ship! But Charlie was still only twelve and had come a long way from home. His loneliness in this grand and demanding new world, his ignorance of what to do or where to go next, the fatigue of his long journey, even the towering masts of *Renown* up which he must soon shin – all combined against his native courage; the cockpit to which he was presently led did nothing to reassure him. This small, sombre, cramped place was to be his habitat, day and night; his sea-chest was his only seat, his hammock, slung aloft every night, his only bed in the close, reeking and frequently tossing darkness. His companions, he perceived, would not only be other boys of his age, but the bitter and disappointed, passed-over lieutenants, thirty or even forty years old and naturally disinclined to be well-disposed towards boys with better chances than their own.

Charlie would not be allowed to drink wine or smoke until he was eighteen, and his food would be scant and disgusting, his only lighting a rag dipped in tallow and put in a bottle by forks set in the cracks of the table. If he misbehaved he would be put to work watch on watch, that is, four hours on and four hours off all round the clock; or mast-headed, sent to the crow's nest up the foremast and forbidden to come down for hours, sometimes for a whole day at a time. For recreation the midshipmen were allowed to dance and skylark on the upper deck in fine weather, and to chase each other round the masts, spars and rigging in dizzying acrobatic games that not infrequently ended in a fatal fall. Visiting foreign ports they were liable to catch diseases for which the medical science of the time could offer no cure; sometimes as many as four out of five midshipmen died of fever after an unlucky jaunt ashore. Even on board a great ship such as *Renown,* the space between decks was so small that if Charlie grew tall he would never be able to stand upright except on the upper deck.

A sense of all that he had left behind overwhelmed Charlie – parents who, however stern, were affectionate and concerned, a houseful of teasing but helpful servants, his own room, his own horse, four square meals a day eaten with splendid silver off good china set on fine linen. At sea his chances of survival into manhood were not much more than evens. Not all of his predicament was immediately made clear to him, but the stench, the darkness, the cramped quarters of *Renown's* cockpit were enough. The dashing sea-officer sat down on his sea-chest and wept bitterly. Was it for this that he had dreamed, planned, fought?

In the gloom of the cockpit the dark-haired Charlie appeared so remarkably swarthy that the other midshipmen added themselves to the number of Charlie's own family who already knew him as Charles the Black, so-called to distinguish him from his three-years-older cousin, Charles Napier, the soldier. (This amongst the sandy Scots was no troublesome distinction in the 1800s.) Before long Charlie dried his tears, cheerfully announced that he was as black as the devil, and rapidly became the life and soul of the party in their reeking habitat.

A tough, spirited, but feeling-hearted boy, he would grow at sea into a fiery, joking, emotional, irascible man, his outstanding ability not always compensating for his abrupt manner. He was a noisier, breezier, less sensitive edition of the soldier Charles, sharing his essential goodness of heart, his energy and will, his ripe oaths and lack of tact, using his same steam-roller tactics in his passionate insistence on the reform of abuses; but spared the other Charles's tugs of personality, his blue devils of doubt. He also lacked the other Charles's percipience, and some at least of his charm. Like him, he enjoyed the confidence of the men he led, because he so evidently knew what he was at. It was a liking that he reciprocated, hating the rough treat-meat to which men in the Navy were subjected, and doing all he could to amend it. Perhaps Black Charlie's most supreme possession was his confidence. After however many setbacks, Charlie's spirits would rise like a cork to the surface.

A day or two later *Renown* put to sea, a process that left Charlie and others far too busy to mope. In the evening, feeling the dark waters of the English Channel moving beneath her, Charlie was relieved to find that he was not queasy. Though horrible smells still affronted his nostrils and the lack of room still fretted his elbows, the stir and movement of the ship exhilarated him. He was where he had so long desired to be – at sea in a man-of-war. And the struggle with Napoleonic France was still on.

Charlie delighted in his profession and, very likely, quite soon became too uppish by half. Captain Eyles was a disciplinarian, and on his orders Charlie was presently flogged. His backside, he recorded, remembered it forever and he was correspondingly tender when it came to inflicting this punishment on others. His offence had been to hack inadvertently at a hawser, while demonstrating to his fellows the smartest manner in which to behead an enemy with a cutlass. Damaging a hawser was almost as grave a sin as not damaging an enemy. Charlie was well liked by his contemporaries and one of them, Augustine Clifford, later remembered him as 'a fine, sturdy, energetic boy, small for his age, but active and very strong'.

Under fire off Elba before he was fourteen, Black Charlie was soon made aware of the realities of war. His enthusiasm was in no way dimmed. Perhaps fourteen is the ideal age at which to wage war; one has no idea of what one will miss by being killed, and very little notion of what will happen to oneself anyway. The Peace of Amiens, that short-lived lull in twenty years of Napoleonic War, sent him back on leave to Edinburgh, to embrace his parents and show off his uniform to friends still at school. Appearing at the High School in fall uniform, wearing a sword nearly as long as himself and listening to a complimentary speech from Professor Adams, he was granted a holiday for his school fellows – rather in the manner of visiting royalty. He led them forth to enjoy it; an episode that did much to enhance a growing confidence, not to say self-esteem. Despite this, everyone noticed his great fondness for, and kindness to, very small children; so much so that he was mocked for being a nursery maid, and replied that he was honoured by the office. Some of his innumerable relations were not best pleased when he called on them, and finding them out, declined to give his name to the servants. 'Tell them someone as black as the *Deevil* has come, and will come again' – the kind of behaviour to which elderly cousins in the Edinburgh area were not accustomed.

Perhaps luckily, he was soon back on board *Renown*; and by the end of 1802 he was serving in the *Greyhound*, a 32-gun frigate commanded by Captain William Hoste, a highly intelligent officer from whom he learned a great deal, and perhaps sobered up a little in his ebullient spirits. He was next serving in the 40-gun frigate *Egyptienne*, taken from the French after the victory of the Nile, capturing French privateers in the Channel, or sailing in convoy to St Helena. He wrote steadfastly every week to his mother, who put away all his youthful letters so carefully that they have never been seen since.

He was already touchy. His captain on board *Egyptienne* once addressed him in language that Charlie considered unfitting, from one gentleman to another, even from captain to midshipman. He did

not forget; and years later as a commander on the same station, he
demanded satisfaction from the insulting Captain Elphinstone Fleeming. Their seconds induced them to shake hands, but it was not until
Fleeming unsaid his earlier words, by a complimentary reference to
Charlie in a public speech, that they really became friends. Such
implacability might bode no good to his career – it was too Scottish,
too clannish. With plenty of friends, he was too ready to snap his
fingers at enemies.

Charlie was next heard of as mate on the *Renommée,* engaging the
Normandy batteries, and going on boat expeditions up the Brittany
River Quimper. In the dangerous spring of 1805, when Napoleon's
Grand Army stood poised to invade England a British squadron
had encountered on 23 April, 'the night being dark and a fresh
wind blowing', thirty-three French gunboats and nineteen transports
which were part of Napoleon's gathering invasion fleet. These were
stealing piecemeal along the French coast, but were thrown into
confusion by a shift in the wind and made for an anchorage between
Capes Blanc Nez and Gris Nez. At break of day on the 24th, despite
aid from the gun brigs and shore batteries, many of them were taken
by the British squadron that had dogged them, and Lieutenant John
Lake in the *Locust* and Charles Napier in the *Starling* captured six
more small ships 'after a spirited engagement', wrote the naval
historian William James.

Charlie was promoted lieutenant in the November of this year and
appointed to the *Courageux,* 74 guns, soon despatched to the West
Indies under Sir John Warren, chasing a French convoy that had
escaped from Brest. They took the French 74, *Marengo,* and their
frigate *Belle Poule,* homeward bound from the East Indies, but it was
across the Atlantic, off Antigua, that Charlie's courage and tenacity
were really to come into their own.

The West Indian islands, that now seem so delectable, were hated by
serving soldiers and sailors in the eighteenth and early nineteenth
centuries, not on account of the French, or the Caribs, but because of
Yellow Jack, the dreaded fever of which men died like flies, and
which compounded its horror in that a man's flesh corrupted long
before his soul departed. The Caribbean Sea was, all the same, a
happy hunting ground for those in search of fame or fortune; and
the robust Black Charlie confronted it without dismay. He was
now nineteen, and was given command of the sloop-brig *Recruit.*

Engaging the French *Diligente* off Antigua, Charlie had his right thigh broken by the Frenchman's second shot, the bone protruding from the flesh. After this, de Willetts, the only other lieutenant on board, was killed, and the master, directed by Charlie, continued to fight the ship. The mainstay was shot away and *Recruit's* mainmast fell, immobilizing the British vessel, so that *Diligente* was twice able to rake her. The end of both *Recruit* and Black Charlie and his crew seemed imminent, but his luck held. An explosion on board *Diligente* caused her to sheer off and make for the safety of Martinique, while the British refitted their mast. *Recruit* lost eighteen men, six killed and twelve mortally wounded. Eleven more wounded recovered, including Black Charlie, who was to have a slight limp for the rest of his life. Rolling gently in the blue seas, with his stricken men around him, whilst the survivors struggled desperately to repair the mainmast before another French sail loomed over the horizon, Charlie fought with his own pain and sought to encourage others. If ever he had been inclined to take war lightly, he did so no more.

It took Charlie three months to recover, but he was in time for the attack on Martinique at the end of January 1809. The *Recruit,* with *Aeolus,* Captain Lord William FitzRoy, and *Cleopatra,* Captain Samuel Pechell, were detailed out of Cochrane's squadron to the upper part of Port Royal Bay. On the night of 30 January they anchored close to Fort Edward; the French, on their approach, had set light to their own frigate, *Amphrite* (whose escape had been cut off), in order to prevent her capture.

Daylight revealed to Charlie an absence of movement in Fort Edward, and he asked FitzRoy for a party of marines to land and storm it. The more experienced captain of *Aeolus* thought it too hazardous; the French were probably foxing; there might be a large garrison concealed. Charlie gained permission to scout. Landing in a gig with four volunteers, he scaled the walls of Fort Edward, found it abandoned and ran up the Union Jack which he had wrapped round him under his waistcoat. On hearing of this, Cochrane landed 800 soldiers, who turned the fortress's own mortars on nearby Fort Bourbon, which rapidly succumbed.

Loss of the *Amphrite* obliged the French garrison of Pigeon Island (Ilot aux Ramiers) to surrender; and at the end of this year poor Admiral Villaret-Joyeuse underwent the un-joyous experience of being broken by the Paris court that tried him – a blow to the general morale of the French Navy. Charlie was soon afterwards made a post captain by Cochrane and given command of the line of battle ship *Jason*, but there was a lucky pause before he could join her. Still in command of *Recruit,* he was sent to Les Saintes, a convenient group of islands enclosing a safe roadstead for ships.

Three French 74s, the *d'Hautpoult, Courageux* and *Polonais,* had made a dashing escape from Lorient. With the frigates *Furieuse* and *Félicité* and under command of Commodore Amable Gilles-Troude, they had evaded the British blockade and were almost across the Atlantic, laden with troops, ammunition and stores for the Martinique garrison, when they learned that this island now flew the Union Jack. They altered course for Les Saintes, awaiting a chance to make another swift dash from this haven to Guadeloupe, where the tricolor still flew.

They had hardly cast anchor before Cochrane's squadron was upon them. The beauty of Les Saintes harbour lay in its many exits. A party under command of the 40-gun frigate *Acasta* lost no time in landing 2,000 British troops from Martinique on 14 February and these, after some sharp fighting, seized the hill that dominated the harbour. They then turned their guns on the French ships. As soon as night fell these were under weigh, stealing out to sea. These handsome vessels had the legs of most of the British ships and, with a fair start, had every chance of gaining Guadeloupe and safety.

The *Recruit* had been lying with the inshore ships, and Black Charlie, alerting Cochrane by the pre-arranged signal, was quickly off the mark. Charlie reported: 'I immediately bore up in the chase, making signals to the squadron, which was also done by the *Hazard* and *Hawke*. The *Neptune* (98 guns), wearing the flag of Admiral Cochrane, and the *Pompée* brought up a strong breeze with them and exchanged a few shots, but they soon dropped astern.' *York* and *Polyphemus* were also part of the hunt, but soon all but Charlie's nippy little *Recruit* were left behind. 'She sailed well, and I took up my position on the quarter of the *d'Hautpoult,* within grapeshot, where I remained the whole night, leading on our squadron, the enemy retreating in line abreast.'

When dawn broke, Charlie was on his own; 'the *Hawke* brig was three or four miles astern of the *Recruit,* the *Pompée* five or six, the *Neptune* seven or eight'. Within range of three enemy 74s, Charlie had every excuse to slacken his pace; but he knew well that the sensible Frenchmen would be more concerned with arriving complete with their reinforcements at Guadeloupe than with pausing to give battle to a comparative midget like himself; a thought which doubt-less encouraged him.

James wrote: 'At daylight *Recruit* began annoying *d'Hautpoult* and her consorts. More than once by her temerity *Recruit* compelled the line of battleships to yaw and fire broadsides at her.' During the long day Cochrane thought *Recruit* in such danger that he several times ordered the signal for Charlie's recall, on one occasion cancell-ing it when *Recruit* made another miraculous escape. Charlie con-tinued to fire at the *d'Hautpoult,*

> yawing under her stern and on her quarter, exposed to the stern guns of the ships of the line, and the occasional broadside of the other two. But being afraid of having their spars knocked away, they seldom rounded to, and they fired in such a hurry that we were only hulled three times.
>
> I once crossed their stern, fired three or four broadsides, and again took up my position on the *d'Hautpoult's* quarter, where they allowed me to remain the whole day, contenting themselves with yawing and firing their stern guns, without much effect, being always in a hurry to resume their course.

His puny efforts were successful: 'As the evening of the 15th came on', wrote James, '*Pompée* had drawn so close to the French line that the three seventy-fours scattered...' Charlie now felt free to leave *d'Hautpoult* and pursue the other two. Darkness frustrated him – 'in the night I lost the enemy'- and he returned to harry the *d'Hautpoult*.

'Early in the morning of the 17th', James continued, 'the other British ships caught up and opened fire and at 5.15 a.m. the *d'Haut-poult* struck, with rigging and sails cut to ribbons, hull riddled, masts broken and ninety men dead.' Like a bulldog at a great bull, skir-mishing round the French 74, attacking, retreating and altogether delaying her progress, *Recruit* had hung on for fifty-five hours. In the end *d'Hautpoult* had put up a magnificent fight; not without honour was the tricolor hauled down and the Union Jack run up. She was renamed *Abercrombie,* and 'for his gallantry Napier was appointed her acting captain. The other ships escaped [James].'

Pompée and *Castor* had behaved well, recorded James, but 'what shall we say of *Recruit*? Her behaviour was gallant in the extreme.' Surrendering his sword, the French captain demanded to know the name of the little vessel that had so persistently and successfully held on. '*Recruit!* No conscript she, but a *very* old soldier!'

After all this Charlie was bitterly disappointed, on arriving back at Portsmouth in command of the *Jason,* to be told there was no ship for him and no prospect but of going on half-pay. To rub salt in the wound, *Jason* was given to Captain King, who had come home in her as Black Charlie's guest. He wrote in protest to Lord Mulgrave, who had become civil First Lord of the Admiralty on the formation of the Portland Ministry in 1807. Charlie wrote probably in an offended and disgruntled vein.

> He prospers who burns in the morning
> The letters he wrote overnight,

the poet was presently to point out; but Charlie had not the benefit of this piece of wisdom. Someone far aloft had hinted to another colleague far aloft that he would very much oblige him by promoting Captain King into the *Jason,* and the thing was done. If he would wait, Charlie was told, he might get another 74. Wait? But for how long? If Charlie had put on a really well-brushed uniform, gone to the Admiralty and uttered smooth words, the tale might have been different. Charlie hated smarminess; but perhaps he carried his dislike of the suave and glib too far. While he was in the West Indies his father had died. Charlie could not even go home as a prodigal son and applaud the better judgement of Charles senior.

His long, long war with the Admiralty was here launched; and he would fight it with the same vigour and persistence as he had shown against the three towering French 74s.

Black Charlie was now twenty. Proved as a seaman and warrior, he was beginning to wonder whether there was something to be said for the further education frequently canvassed by his father and by the Revd William McCall. Chaplain Richard Walter, returning from Anson's voyage round the world and writing his account of it, had come up with some very firm and novel ideas about naval officers which during the eighteenth century began, very slowly, to take effect. In the 1740s he wrote:

> Tho' some have been so far misled as to suppose that the perfection of sea-officers consisted in a turn of mind and temper resembling the boisterous element they had to deal with, and have condemned all literature and science as effeminate and derogatory to that ferocity which, they would falsely persuade us, was the most unerring characteristic of courage; yet, experience

has proved that a proficiency in the arts is extremely consistent
with the most exemplary bravery, and the most distinguished skill
in every function belonging to the duty of a sea-officer.

At twenty, keen though he was in his chosen profession, Black
Charlie felt very differently from the twelve-year-old who had cared
little for his books and had wanted only to be at sea, fighting his
country's battles. After eight years at sea, Edinburgh University beckoned; and so, more powerfully, did Scotland. By the end of 1809 he
was on half-pay, buckling down to it at Edinburgh University with a
true Scots passion for self-improvement; going to classes in history,
chemistry, mathematics, moral philosophy, French, Italian, Spanish
and German. He had never been one for half measures.

2

Tom Tiddler's Ground

How much learning he actually acquired is uncertain; for one who downed tools, academically, at twelve there must have been a long way to go. His fellow students, though of the same age, may have seemed to him a little infantile in their inexperience of the world. Many pleasures beckoned. 'Auld Reekie' had now largely ceased to reek, expanding northwards to the other side of its filled-in Nor' Loch into a brave new world of well-laid-out crescents, terraces and broad streets; as if Edinburgh, no longer a capital city, were determined to look more than ever like one. Black Charlie had private means (mostly through his mother) and drove a handsome curricle, bowling along recently-built Princes Street and through the fine, elegant squares of the new city, for whose houses the genius of the brothers Adam had designed fanlights and columns and great garlands of stone flowers. He loved to dance, and at Scottish reels he could dance everyone else off the floor. In the long light of Edinburgh's summer evenings, the fiddles sang through the high houses, while Black Charlie, broken thigh or not, leapt to their call, fronting the shy Jane Austen girls with their bobbing ringlets and high-waisted Empire dresses of Indian muslin, who loved him for the perils he had passed, while he loved them that they did pity him.

He was often to be seen out hunting this winter, generally in his rather peculiar, inherited hunting clothes, which had suited his tall father but sat less well on Charlie's square frame. He rode 'a great long-legged bay mare', who was not an enthusiastic jumper; often enough Charlie would shoot across the fence whilst the bay mare remained behind. He rode hard, very nearly broke his neck several times and altogether was doubtless a bit of a menace to the rest of the field. But they liked him for his hard riding, his enormous enjoyment and his sporting goodwill, though Christian Napier, his mother, was relieved when the hunting season ended.

The girl on whom he had set his heart did not love him enough and married someone else. Black Charlie in his pain could not, of course, console himself in the foreknowledge that her husband would die, that he would marry her in the end and bring up her four children as if they were his own. Perhaps he got on with his studies all the more for this setback, or maybe not. In any case, the war was still on; and though no ship for him was yet available, when his year at Edinburgh University was over by the summer of 1810 and he had finished his courses, he felt he had had enough of civilian life and sailed with a friend, Captain William Pakenham, to have a look at the Peninsular War. The soldier Charles wrote home to his mother (the famous Lady Sarah who had nearly married King George III):

> Black Charlie is as queer a fellow as ever crossed me and as honest a one. He is the delight of my life, and should live with me and be trusted with any enterprise, if I were a great man, he just being fit for a sailor; that is bold, decided and active – he will make a figure yet.

A harsh critic might have considered Black Charlie a bit of a figure already, with his tendency to wear spurred hunting boots on board and a naval coat when hunting – not from swank but from a general vagueness about what clothes he actually had on. The brothers Charles, George and William Napier, his first cousins and all in the Peninsular Army, had received Charlie with enthusiasm when he appeared near Coimbra. On the route south, riding where George had told him not to, Charlie was shot in the leg by a French sharpshooter; 'only slightly and well he deserved it, the obstinate dog' was George's comment. The brothers shared their meagre rations with Charlie and took him into action with them for a front-row view of the Battle of Busaco, fought on a hot September day along a mountain ridge on the route to Lisbon, along which Marshal Soult, with a great army of experienced French soldiers, was pursuing Wellington, in charge of England's small and solitary force.

Busaco's battle thrilled Black Charlie. It had been a wonderful sight to see Wellington handling his small, brave, inexperienced army with such skill against the mass of doughty French veterans, and holding the ridge to such effect that he delayed their advance and gained vital time. All three of the brothers had been wounded in the battle, Charles so badly that they nearly buried him on the spot. 'Busaco, where I was hit in the stem and George in the stern; that was burning the family candle at both ends,' he commented.

From then on Black Charlie was inspired by a compelling wish to command a shore enterprise and even fight a land battle. Oddly enough, he did.

With the coming of autumn Wellington established himself behind the lines of Torres Vedras and waited for the French army to run out of food. This policy caused Black Charlie to ask, when dining with the then Sir Arthur Wellesley, why, with the French so near him, he failed to attack? What about 'a boarding dash'? For at sea the British almost invariably attacked the French; their difficulty was to get near enough to the enemy ships. Wellington patiently explained to him that England had only one army, that it would cost him 10,000 men to defeat the French and that 'he must fight in a position where the French must lose more men than he'.

Expressing the opinion that campaigning was 'a damned rum concern', Black Charlie left Portugal to visit his younger brother, Thomas, in Spain. Francis, his eldest brother, was now in India, and Tom, a tall, fair soldier, was just now seconded to a kind of Free French regiment called the Chasseurs Britanniques, manned by those who couldn't stand the French Revolution. They were stationed at Cadiz, with a view to an occasional prod at the soft underbelly of Marshal Soult's Andalusian domain. Here Black Charlie halted awhile to brush up his Spanish in dalliance with the senoritas, while he waited for a ship. The two brothers' extreme unlikeness to each other caused many a Spanish joke; what had their mother been up to? The southern Spaniards, almost uniformly dark, were unaware of the range of colouring existing in the British nation and still less acquainted with the stern sexual mores of a Miss Hamilton of Lanarkshire. 'Ah de mi,' they mocked, 'caballeros, que habra entonces hecho su madre de Ustedes?' Charlie and Tom could laugh and pretend not to understand, but the best fun was provided by Charlie's determination to speak French to the Chasseurs Britanniques in their mess, with his Winston Churchill accent and his unflagging determination to get his point across.

Charlie's next two years as captain of the *Thames*, a 32-gun frigate, in the Mediterranean, were the happiest of his life, professionally at any rate. Here was one of the reasons why young men joined the Navy, for a break like this in the midst of the comfortless monotony, the ceaseless danger, the cold, the long watches and the close, pestilent life between decks where only those well under six feet tall could ever stand upright. (In the twelve years between 1803 and 1815 the Royal Navy lost ninety ships by enemy action and one hundred and eighty-three by shipwreck, while fifty-six of their vessels foundered; and these were the prime seamen of their age.)

HMS *Thames* was an ill-found, slow-sailing, often-leaking tub – 'more like a candle box than a man-of-war,' an officer complained; but to Charlie she was the zest and glory of life. And here, let loose into the summer Mediterranean on his own, Black Charlie could simply be a pirate. With all the power of sea-victorious Britain behind him, and only a stern upbringing on the Gospel according to St John to civilize his wrath, coupled with the King's Regulations and Admiralty Instructions which forbade him, among other things, to do anything 'to the derogation of God's honour', Charlie could work his will. 'The nations not so blest as we, Must in their turn, To tyrants fall,' sang Black Charlie and his shipmates; and glancing round Europe under Napoleon it certainly looked that way. The luckless Neapolitans were now under French sway, so that British frigates were at large in these delectable waters to capture everything in sight.

The game as they saw it was to take as much shipping and blow up as many forts as possible while losing the minimum number of lives – and Charlie lived on Tom Tiddler's ground, picking up gold and silver, while it winked back at him from every ripple. He would trail his coat past Naples harbour, a great blue ensign flying from his main masthead with the legend '32 guns and 216 men' inscribed on it, hoping to lure out some more powerful vessel for the best of three rounds with him. This enterprise was spiced by the fact that the wind drops very suddenly in the Mediterranean and might leave him becalmed and at the mercy of a large fleet. Or he would run the *Thames* frigate close in under the cliff at Palinuro, and shin up to the top like a goat, to distract Italian General Pignatelli onto the headland while he covered the landing of Major Derby and 250 men of the 62nd Regiment. He would then swing down in a basket to go back on board, sail into the harbour, silence the forts, capture eighteen ships and re-embark the soldiers with a loss of only five men. In the glassy dawn he would float past the Aeolian Islands on the lookout for French gunboats, the *Thames* frigate like some huge, ruffled, white bird asleep on its own reflection. Cruising by Ischia, he would whip off a dozen iron-ore *feluccas,* or, in company with *Impérieuse,* Lieutenant Duncan, capture the island of Ponza as a base from which to keep watch on French comings and goings from Naples. Best of all was the return to Sicily, on a dreamy September

Sunday, towing a string of prizes with the Union Jack flying at their mastheads above the French tricolor, while bands played and the pretty girls of Palermo were about on the Marino to see, and all the bells of the city singing out across the still water:

> Rolling, harsh, holy,
> Slow, mellow, melancholy.

In a week, revictualled, they would be off again, to 'stretch across to Sardinia', or sweep the coast from Capri to the Gulf of Salerno. The glories of the Mediterranean never ceased to delight him. 'It is impossible', Black Charlie thought, 'to conceive anything more beautiful than the whole coast from Naples to the Faro point', and it was tantalizing that they could only occasionally dash ashore to get fresh water. 'The temples of Paestum are clearly discovered from the sea, and could we have found an excuse to land, we could easily have visited them under an escort of marines.'

The temples of Paestum would have to wait; but Black Charlie could enjoy yet another joyful return to Palermo and the blessings of the land at evening, with Mount Pellegrino lit by a setting sun, the bright light slanting across the Conca d'Oro – the golden shell of Palermo's sea-fronting plain – while *Thames*, his beloved old tub, threaded her way through the fishing boats to her anchorage. Not all that went on in this city met with Black Charlie's approval and he was shocked at Sir John Acton, Prime Minister of the two Sicilies, who at the age of sixty-four had married his fourteen-year-old niece, Mary Anne, with full papal consent. Acton was an Englishman and should have known better, Black Charlie concluded severely.

When winter came on, the trading vessels and supply ships of the enemy sought harbour and the *Thames* frigate and her ship's company could return to Malta (newly in British hands after her conquest by Napoleon). There they could enjoy the football and the dancing and the racing, the bowling along the stone-walled lanes in fast curricles, the opera and the dalliance, the serious Scottish reeling and the light-hearted loving, to see the yellow bastions rise in the pearly mists of dawn, the clusters of brightly painted boats, the harbour lights at evening streaming out over still, black waters. It was all a far cry from Edinburgh.

The ship's company of *Thames* had soon found Black Charlie 'a precious taut hand'. His nose, one of them reported, was into everything as soon as he joined and he had been up all mastheads before nightfall –

> ... a black ugly-looking fellow who halted considerably from a wound he had in the West Indies, but seemed tolerably active on his pins. His clothes were good enough but looked as if they had been hove on with a pitchfork and he wore a three-cornered hat right athwartships.

Success continued when he became captain of the bigger and faster frigate *Euryalus,* in which, with *Undaunted,* he destroyed the batteries of Cavalaire Bay and captured twenty-two vessels; one man lost, one wounded. He was blockading Toulon in 1814 when the blaze of illuminations at Marseilles announced peace.

Strangely, in that epoch of intense patriotism, far less resentment was harboured between foes than in these days of alleged international good will. After twenty years of bitter war Black Charlie was ashore in France in a trice, plunging with weather-beaten concentration into the intricacies of the quadrille and learning the latest French dances from hospitable local families who had had enough of the dourness of revolution. At all the local balls Black Charlie was to be seen, partnering the charming mademoiselles whose brothers he had recently mown down with his round shot, chatting agreeably in his Scots-accented French and spinning round the floor 'with all the awkwardness of John Bull, quite unacquainted at the time with French dancing'. Self-consciousness had never been his problem.

All too soon the kissing had to stop. In 1812 there had been one of those terrible trans-Atlantic failures in communication and, by midsummer, America had declared war on Britain. For the British then, still locked in combat with Napoleon, it was like being stung on the backside by a hornet while engaged in a twenty-year death-struggle with a tiger. For Black Charlie and the ship's company of *Euryalus* it was a damned nuisance – goodbye to the immediate hope of England, home and beauty; to the chandeliers and the quadrilles; to the lively waterfront of Marseilles; and away across the Atlantic once again, to the flat, dull coast and the New England fogs. And then bump, bump up the Potomac river, hauling off one shoal only to stick fast upon the next.

3

Potomac

'Always keep a hold of Nurse for fear of meeting something Worse' had been the prevailing dogma in the States up until 1775 – Nurse being the British and Worse being the French. British intransigence leading up to the American War of Independence and French help in achieving it had altered this creed, until in 1802 President Jefferson, hitherto starry-eyed about the glories of the French Revolution, had had the stars finally knocked out of his eyes by the sale of Spanish Louisiana to France. Who needed Napoleon on their doorstep? The old view of Nurse as at least the lesser evil began to prevail.

'The day that France takes possession of New Orleans,' Jefferson told his envoy in Paris, 'we must marry ourselves to the British fleet and nation.' But Napoleon, his soldiers defeated in the French West Indian colony of Haiti, performed a characteristically lightning switch of plan. Abandoning hopes of an American Empire he sold Louisiana to the States for fifteen million dollars and turned his attention elsewhere. Worse no longer menaced; the British fleet and nation, far from wooing America with a view to re-marriage, contributed in a very highty-tighty manner to seize erstwhile British subjects and even native-born Americans off American ships on the high seas and sometimes within American waters, in desperate attempts to man a Navy that had now been at war for nearly twenty years.

This was naturally intensely irritating and galling to a nation not thirty years independent, and indeed would have been to anyone else; rather as if, in 1914, Britain had compelled Charlie Chaplin to quit a still neutral America to fight in the trenches or had conscripted the newly-arrived English parents of Gary Cooper into their munition factories.

The build up to what Winston Churchill was to call 'this futile and unnecessary conflict' had, all the same, been slow. When Napoleon issued his Berlin decrees, closing to British trade the ports of a continent he now controlled almost in its entirety, Britain had countered by their Orders in Council blocking all neutral imports into France.

America, and particularly her eastern seaboard, suffered badly in trade, and her feelings of bitter resentment were increased by the stopping and searching of her vessels on the high seas. She invoked the Freedom of the Seas, the right of all neutrals to trade impartially with belligerents. Most Americans knew little of what Napoleon was up to, and cared less, so long as he kept away from the Western hemisphere.

Besides this nationwide resentment there was a powerful party in the West that wanted to expand northwards, and now that Britain was at full stretch trying to contain Napoleon in his native land, found the chance to conquer Canada irresistible. The views of this powerful party prevailed and the usual failure in communication, enforced by the wide Atlantic, bedevilled the business. England too was feeling the loss in trade and Castlereagh had cancelled the Orders in Council, but the news reached America too late. On 12 June 1812 Congress declared war on Great Britain. A graver midsummer madness possessed Napoleon; three days later he crossed the river on his fatal invasion of Russia.

Euryalus had been longer in the Mediterranean than any other frigate and every man jack on board had counted on home and leave. Refitting at Minorca they found *Iphigenia, Bacchante* and *Furieuse* and set sail for Bermuda, pausing at Gibraltar to pick up a convoy of 3,000 soldiers, sent to cross the Atlantic without enough food and water to last them to the other side – a foretaste of further ineptitude to come. 'Who was to blame I do not know,' wrote Charlie. 'All that our commander could do by way of remonstrance and application was done, and yet we sailed in this manner.' They had to put in to Santa Cruz for more water for the troops, and were extremely lucky to meet favouring winds.

At Bermuda they found Sir Alexander Cochrane, Commander-in-Chief on the America Station, in a rare taking. The 44-gun American frigates had proved themselves able to out-range and to out-sail the smaller British frigates. Manned in part by ex-British seamen and captained by skilled officers, their excellent American gunnery put paid to a number of British ships. Although this had little effect on the course of the war, it had a considerable one on American morale, and her privateers continued to harry British shipping. Ashore things went well for the British at first; an American expedition into Canada was driven back, and by August of 1812 the Union Jack was flying over Detroit and Fort Dearborn (now Chicago).

'I have much at heart to give them a complete drubbing before peace is made,' Sir Alexander Cochrane told the Admiralty; though if the impressment of American seamen had ceased at this point early in 1813, the war might have stopped. But it went on. Tempers were up. Since the American invasion of Ontario and the burning of its entire little capital of Toronto in midwinter by US militiamen, a state of feeling had crept in described by Admiral Mahan as 'acrimony amounting almost to virulence'. The Royal Navy in particular was smarting under its unaccustomed reverses; and although HMS *Shannon* had retrieved respectability by forcing the USS *Chesapeake* to surrender after a fifteen-minute fight, and command of the seas all down the eastern seaboard of the States was now in British hands, as well as the state of Maine, this resulted in nothing more than stalemate. With a 'complete drubbing' in view, an expedition against the city of Washington was set in motion, anchoring in the Chesapeake. *Eurayalus*, sailing with it, was destined for Captain James Gordon's sally up the Potomac. The soldier Charles Napier, stationed with his regiment at Bermuda, and accustomed to serve under generals such as Sir John Moore and the Duke of Wellington, could hardly believe his eyes at the ineptitude with which operations were being conducted; at the delays, the rivalries, the absence of clear direction and overall command. He longed to take charge himself, yet knew that he was too young to hope for the command of more than his own regiment.

'An American war is a miserable thing,' he wrote. 'Though much abused, they really are fine fellows.' And besides, they were relations. Beckwith had cousins in Virginia of whom he was very fond, some of the officers had American fathers and many had American cousins. 'It is a most unnatural war . . . a sort of bastard rebellion. . . This transatlantic service sickens me.' Years later he was to recall it as 'a war of folly and piracy, uniting all that is bad without a redeeming point, not even that of success'. He protested throughout, but nobody listened.

Numbers of Frenchmen who disliked Napoleon had joined the British Army simply for a free trip across the Atlantic, and deserted as soon as they were set ashore in the States. But not before the disgraceful sack of Hampton. Troops known by Charles as 'the dubious foreigners' had been stranded during the botched attempt on Craney Island and were all killed by the Americans: their mates had taken it out on the luckless people of Hampton. Charles was very glad that his own regiment, and the Marines, had refused to take part in this. A Frenchman had later 'robbed a poor Yankee and then shot him in the back: I would rather see ten of them shot than one American,' Charles raged. 'It is quite shocking to see men who speak our language brought in wounded: one feels as if they were English peasants and that we are killing our own people.' When it came to 'the perhaps necessary part of our job', which was driving off their cattle, he felt it 'hateful to see the poor Yankee robbed and to be the robber. . .'

'Wherever we land the Yankee runs away . . . he is quite right,' thought Charles. The American had, after all, plenty of space to run to: to chase him across a continent would be both futile and dangerous. He was no fool, and knew this. In any case, Charles feared the stupidity of the British generals would do their work for the Americans in the end. Cockburn was 'a little lacking in gumption' he reported mildly; 'no doubt an active good seaman but he has no idea of military arrangements . . . before an active enemy he would get his people cut to pieces.' Then Beckwith also was indecisive – 'I would have attacked three times our numbers of Yankees with confidence, but Beckwith was resolved to let nothing take place.' Denied his own way, the general had 'run sulky' and let a fine opportunity slip.

We seemed, Charles thought, to take care to let the Americans know exactly when and where we were coming. 'If the Yankees are worth their salt they will give us a thrashing yet in one of our own landings, going ashore as we do like a flock of sheep.'

The come-uppance duly came up at the landing below New Orleans, when the British under command of Sir Edward Pakenham, 'most delightful of men' thought George Napier, but not the most apt of generals, bit the dust; or, more accurately, the Mississippi mud. The general picture of unrelieved stupidity was underlined by Mr Croker, Civil Lord of the Admiralty. Some British ships, hastily built and manned on the Great Lakes, had failed to defeat the American vessels and were thus unable to support an advance from Canada down the Hudson valley, which accordingly ground to a halt. Shrugging aside the tiny difficulty of getting a fleet up the Niagara Falls, Croker demanded to know why we did not send the seagoing British ships to operate on the Great Lakes?

But before this debacle, Charles's cousin and namesake was to have a run for his money, though not so complete a one as he had hoped. Black Charlie's experiences were happier and less disillusioning. Arrived at Bermuda in 1814, *Euryalus* was sent on the expedition to the Chesapeake, where General Ross landed his 4,000 troops and marched to the federal capital. Brushing aside the 7,000 American militiamen, Ross entered Washington on 24 August, sending President Madison fleeing to Virginia. The naval yard and civic buildings, including the White House, were burned, though no hardship was inflicted on any private citizens. It was customary for British soldiers taking the enemy's capital in wartime to be given a medal; but Washington had been such a walkover that no medal was awarded.

Sailing up the Potomac meanwhile, the British squadron under Captain James Gordon in the 38-gun *Sea-Horse* had a rather more difficult time. Second-in-command was Black Charlie in *Euryalus*; they were followed by three bomb ships, *Devastation, Aetna,* and *Meteor,* the rocket ship *Erebus* and a small tender named *Anna Maria.* They sailed from the Chesapeake anchorage on 18 August. Black Charlie wrote later in the *United Service Magazine*:

> The River Potomac is navigable as high up as Washington, but the navigation is extremely intricate, and Nature has done much for the protection of the country by placing, one third of the way up, very extensive and intricate shoals, called 'the Kettle-Bottoms'. . .
>
> The charts gave us mostly very bad directions, and no pilots could be procured. . . The American frigates themselves never attempted it with their guns in, and were several weeks in the passage from the naval yard at Washington to the mouth of the Potomac.
>
> The evening of the second day brought the little squadron, without any accident, to the entrance to the Kettle-Bottoms . . . *Sea-Horse,* keeping the Virginian shore, led . . . the wind was light and several boats were ahead, sounding, when *Euryalus* opened the ball [being the first to ground]. No-one could tell where she hung, there was an abundance of water astern, ahead, all round, and yet the ship was immovable. [A diver discovered] an oyster bank not bigger than a boat, under her bilge.

She was hauled off, and the next to ground, more seriously, was *Sea-Horse,* on a sandbank.

This involved unloading stores, and eight or ten of her guns, and re-loading them next day when they had hauled her free. Several of the smaller ships had brief encounters with the river bed, but with a fair breeze they were clear of the Kettle Bottoms before dark. Next morning the wind was foul; and for five days the ships warped for the next fifty miles up the river, still amazed that no rifle fire opened up on them from the wooded shores.

On the fifth day they anchored off Maryland Point and Black Charlie went ashore to see how the land lay, visiting a substantial farmhouse. The American farmer with two daughters (disappointedly described by Black Charlie as 'rather uncouth and homely'), invited them in for some peach brandy, 'and seemed to know and care very little for what was going on, though he begged the Britishers not to make off with his negro slaves'. These were an unlikely piece of loot to make, as the negroes would be free the moment they set foot in an English ship; but this the farmer, with the ignorance of Americans for English ways, did not know.

That night a great glow in the sky was visible from all the ships: Washington's arsenal and her civic buildings had been set alight. Next morning, as the ships were beating up Maryland Reach, a violent squall struck them as if in revenge for the burning. Black Charlie had strongly disapproved of this fiery proceeding; even if the American militiamen had burned the whole township of Toronto, rendering its inhabitants homeless in a Canadian winter, being barbarous ourselves was no way to teach others to be less barbarous. In the violent squall the *Sea-Horse* had her mizzenmast sprung, while *Euryalus* had both bowsprit and the head of her foremast badly damaged, and the heads of all three topmasts carried away.

Captain Gordon thought the game was up,' wrote Charlie, 'but he was assured we should be refitted before the other ships joined.' And they were. 'Such was the state of discipline on board the ship, that in twelve hours the *Euryalus* had refitted herself and was again under way, ascending the river [James, vol. 5].' 'Although we did not work after dark, by next day at one o'clock we were all a-taut and weighed as the two sternmost vessels passed,' wrote Charlie. It was calm, and the boats, manned by marines, towed the ship as the seamen were setting up the rigging. At dark the squadron anchored for the night.

The following morning to our great joy the wind became fair, and we made sail up the river, which now assumed a more pleasing aspect. At five o'clock in the afternoon Mount Vernon – the retreat of the illustrious Washington – opened to our view, and showed us [Charlie added patronizingly], for the first time since we entered the Potomac, a gentleman's residence.

Higher up the river, on the opposite side, Fort Washington appeared to our anxious eyes, and to our great satisfaction it was considered assailable. [They proceeded to assail it when they anchored before sunset, out of gunshot; the bombships lobbing shells into the fort and the frigates preparing to attack it next morning, when to their great surprise a huge explosion destroyed it.] Whether occasioned by one of our shells or whether blown up by its garrison. [The populous town of Alexandria then surrendered: had they blown up their own fort?] We were at a loss to account for so extraordinary a step. The position was good, and its capture would have cost us at least fifty men, and more had it been properly defended; besides, an unfavourable wind and many other chances were in their favour.

At dawn the ships moored under the fort and completed its destruction. The guns had already been spiked by the enemy, and their complete mutilation, together with their carriages, was effected by the seamen and marines of the squadron.

A deputation from the Common Council of Alexandria arrived, under a flag of truce, with a proposal for capitulation. On 28 August the squadron anchored abreast of the town, in a position to enforce the tough terms imposed by Captain Gordon. The twenty-one American merchants' ships in the harbour had all been sunk by their owners, after their merchandise had been put ashore. The citizens were ordered to raise all these, restore their provisions and merchandise, and hand them over to the British, which they did with briskness and efficiency. In three days all were ready.

Meanwhile, having made their point, the British soldiers had left Washington, hardly expecting to hold their capital with 4,000 men and a possible reinforcement from the squadron of two or three hundred seamen and marines against potential millions of Americans, however scattered. On 1 September HM Brig *Fairy* arrived up-river, with orders for Gordon to return to the Chesapeake anchorage. *Fairy* reported having been fired on from below Mount Vernon, and noted the furnishing of batteries from strategic points down the river. The return of the squadron towing their prizes would be no picnic.

On 4 September the squadron and prizes set sail. Passing Mount Vernon, Charlie noted with satisfaction that it had been placed under a strong British guard; it was, after all, a gentleman's house, and the Washingtons were respectable squires from Sulgrave in Northamptonshire whose modest coat of arms contained the stars and stripes, now, in honour of their great scion George, become the national flag of his country; and if ever any man deserved such an honour it was he.

Again there were contrary winds, again the laborious business of warping the ships down the channel of the river. The grounding of the *Devastation* delayed them for a day; that night the Americans attempted to destroy her with fireships, and were thwarted by her captain, Alexander, who pushed off at the head of his boats and drove them back. The luckless *Devastation* was still grounded and again attacked, and though *Fairy*, sent to her aid, was able to drive away a fresh fire-boat attack, riflemen were by now active in the woods and she lost a lieutenant and eight men before *Devastation* was brought up with the rest of the squadron.

The British squadron, grounding, warping, landing to attack shore batteries, anchoring at dusk and weighing in the morning, was clear of the river in twenty-three days; 'each ship was ashore at least twenty times'. The Americans had rallied from their Washington panic and under Commodore Rodgers of the *Guerrière*, Captains Porter and Perry, others of Barney's flotilla and regulars from the *Constellation*, ranged themselves along the shore of the Potomac river, 'to punish the base incendiaries'. 'It is impossible', the American newspapers announced, 'that ships can pass such formidable batteries, commanded by our naval heroes and manned by our invincible seamen.'

On their way down river the British squadron were several times attacked. 'The Americans fought under a white flag bearing the words "Free Trade and Sailor's Rights" and behaved remarkably well, but their efforts were useless,' Black Charlie reported rather dismissively; and by 27 September the squadron and prizes were well away at sea. Gordon received a KCB, and Black Charlie a glancing bullet in the back of the neck from an American battery.

In the attack on Baltimore that ended the expedition – the American militia were now at the ready and General Ross was killed in the first assault – Black Charlie with nine boats under his command was up the Ferry branch of the River Patapsco with orders to create a diversion that might relieve the pressure on the British forces assaulting the entrenched camp. He reached some way above Fort McHenry where his feint of an attack drew down a considerable number of troops to the shore; a useless effort as the retreat had already been ordered.

Wellington, with his usual common sense, had refused to take command in this pointless war, which was as well, as he would hardly have been back in time to defeat Napoleon at Waterloo. For the Navy, with no American warships leaving port, the war had become increasingly desultory. Refitted at Halifax, *Euryalus* had spent the autumn cruising off the North American coast, hoping that an opponent might creep out under cover of the Cape Cod fogs. Black Charlie, bored and cruising off Norfolk Island, sent a challenge to Captain Charles Gordon, commanding officer of the USS *Constellation* lying in Norfolk harbour.

> ... I request you will inform me your time and place of meeting, which I shall accept if in my power. Our force is twenty-six 188 pounders, twelve 31 pounders, cannonades, one 29 pounder. Complement 294 men and boys. I trust, sir, you will believe I have no personal hostility towards you, and I have no wish than to perform a grateful service to my country, and from what I have heard of Captain Gordon, I give him full credit for the same feelings. I have the honour to be etc. CHARLES NAPIER

The challenge was accepted with alacrity, and the arrangements, as if for a tennis tournament, were entrusted to an American gentleman, a Mr Littleton W. Farrawell of Norfolk, Virginia. But at this moment, greatly to the annoyance of the players, peace broke out. Black Charlie was obliged to switch his energies onto Napoleon, lately skipped from Elba, and the *Euryalus* was ordered to support a British army landing in Belgium. Keen to repeat his experiences at Busaco, Charlie scoured Hampshire for two suitable horses and had them loaded into *Euryalus*. Extra officers were appointed, and a picked body of sailors sent on board. Charlie was just weighing anchor from Spithead for Antwerp when the naval part of the plan was shelved. He was quite unable to resist protesting to the Duke of Wellington, from whom he received a polite but firm request to mind his own business:

> The Duke of Wellington presents his compliments to Captain Napier. The Government and the Admiralty are the best judges

whether any part of the Navy shall be employed with this army. . . Brussels, 23 May 1815.

Black Charlie's much-loved mother had died while he was in America and his home, Merchiston House, had been sold. The town, advancing to surround it, had destroyed its charm and its point. He no longer had a home to which to return and be cherished. *Euryalus* was paid off; her captain, though given the CB, was put on half-pay. Baulked in every direction, Black Charlie was obliged to go ashore to find something to bite on; and here he immediately married a penniless young widow with four children under six.

4

Charlie Ashore

Elizabeth Younghusband had been the love of Charlie's youth. Her father, like his, had been a sailor, as were two of her brothers, George and Delaval. So much the better; she would be accustomed to the difficulties. She had, it is reported, great charm, and her rather too full face was redeemed by a bright, clear complexion, large hazel eyes and neat regular features. Her mouth looks tight and a little alarming but she does not seem to have been an alarming person. She was married very young, to Lieutenant Elers, RN, a young man of Dutch extraction whose forebears had first introduced salt-glazing into the Staffordshire potteries. Apart from being the uncle of the novelist Maria Edgeworth, Lieutenant Elers had no time for fame. He died young.

His four little children were lucky in their stepfather; Charlie embraced them warmly, presently changed their name to Elers-Napier, and furthered their interests in all directions. They in their turn gave him plenty of occupation when it was most needed. For peace brought to naval as to army officers a dreary time of half-pay and unemployment, of idleness and hopes frustrated, of ships laid up and regiments disbanded. No one in authority took the smallest account of their plight. Discharged and limbless soldiers, whose shoulders had so recently held the skies suspended, stumped the seaports and the garrison towns, and except for a lucky few at Chelsea and Greenwich, unpensioned and neglected. 'This subject requires much attention,' Charles the soldier wrote now; 'Most soldiers' widows and children starve.'

Luckier than most, Black Charlie was not dependent on his naval pay. Prize money had added itself to his considerable inheritance. He made the most of his happiness and his freedom, first setting up house at Horndean with his large new family. After so long at war and at sea, he felt himself entitled to a jaunt round Europe with his wife, who had had a sad time of it latterly, hard up and bereft. She was not strong; a winter in a milder climate would do her good.

Charlie had a special curricle built for him at Fareham and, persuading his wife to bring a nightgown with her in order to spend a couple of nights at Brighton, he spirited her on board ship and whizzed her across to Paris, with curricle, horses and all, where they set up house in a château at Viroflay, near Versailles, surrounded by beautiful woods. This charming place was rather less charming than usual – in the few months since Waterloo it had been visited by both Russian and Prussian soldiers, who had removed all the furniture, smashed the chandeliers and looking glasses, riddled the ceilings with bullets and slashed the family portraits with bayonets. In these *vae victis* surroundings Black Charlie left his wife in the care of her brother, George Younghusband, and of his own cousin, William Napier (both in the allied army of occupation in Paris), while he went back to fetch the four little Elerses and their nanny. His precautions did not prevent five Cossacks from forcing their way in one night. Having sent out a plea for help while calling a servant for wine, Elizabeth sensibly kept the Cossacks happy with a good dinner and just enough wine until aid arrived.

Autumn found Napiers and Elerses on their way to the milder climate of Naples, nanny and the children following steadily in a carriage while Charlie and his wife bowled dashingly ahead in the custom-built curricle, swinging round the Alpine valleys and down hills still warm with the sun into the Italian plain. Known by the Captain as his 'three-decker', the curricle was handsome and roomy, with a dicky behind, huge boxes in the sweep, a large imperial on top and a blue lining. Painted sky blue with red wheels, it was drawn by four horses and driven by an argumentative but unusually sober French coachman known as Petit-Jean. Surviving a snowstorm in the Simplon, during which nanny (Mary Branscombe) was all but lost in a snowdrift, several bands of brigands and a row in a Roman *albergo*, the family spent a happy year at Naples, from whence Charlie was at last able to see the sights that had so often tempted him from the sea.

They visited Capri, Vesuvius, Pompeii and Herculaneum, sailing to Ischia in an open boat which was later becalmed and in which the youngest Elers would certainly have died of croup had not Charlie galvanized the crew into rowing them back to Naples, taking the stroke oar himself. Next year a son, the third Charles, was born, and the family moved on, by slow stages, to have a look at Rome. Sometimes they would spend several days at a place that took their fancy. What the nanny thought of the food, the accommodation and the sanitary arrangements provided for her charges was probably quite unprintable.

Charlie and Elizabeth had brought their own saddles, and they would leave the children to their nanny for long, enchanted days, riding out in the cool of the early mornings and returning when the shadows of evening were long. For Charlie, after his many seagoing years of abstinence, lonely nights and the lack of any female company, his life with Elizabeth seemed like paradise. Much as he delighted in his ready-made family and his own chuckling baby, such solitude with the woman he had always loved was an unimaginable bliss. Having been under strict orders and bound to hard duty since he was twelve, the months of freedom to act on impulse were intoxicating, going home at the end of the day from the Apennine foothills and through the olive groves and the vineyards.

Whether it also seemed paradise to Elizabeth is not to be known. Wedded to Charlie's incurable activity, she may sometimes have felt slightly exhausted. She left no letters. Charlie wrote to her always with the candour and warm affection rarely displayed by men whose wives do not love them. Whenever he could he sent for her to be with him; she invariably came. And even Victorian wives were capable of thinking up excellent reasons for not going where they did not wish to go. Her affection must have been sternly tested during their next winter in Pisa.

Charlie loved Rome – antiquities, pictures and, above all, its sculpture. He drew the line at the bloodier religious paintings. His heart rebelled against the crucifixions and martyrdoms where the artist himself seemed to be enjoying the pain. These pictures he thought sadistic – 'Black ugly-looking daubs as unpleasant to behold as to see a poor devil tied up to the gratings and writhing under the boatswain's lash'. (Charlie's hatred of brutal punishments had increased over the years; he never allowed floggings in his own ship.) But he was unable to resist making Eliza laugh with his imitation of 'an ecstatic amateur, throwing himself into all the attitudes of a dancing master' in front of an alleged masterpiece.

Before leaving Naples they added another horse to their equipage, called Murat; he had been the battle charger of Joachim Murat, Napoleon's King of Naples, and he charged along merrily with the three-decker; it was heavier than Murat but less alarming. Reproved by Charlie at the end of a long drive for feeding and watering himself before feeding and watering his horses, Petit-Jean came back at his

master with great firmness. There were, he pointed out, plenty of
horses in the world, but only one Petit-Jean. He had discovered by
experience that if you could make Black Charlie laugh, you could
generally turn his wrath. Ashore, that is; though not at sea.

Turning north, as summer ebbed, they visited Florence, and went
on to Leghorn and Pisa. Edward, eldest of the little Elerses, remembered how Charlie never forgot his real job in life. Whenever they
touched the coast he took note of the terrain, looking for suitable
landing beaches, and drew sketches of fortifications with a view to
possible later use.

At Pisa he was involved in a smaller and less complicated dust-up.
Two *vetturini,* dissatisfied with what he had paid them, although it
was what they had agreed to, forced their way into the house at Pisa
after Charlie, and went for him.

Charlie was to tell the judge:

I liberated myself, and . . . went to the chimney . . . brandishing
my weapon for a considerable time, keeping them at bay without striking, and calling on them to leave my house. [The *vetturini* renewed the attack.] I was obliged to use my weapon,
and in consequence broke one man's arm. . . I used the weapon
solely to defend myself against attack. . . Though I have been in
many actions, I never was before in such fear of my life.

He had gone out at once to cross the river and explain what had
happened to the local tribunal. Elizabeth persuaded him to take her
seven-year-old Edward with him, on the grounds that Italians were so
fond of children he would be a sort of protection. These Italians
turned out not to have heard of their reputation. The little boy
remembered feeling 'very queer' at the shouts, curses and threats of
the crowd that quickly surrounded them. Charlie, taking him by the
hand, forced his way firmly through and told his stepson 'to walk as
fast as I possibly could, but not to run'. The boy complied – 'never
did I walk with such a will.' Glancing over the parapet at the dark,
swirling waters of the Arno, he feared 'that we might in a few
seconds be struggling in the deep and rapid waters below'.

The crowd had halted before Black Charlie's determined sally
from the house, but when he and his stepson were halfway across the
bridge, they took heart and made a sudden rush. 'Now hold onto me
and run for your life,' Charlie commanded. Since one of them was
lame and the other was only seven, they only just made it to the doors

of the town hall. Here a carabinier was leaning on his musket and regarding the scene with detached interest; he was guarding the town hall, not tourists. 'Captain Napier, with a sudden jerk, swung me behind him, wrenched the musket out of the soldier's hands and brought it down to the charge,' his stepson remembered. 'It effectively arrested the charge of this savage and cowardly mob,' and in that moment they were safe inside.

The Chancellor of Pisa strongly advised Black Charlie to pay the damages for the broken arm and have done – a piece of advice that many would have taken. But Charlie saw that, though 'violently attacked in my own house', the authorities regarded him as the aggressor, and he was determined to bring the matter to court. 'No man who had any regard for his own honour and character would suffer himself to continue under such an imputation,' he thundered. As a result of this stand, while waiting trial for 'assault and battery', Charlie and his family were obliged to stay in or near Pisa for almost the whole winter of 1816-17. He took a house at the Baths of St Julian, and diverted himself with a series of indignant letters to the Admiralty about the deteriorating state of the Navy. On acquittal at the trial, he immediately gave a handsome sum of money to the battered *vetturini;* and probably nobody in Pisa had the slightest idea why he hadn't done it in the first place – another eccentric *Inglese* occupied with his honour rather than his purse.

However much Black Charlie enjoyed domestic life, he was not prepared to leave the Admiralty unperturbed by his own perturbations. Though he had been patronizing about the lukewarm efforts of the Americans around the Potomac to defend their native land, he was openly admiring of the efforts of their seagoing frigates, from whom, he pointed out, we had plenty to learn. 'Formerly', he told Lord Melville on 1 January 1816, 'we had to contend with nations that we believed to be less brave and that we knew to be less skilful than ourselves.' But in the Americans, as the soldier Charles observed, we had been up against our own flesh and blood, and 'from want of discipline in our Navy, and the inattention to the main point – the guns – we have not only taught the Americans to despise us ... but have opened the eyes of other nations, and shewn them that we are not invincible at sea.' America was now naturally 'proud of its young Navy, and the glory it has acquired. I say glory, because I look upon the taking of our ships, though much inferior to them, a great glory in so young a Navy. . .' And he added fairly: 'I do not think that the three frigates and the numerous brigs we lost ought to have taken the American ships, who were much superior to them; but they ought either to have beat them off, or have made them pay much dearer for their victory.'

He would not go into the better construction, manning and arming of the American ships. The main trouble, he considered, was in our poor system of promotion, which meant that the men who reached command were much too old for it. 'An officer of merit will have great luck in future if he is posted before thirty'; and the average age of a rear-admiral would be between fifty-five and sixty. Black Charlie, who rarely suffered from hesitancy, went on:

> I have no hesitation in saying that in the latter years of the war, zeal and energy were nearly extinct in the breast of the greatest part of the officers and men. [Some attributed this to war-weariness after twenty years of continuous patrol and blockade, but] I am of the opinion it proceeded more from the age of the officers commanding the fleets and the ships of the line. . .
>
> I served in the Mediterranean Fleet three years [and although there were exceptions] I don't believe there was one fourth of the line-of-battle ships in that fleet that had been exercised in firing powder and shot (and without that, all exercise, even with powder is of little use, for if not accustomed regularly to load their guns, the seamen will know nothing of it; and if powder alone is used in exercise, one half of the crews will forget to put in their shots when in action); and as for firing with precision, they know nothing about it. Had Lord Exmouth gone to Algiers direct from Toulon, with five ships and without any previous preparation, the chances are he would have been beat. . . The Government also were not without their share of blame, for allowing so small a proportion of powder and shot for exercise. . .

Charlie went on to propose a detailed plan for the promotion and retirement of ageing post captains into the relatively comfortable position of half-pay rear-admirals, thus allowing the bringing forward of 'men with superior talent and merit' – this to be judged not by the Board of Admiralty but by serving admirals. Aware of having stuck his neck out a considerable way, Charlie excused himself:

> A sincere desire to improve the state of the Navy, and prevent its

ruin, the fore-runner of the fall of this country, has called forth this letter. Something must be done, and that speedily, or a new war will see our fleets and ships commanded by worn out old men, and the British flag, which has so long been triumphant, will be disgracefully driven from the seas.

No reply. By March he was at it again. What was being done for all the young men who had been taken on as boys during the war? At the end 'they found themselves without any profession, when too old to embrace another line of life'. In April he took up the cause of the seamen. Although these did now qualify for pensions,

> Fourteen years is a long while for a man to look forward to, particularly a seaman, the most unthinking man in the world; it ought at least to be reduced to ten, and British seamen would then see that their services, when no longer wanted, were not forgotten; and it would in some measure do away with the great injustice of impressment. . . I would throw open more situations to the seamen, and make those already open more lucrative and distinguished. . .

On he went – there must be no corporal punishment for petty officers, and great attention should be paid to the training and welfare of seamen boys.

> The confinement that seamen are liable to on board a man of war ought to be entirely discontinued, and their pay, instead of being kept back until the day before they sail, when it is of little or no use, ought to be given when the ships are ready for sea, and several days allowed to spend it on shore. . . nothing but the most urgent necessity should ever send a ship to sea until every man has had his turn on shore. . .
>
> The punishment of flogging round the fleet should be entirely discontinued. The worst character subject to such treatment receives commiseration from all seamen, and the feeling uppermost in their minds is disgust at the brutality of officers sentencing him to such a punishment.

All of which, though obvious enough now, was startlingly radical in 1816, and received by the Admiralty in disdainful silence.

Next it was the turn of the Marines,

> that gallant and neglected corps, who instead of the first to be

turned adrift, ought to have been the last. They are a body
of men, without exception, more useful than any other that
receives the King's pay – they have always shewn themselves fit
for any description of service.

Now they, as well as seamen, could be found starving in every
seaport town and Charlie felt moved to quotation –

> Then, oh protect the hardy tar,
> Be mindful of his merit,
> And when again you're plunged in war
> He'll show his daring spirit.

Marines, Charlie pointed out, 'would be on shore and in possession
of a place, before the soldiers had recovered their sea sickness'.

Having got this off his chest he could be happy, waiting full of
hope for an answer that never came. It is to be doubted whether
anyone at the Admiralty ever read his letters or, if they did, thought
for a moment about acting on them. Indeed their immediate reaction
would have been to take offence.

The matter of the injured *vetturini* once settled, the family set out in
the spring weather, pausing at Lucca and Bologna on their way to
Venice. Charlie's appreciation was still tinged by his ruling preoccupation. He located the batteries of the sea approaches to Venice,
took cognizance of the forts and estimated the chances of a fleet
reducing them. Summer heat increased as they travelled slowly to
Lakes Como and Garda, over the Alps into the Tyrol and thence to
Vienna, continuing through Bohemia and Bavaria and coming to rest
in Switzerland, in a villa at Vevey on Lake Geneva, looking across to
the snow-capped and serrated peaks of the Dents du Midi.

Neither Charlie nor Eliza had ever known Europe at peace, and it
seemed strange and wonderful, as well as illuminating, to traverse
countrysides now quiet that had so recently shaken to the tramp of
the huge armies of Austria, Russia, Prussia and France. An idea of
Napoleon's scope, never very evident at sea, made Charlie understand, for the first time, exactly what his country had been up against
in all those long years of fearful struggle. Britain alone had fought the
whole thing, while Spain, Italy, Austria and the Netherlands, Prussia
and the German small kingdoms had lain beneath Bonaparte's yoke,
and Russia had at one time joined in on his side.

Though there was still much misery and poverty, it seemed amazing to behold the tranquil beauty of the scene, the unchanging lakes and mountains, the wide valleys with their prosperous farms, the lovely medieval, baroque and Georgian towns where, as yet, no factories fumed round the outskirts and no ugly buildings rose up to affront the eye. The discomforts of travel were considerable – no roads were metalled, no iron railways cut the landscape. Europe perhaps had never been so beautiful and would almost certainly never be so beautiful again. To Charlie the still-standing walls of Vienna were splendid fortifications; he could not foresee how soon they would be pulled down, now that the Turks were no longer a menace, and the capital of the Austrian Empire no longer Christendom's frontier fortress.

A daughter, Fanny, was born next summer by the lake, and Eliza was so far moved by seeing the site of Jean-Jacques Rousseau's *Nouvelle Héloïse* as to endeavour to christen the baby Héloïse, an attempt frustrated by the indignant Swiss pastor who firmly wrote her down as Frances Elise. They were happy, driving out together, watching the changes of light on the lake, playing with the two babies, sturdy Charles and elegant little Fanny. Charlie bought a few hundred acres of land near Vevey, and started to farm them. When their lessons were done, Charlie would row his stepsons out and teach them to fish. He took lessons from a local artist and, seated in front of an easel, could be seen painting watercolours of Chillon Castle or sunset on Lake Geneva, with absorbed attention. But Art, at least for Charlie, could not be Life.

Nor, it seemed, could farming. Very much later Charlie was to take to it with zest, but at thirty years old his energies were too restless. Nor could he ever forget his profession. From time to time during these years he made swift journeys home to England, to see what was doing at the Admiralty and whether there was any chance of a command, and to follow up a pet project and investment in steamships. Even amidst the calm beauties of the Vevey lakeside he did not cease to torment the current First Lord with his pleas for reform in the Navy. In March of 1816 he was pleading the cause of 'grey-headed lieutenants'; what hope had they of promotion, what incentive to bring their ships up to scratch?

No First Lord of the Admiralty, and no Commander-in-Chief ever dreamt of promoting a First Lieutenant whose ship was a

credit to the Navy, Lord St Vincent excepted, notwithstanding the severity of his discipline, which he certainly carried too
far. . . Under him, an officer who had zeal for the service, was
sure of being taken by the hand. . . He was not afraid to speak
to the Admiralty, and he would have his recommendations attended to. [But now] the Admiralty, or rather the First Lord, has
too many friends of his own to provide for to attend to merit.

Your Lordship will excuse my speaking plain, the state of the
Navy requires it, and the safety of the country demands it.

But of course his lordship did not; and Charlie himself was aware
of how much he was sticking out his neck. Perhaps he felt that he had
already burned at least some of his boats; he may even have felt that,
with so few ships still in commission, those that existed should more
fairly be given to those many officers who were wholly dependent on
their naval pay, and who could enjoy full pay only on appointment to
a ship. Later he was to point out:

I had no interested motives in writing these letters. The Service
knows well enough that when a man puts himself forward to
censure the Admiralty, he will inevitably bring down on himself
their wrath; while, on the other hand, if he shuts his eyes to their
follies, and exaggerates any good they do, he gets into favour. I
have done what I thought my duty, regardless of frowns and
favours, and I hope I have done it with moderation.

Many in the Navy and outside it applauded when, years later, he
finally published his disregarded letters. Those in power did not.

Vevey and farming were too peaceful. At the end of 1818 the pretty
house and the acres were sold and the three-decker once more set in
motion. The family set out for Paris through what proved to be the
coldest winter on record, that of 1818-19; the eldest of the Elers
children remembered all his life how freezing the journey had been.
Arrived safe and sound in Paris, the Napiers took up their abode in a
house in the Rue Pigalle, in which they lived for two years, entertaining on a lavish scale.

In France, Charlie's famous luck deserted him.

5
Steam

From Paris, as from Vevey, Black Charlie continued to plague the Admiralty and to finance his steamboats. To his wife Eliza, and her softening effect upon him, Charlie's renewed efforts to make the Navy a less unthinkingly cruel organization can perhaps be in part attributed. He had always hated and avoided cruel punishments in his own ships; now he made it his life's work to put a stop to flogging and impressment. In matters in which he could wholeheartedly join with his brother officers, he did – signing a letter from the Navy Club asking that a memorial to Sir William Hoste should be erected in Westminster Abbey: 'we conceive that such a desired object may be spontaneously effected'; in other words, we'll raise the money among ourselves. To pay honour to those meet to be honoured was one thing; but how to prevent the Navy itself from falling into dishonour?

Nothing to do but write letters and lodge protests, while the Navy that he loved appeared to go steadily to the dogs. The Board of Admiralty was at this time composed entirely of civilians, changing frequently as one political party succeeded another, and with very little time for Charlie and his complaints. Not that this persuaded the Captain to let up. From Bury Hall, at Stoke, he was at it again in June of 1817, promoting the better treatment of seamen – 'they may be abroad for five, for ten years, or during a whole war, without receiving a farthing.' Sailors were ill-managed as well as unpaid, and 'when they go ashore, clothed in pursers' slops, a laughing stock; and yet we are astonished at their getting disgusted and deserting.' If officialdom thus took away a man's self-respect by leaving him penniless and miserably clad, it took also his pride and his honour, and set at risk his love of country and his sense of duty.

The Government have certainly forgotten that Great Britain is an island . . . it was the bravery of the English army that taught the continentals the French were to be beaten; take care that the

Americans do not show the maritime powers that the English
navy can be beaten also. When that sad day arrives, farewell to
old England's glory, her power, her riches, her proud station in
Europe – all, all will be lost. To maintain her where she is
depends entirely and alone on the skill, bravery, and discipline
of the British seaman. . .

From Paris, on 1 November 1819, he struck another blow against
impressment, detailing a plan for registering all seamen:

they should never be kept like prisoners in a receiving ship. . . a
liberal bounty should be paid each seaman being called upon. . .
Men-of-war, on falling in with merchant ships at sea, should on
no account whatever be allowed to impress their men . . . the
term of service should be limited as low as possible. [If seamen's
lives were made better, the time would come] when the naval
service would become the pride, instead of the detestation of the
lower orders.

The present system, Charlie pointed out, in terms little likely to
sound sweetly in the ears of those now operating it,

is little better than seizing slaves on the coast of Africa. Anyone
who believes in it should be on board a man-of-war on the
impress service, I think they would soon be disgusted. There
they would see sailors coming from a long voyage, with the
hope of seeing their wives and families, dragged from their
hiding places, many without receiving their wages, which their
masters are often too well pleased to make excuses to keep, and
the Captain at other times too impatient to wait for, sent like
slaves, on their arrival in port, on board a guardship, and
though just returned from abroad, perhaps drafted into some
man-of-war on the point of sailing for the East or West Indies,
leaving their wages for ever in the hands of their former masters,
and most probably leaving their wives and families, if they have
any, to starve. . .

Charlie wrote on, his indignation carrying him on into an ever-
lengthening sentence.

As it is impossible to man the fleet by volunteers, when the
merchants pay four times the wages of the Government, the
question is shall we have a systematic plan for completing the

Navy, or allow it to be manned in the disgraceful way it has hitherto been...

There was nothing arcane or mysterious about manning the Navy; offered the same pay as merchant seamen, paid regularly and given reasonable conditions, the Navy could be manned overnight. Impressment was manifestly unfair as well as cruel, and degraded the officers who had to enforce it as well as the men subjected to it. All this seemed as clear as daylight to Charlie and he was simply unable to understand the doubts and hesitations, the prejudice of those happy to continue impressment, many of whom were otherwise civilized and moral men. Why wouldn't they come and see for themselves how brute and beastly the system was? Barely excusable even at the height of the Napoleonic War crisis, it was totally unacceptable in peacetime conditions.

Charlie continued belligerently:

I shall continue to trouble your Lordship with my sentiments from time to time though I have little hope of seeing any good done for the naval service, till someone of the profession, in the House of Commons, has talent, perseverance, and independence, sufficient to bring its real state under consideration.

These qualities he certainly had himself, and nothing was going to stop him, though Lord Melville never answered his letters, and probably never read them. Surely, touched in their pride, they must take notice?

The superior discipline of the *Shannon* showed at once what could and what ought to have been done; had Sir Philip Broke fallen in with the first American frigate, I don't apprehend they would ever have sent another ship to sea.

Charlie went on to beg for the retirement of old captains,

and give them the rank of Rear-Admirals; the expense would not be great, and it would be gratifying to the feelings of old officers who had long and faithfully served... to retire on something comfortable, and with a superior rank; seeking in the bosom of their families that repose for which they are more calculated than the fatigues of active employment.

These were the men, though Charlie did not mention the point, who had borne the burden and heat of the day in the twenty-year-long struggle with Napoleon, and whose shoulders had held the sky suspended when even the Russians packed it in and allied themselves with Bonaparte. Surely they were entitled to a decent old age as the village admiral, respected and listened to by the rest of the parish? He concluded:

> Our apathy is unaccountable. We repair our ships and arsenals it is true, but there our exertions end; the few ships we have in commission are half-manned... Till lately, our seamen were starving in the streets, and many of them have taken refuge in foreign countries.

He was wasting his breath; but this afforded him no lasting discouragement. Meanwhile, he turned his attention to steam.

Fortunately Black Charlie, like a steamship, 'possessed within himself the means of moving'. He was still a well-to-do man. From Paris in 1818 he had come back to England to interest himself (and thereafter, he hoped, the Admiralty) in ironclads and steam vessels. On arrival with his family in London in 1820, the famous three-decker curricle, its following carriage and the family were all but mobbed by a London crowd. The Italian servants who came with them, the swarthiness of Petit-Jean the coachman and the 'blackness' of Black Charlie himself, had laid the party under suspicion of being a further bunch of bloody foreigners brought to bear witness against Queen Caroline at her trial (this luckless and irregular lady having acquired a solid body of cockney support).

Failing to involve the Admiralty in his enthusiasm for steam or for ironclads, Black Charlie had embarked on a project, in conjunction with a Mr Manby, to establish iron steamboats on the Seine. Crossing the Channel in one of the earliest of these ships, financed by him and built largely to his own design, he steamed up the river and arrived in Paris to the plaudits of large crowds. Many of them, nonetheless, insisted that the whole thing must be an imposture, as an iron vessel could clearly never float.

Charlie was plainly not designed for the world of business. He built four more boats, which were to run for years, but was quickly outsmarted by the French, and lost nearly all his money – the everlasting story of English inventiveness exploited by the sharp rapacity of foreign entrepreneurs. Some of the visitors to the hospitable house in the Rue Pigalle had proved false friends. A few more thousands invested, they told him, and the Seine steamboat enterprise would be a gold mine. Upon Charlie's sanguine spirit the familiar arguments prevailed. The steamboats did indeed run for twenty years, but they ran at Black Charlie's expense. Soon the family were out of the Rue Pigalle and into a more modest house at Versailles. The steamboats were, it is true, rather awkward vessels and not seagoing, although Charlie had crossed the Channel in them. The smooth individuals who had induced Charlie to plunge on them continued to extract more capital from him; and steamboats were certainly an enterprise after Charlie's heart. By 1821 the family were in an even smaller house at St Cloud, entertaining scarcely at all, and by the end of the twenties they were in a cottage at Rowland's Castle, Hampshire, where Charlie could only occupy his energies in the garden.

The summer of 1821 had brought a far sadder loss. Little Charles Napier, Black Charlie's own only son, died at the age of five from a fall off a haystack.

In London he once again pursued the Admiralty with his hopelessly cranky notion that iron steamships were the vessels of the future; and failed to evoke a response. His trip to France in such a vessel had only enhanced his reputation for eccentricity.

In 1828 Lord Melville, Civil Lord of the Admiralty, officially pronounced that: 'Their lordships feel it their bounden duty to discourage to the utmost of their ability the employment of steam vessels, as they consider the introduction of steam is calculated to strike a fatal blow at the naval supremacy of the Empire.'

Unluckily for Lord Melville, the French and the Americans felt differently and went ahead. Black Charlie's chagrin was boundless: 'It may be said "We have beat all the other nations under the present system – then why alter it?"' But in those days British ships had been under young captains; now they were under old. 'The Americans have opened our eyes too, and have shewn us what it is to contend with a well-manned and disciplined enemy.'

Now a comparatively poor man, Black Charlie was delighted, after fourteen years ashore, to be given a command. Apparently forgiving him his extraordinary obsession with steam and iron, the Admiralty appointed Charlie captain of the *Galatea*. This vessel was widely believed to be one of the worst ships in the Navy, and guaranteed to sink in the first gale. Perhaps the Admiralty thought that Charlie's skill as a seaman could well be employed in keeping her afloat.

Undiscouraged by the age of his command, the new captain rigged the *Galatea* with paddles, which could be shipped and unshipped in a quarter of an hour, and which he worked on a new system of winches. With these devices he startled his colleagues by entering and leaving harbour without a tow, whatever the state of the wind. Would the Admiralty take up this idea? No, they would not, and even Charlie had to admit that the paddles could only do three knots in a dead calm.

There was not much going anywhere. Charlie had to content himself with long letters to naval Members of Parliament, criticizing the unwieldy and inefficient design of the naval ships under construction. At least he himself, whatever else he had lost, had lost none of his tautness. Though grumbling slightly – *Galatea* was an ancient 42-gun frigate, and his last command, *Jason,* had been a ship of the line – he was determined that his men should be trained to a hair. At 6 a.m. on 2 March 1829 the *Galatea* had only her lower masts in, and although sixty men short of her complement, by 6 p.m. she was completely rigged, with royal yards crossed; and even the ranks of Tuscany, represented by the dockyard admiral, could scarce forbear to cheer.

Though often away training his men in boat landings and the like, Charlie was determined to have the best of both worlds for as long as he could. His eldest stepson was now at Sandhurst, but he accommodated the rest of his family on board; and a very snug time they had of it. Early in June they had to say goodbye, and on the 12th *Galatea* sailed for the West Indies. Charlie was happy enough at sea, sharpening up the senior officers, encouraging the midshipmen in their duties, and brightening the seamen's lives by 'calling all hands on deck to dance and skylark' in the tropic nights as often as possible, and organizing parties for them in the Barbadoes.

Harry Keppel, who served under Black Charlie in the *Galatea*, found him 'an irascible Scot'. He had no misunderstanding with the captain, he wrote; and when his relief arrived on board *Galatea* had been 'sad to part' with Fanny Napier and with the young Elers-Napiers. On a cruise to the West Indies, Black Charlie had put Harry Keppel under arrest for refusing to obey an order from the first lieutenant, but while confined to his cabin Keppel had disguised himself as an officer's servant and gone ashore to a dance, only to be put to flight by Black Charlie, arriving onto the dance floor in full fig. Keppel fled, but not quite quickly enough; Black Charlie spotted him and he was all but brought to a court martial. He was let off with a caution, but probably not without receiving the rough edge of Charlie's tongue. The captain did not, of course, expect the same 'zeal and energy' as had prevailed in war; but he disliked amateurism and found some of the young officers extremely lackadaisical. 'As for seamanship, they know nothing about it: should a ship be taken in a squall, unless the Captain and the First Lieutenant sleep with their eyes open, she must inevitably be dismasted; all they can think about is dancing on shore as much as they can.' But Harry Keppel, whatever else, was not slack; and perhaps Charlie remembered that he himself in youth had not been at all behindhand in dancing about on shore whenever he got the chance. Harry Keppel got away with it.

On a trooping trip to Edinburgh, Charlie found it fine to work the *Galatea* into Leith Roads with his paddles (the regiment supplying additional manpower), and to step ashore to use and hear again the speech of youth from old Lady Duncan and the two Miss Hendersons – 'Hoo is aw wi ye? Dinna ye ken Charlie Napier?' All too soon they were back in Portsmouth Harbour; 'it is precious dull work sitting by myself in my cabin,' he mourned to his wife on 9 April 1830, like many another before and since. 'It makes one feel so lonely and deserted, and a thousand times have I wished myself at Pulbrook where I trust and hope you are safe and settled. It is horrid work and no prospect of doing anything, not even a smuggler.' It was deadlock on all fronts.

When the administration had changed in 1827, Black Charlie started all over again on Lord Althorp – surely a Liberal must hate impressment as much as Charlie did himself? 'It is at once disgraceful to a free country, injurious to its commerce, and cruel and, unjust in its execution.' Admittedly the French too impressed men, but in a more systematic and milder way; men were not hunted by press-gangs, and torn from their ships and families, like felons. And they were all seamen already.

> In our seaports a general sweep of everybody takes place – seamen, landsmen, tradesmen etc. – all are hurried indiscriminately on the tender and confined like slaves in the press-room; if a wife wants to get rid of her husband, a father of his son, or a son of his father, the press-gangs are always at hand to accomplish it ... and no kidnapping slaves on the coast of Africa is more infamous than the system followed in the seaports

of England. [And let no statesman shelter behind the hope that the men didn't mind.] Sailors are made of rough materials it is true, but still they have some feeling, and their families have more.

Charlie then went on to propound a thirteen-point system on how to man the fleet with justice and fairness – all seamen to serve a certain term in the Navy, and when called up for war should receive a bounty, and when leaving, a pension. Pay should be available during the commission, and leave to go ashore, and maritime districts should be exempt from the militia call-up. First-class petty officers should have double a seaman's pay as an incentive, and there should be widows' pensions.

Lord Althorp did at least send an answer, though it took him six months to get round to it, and when it came it was a polite refusal to act. He thoroughly agreed in principle, he told Charlie. 'But the question is one which requires much delicacy in managing.' It would run counter to the prejudices of some, and engage the passions of many more, so that 'I have a very great disinclination to put myself forward upon it.' No joy; but Black Charlie had meanwhile been in correspondence with the Chairman of the Finance Committee on more and better-trained marines; to the Lord High Admiral on how to construct a steam-driven man-of-war – 'I have had a considerable degree of experience, but I write with great diffidence,' Charlie began, continuing the rest of the letter on a highly authoritative note. Three months later he launched upon a discourse to the same office, on the necessity of amalgamating the Admiralty and the Navy Board.

With his incessant letters and his strange addiction to steam, Black Charlie was slowly convincing the authorities that, in spite of his successes at sea, he was more than half out of his mind. Yet, undiscouraged by his failure over the abolition of press-gangs, in a long letter written this year he besought the Admiralty to train men in steamships and, if possible, to put him in command of one. Steam, to him, seemed to have everything to recommend it. There would be no more of those wearying and expensive blockades, 'a few steam vessels could watch and in any weather report rapidly upon enemy movements. Never again would light airs enable the French to escape.' A steam vessel would be despatched to keep sight of them.

Greatheaume's squadron would never have escaped from Sir John Warren, Jerome Buonaparte from Sir John Duckworth, or the two sail-of-the-line from Sir Alexander Cochrane in the West Indies, had there been a couple of steam vessels in company... The enemy will find no safety in their outer roads... Steam has gained such a complete conquest over the climate...

We are now in possession of all that was required to make maritime warfare perfect, and such a field is open to the enterprise of officers and seamen, that I know of no place the enemy will be safe in. [Landing troops on an enemy's coast would be comparatively easy; and never again would a fleet be bottled up by contrary winds –] I forget how many days Lord Nelson lost by not being able to get through the gut of Gibraltar. [Other nations, of course, would build steam fleets, but] I hope the superiority of our sea tactics, combined with the excellence of our machinery and the innate bravery of our officers and seamen, if well experienced and on their own element, will always give us the advantage. Our coals are also better.

But none of this was any good unless men were trained in steam. He was to write later: 'Had we employed nothing but steamers, and fast steamers on the coast of Africa the slave trade would have been put down long ago.'

Though pleading vainly, he was writing from practical experience. Directly the war was over, in 1823, he had written:

Upwards of eight years ago Mr Manby, late of Birmingham, and myself, constructed an iron steam vessel of one hundred feet long, seventeen feet broad, and eight feet deep. She was followed by four others... These vessels have been running ever since on the river Seine, and have never cost a sixpence for repairs... They have been aground on shoals and stones, have been at sea in all weathers, going in and out of Le Havre, have been knocked against bridges in all direction.

Yet they were still as sound as bells. Whereas wooden vessels in the same service...

Soon he was begging to be allowed some say in the construction of these ships. The Admiralty had at long last sanctioned some, but on present designs

it does appear to me that neither the engineer who makes the engine, nor the builders who construct the vessels have the least idea of what is necessary to construct a steam man-of-war. . . It would be just as easy to secure the boilers as it is to secure the magazine. . . The vessels are all too shallow either to house their boilers and engines as they ought to do, or to carry a sufficient quantity of fuel. . .

Charlie appealed to the new Civil Lord, Sir James Graham:

If I could see you on board a steam boat half an hour I should have no difficulty in showing you their defects, and how easily they might be remedied. I have spoken to Sir Thomas Hardy and Admiral Dundas on the subject, and have urged them both to allow me to fit one out. . .

I trust you will do me the justice of not supposing I am searching for a job for myself. I can assure you I am only actuated by a feeling to do good; many officers have been allowed to put their plans in execution, and even to build ships: now I do not pretend to do this; all I wish is to put them in the way of building an efficient ship.

To this letter he received no answer. But he noted with pleasure that Sir James Graham had at least sent the home fleet on a cruise. 'It is almost incredible that during a peace of sixteen years we have had only one squadron before this at sea', (except, of course, in the Mediterranean). In twenty close-written pages he called the attention of Sir J. Pechell, a naval MP, to a varied list of matters crying out for reform, and to 'the evils that press so hard on the Naval service of this country'.

In 1831 he was writing again. He was now in his forties, beginning to get more irritable, more difficult, aware of getting nowhere, more critical of the young. Where the good of the Navy was concerned he would not let go; he held on like some black-pointed bulldog, and with much the same stance.

Anyone who fought in the late war would find catastrophic changes, he told Pechell. Could nobody wake the Commons from their slumbers?

The Navy now is like a painting that has been copied and re-copied, and lost all the appearance of the original. Since the peace, interest has taken the lead in the employment of officers to the almost entire exclusion of merit. Young men take ships solely for their promotion and amusement, to bring up a set of youngsters (who consider all duty a bore) with the same ideas.

He suggested special training cruises for midshipmen:

in a 28-gun frigate commanded by a smart and strict Captain, with a chosen set of officers and a crew of a hundred picked men ... they should be divided into 3 watches and the topmen's duty should be done by them night and day, with a certain number of seamen to assist and instruct them. The watch below should go on with their studies... This ship should not be kept laying in harbour, but should be sent to all countries and all climates, [so that the boys should really learn their job].

The Mammas in all probability would make objections: those that did, might keep their boys at home, which would be the greatest favour they could confer on the British Navy.

Some hundred years later, his training cruiser plan was adopted.

The luckless Pechell underwent a steady bombardment – complaints about the hopelessness of trying to run the Navy with four different boards, about the shortage of powder and shot for exercising the guns, about mistakes in construction – 'the *Euryalus,* the parent of the 42s, was a sweet and beautiful ship,' Charles recorded fondly, 'far superior in qualities and appearance to the others.' The rest of the 42s were 'crank, because over-masted'. He complained about victualling, about clothing for sailors in tropical or icy climes, about doctors, about small arms:

The arms that are supplied are of the worst kind, many of the muskets go off at half-cock, many won't go off at all, and all are of so bad a form that after firing a dozen rounds, the men's shoulders are black and blue... The gun carriages in many ships are so ill-fitted and depress so little [that in many weathers there was no chance to hit lower than the masthead].

Though it is an Herculean labour to change old establishments, still, it is to be done by perseverance: the Slave and Catholic Bills were both carried by the same means.

By 1831 Black Charlie's prolonged war on the Navy's maladministration had become almost a way of life; and it was not one which made friends. Nor, alas, did it appear to influence people; at any rate, not immediately. The turmoil of major Parliamentary reform absorbed all the political attention that people had to spare; and in the early thirties the international situation appeared less threatening than usual. Even the French had had another revolution that would, it was hoped, keep them at home for a while.

But Charlie declined to let up. In a ten-page letter to Sir James Graham, Civil Lord, he again attacked the iniquities of the promotion system, the lack of proper training for midshipmen, the folly of employing ageing captains and seventy-year-old admirals.

> Most men of sixty are too old for dash and enterprise. Lord Nelson fought the battle of the Nile at thirty-nine, Copenhagen at forty-two, and was killed at forty-seven. Had he been seventy, you would probably not have heard of either one or the other. When a man's body begins to shake, the mind follows, and he is always the last to find it out.
>
> By Lord Collingwood's own account, he was beginning to fall off; and by everyone else's account he was done up long before he died.

Naval affairs, Charlie considered, were in a bad way; and he was never one to mince matters in saying so.

> If we see a general relaxation, no emulation, no zeal, and the generality of our ships in bad order, or in no order at all, we may pronounce without hesitation that the Navy has been ruled with injustice and partiality, and that promotion has been sacrificed to political purposes, and consequently bestowed on men without talent or experience, to the total exclusion of meritorious and old officers, who are left to pine in penury and neglect, or if employed, are disgusted at seeing ignorant and foolish young men put over their heads, who are totally incapable of keeping their ships in the order that British men-of-war ought to be.
>
> . . . I have been thirty-two years in the service and during that period, with the exception of commanders of sloops, first lieutenants, and senior midshipmen of line-of-battle ships and frigates being promoted in consequence of the capture of an equal or superior force, I have never observed anything like common justice in the distribution of promotion; a first lieutenant might be the best and most zealous officer in the Navy – that was no recommendation whatever for advancement.

And what was the result? Black Charlie wrote on indignantly:

[The Navy was now] glutted with inexperienced officers . . . who know more about driving a tandem or hunting a fox than taking in a topsail or reefing a course in a gale of wind . . . we beat the French and Spaniards last war, not because we were in good discipline but because they were in bad; and the moment we had to do with the Americans we were disgraced. . .

At present all the old Captains are worn out; they are tired of the detail necessary to keep the ships in order. What was a pleasure in their youth is a pain in more advanced life. . . I was in a three-decked ship last, commanded by an old man. The lower deck guns had not been run out for seven months; the men were so badly stationed that some guns had only two or three men, while others were fully manned; and as for instructing them in gunnery or even exercising, I never saw it attempted. Had that ship been fallen in with at night by a small 74 she would have been taken . . . and I daresay Sir Thomas Hardy will tell you she was not the only one. Many of our frigates were also very bad; and the action of the *Guerrière* and *Macedonia* showed that they inflicted small injury on their opponents.

He went on to detail a comprehensive study of reforms – greater fairness, promotion based on merit – and ended up: 'Any man acquainted with human nature will at once see the immense stimulus to exertion such measures would create, and the advantage the country would reap from it.' He had 'the honour to remain the Civil Lord's obedient servant, Charles Napier, HMS *Galatea,* May 17, 1831.'

By September he was pressing for a fair trial for *Galatea's* paddles:

I proposed to the late Admiralty to pay the expenses if the *Galatea* did not go three knots with her paddles. I made the same offer to move a three-decker at the same rate; and really at the time that steam is getting such a pitch, a fleet ought not to be exposed to lay in a calm like logs, when they possess the means within themselves of moving. . .

At sea that autumn of 1831, the *Galatea* riding in the Downs, Charlie was cheered by a visit from the Duke of Wellington and his invitation to dinner, where 'he was most civil: and talked a great deal about the Navy. I was quite at home,' Charlie told his wife delightedly, 'and asked him many questions, which he answered with the greatest freedom.' The Duke, who could be as good a listener as any where he was interested, had questioned Charlie closely about the paddles he had mounted in *Galatea,* and asked for a demonstration.

> If we go to Woolwich, he is to come down to see them. He was astonished that nothing has been done about them; and I said I had never been able to get the last Board of Admiralty, or this one, to look at them. [Encouraged by Wellington's interest in his technical innovation] I opened out with him as I do everywhere, and I think he was much pleased. He shook hands twice when I came away.

Perhaps Charlie had at last caught the ear of someone influential.

It seemed not. Charlie could open out as much as he liked, but to no avail. Had he been too talkatively effervescent for the Iron Duke, too guilty of the misdemeanour of enthusiasm? More likely the Duke had too many other things to think about, matters of greater moment. Charlie and his paddles went by the board.

All his letters and protests – against maladministration, against impressment, against flogging, against going ahead with the construction of untried ships and then scrapping them all next year – had made no impression; he was faced with glazed eyes and unhearing ears. *Nil desperandum* – why should he not press home his points by going into politics himself? The *Galatea* was paid off in 1832, and in the General Election that followed the passing of the Reform Bill, Black Charlie, feeling that now if ever was the opportunity for a good shake-up in the Navy, stood as an Independent Liberal.

> I have been told I am a bold man to canvass Portsmouth; so much the better. I love enterprise, and the inhabitants of Portsmouth will not like me the worse for that... Now, gentlemen, for my profession of faith without further palaver; my principles have been liberal all my life: I am favourable to reform and to the correction of all abuses... I wish to see all sinecures and useless situations abolished, whether in the Navy, the Army, or any other branch; I wish to preserve useful institutions, to keep up as large a Navy as the finances of the country will allow, and to keep that Navy efficient and always ready for work.

This programme found insufficient favour with the voters of Portsmouth, especially those considerable numbers who were themselves happily occupying sinecures and useless situations; and Bonham-Carter, the Conservative candidate, had been well bought in in the constituency by some judicious jiggery-pokery of the accepted sort. Black Charlie found himself at the bottom of the poll.

Untroubled by false modesty, Charlie on the hustings when asked who he was, had answered:

> I'll tell you. I am Captain Charles Napier, who twenty-five years ago commanded the *Recruit* brig in the West Indies, and who had the honour of being twenty-four hours under the guns of three French line-of-battle ships flying from a British squadron, the nearest of which, with the exception of the *Hawke* brig, was from five to six miles astern the greater part of the time. I kept flying double-shotted broadsides into them. . .

And so on, through a brief account of his naval career. It did him no harm with the generality, none of whom, to Charlie's undoing, possessed votes.

'Bonham-Carter 825, Baring 706, Napier 260' the poll read. When the successful candidates attempted to return thanks from the hustings for their election, a body of stalwarts approached Charlie with 'Captain, shall us board 'em and cut short their damned yarn?' A firm believer in free elections and free speech, Charlie declined this tempting offer, but had some difficulty in preventing its being put into effect. The stout forearms and commanding personality of the defeated candidate alone saved his successful opponents from some very rough handling from the disappointed and voteless people of Portsmouth. Francis Thornhill Baring was in particular danger; the foolhardy fellow had married the Prime Minister's niece.

6

Portugal

A higher authority than Black Charlie was equally fearful that the country was going downhill. 'The Revolution is made,' the Duke of Wellington wrote gloomily to Croker in March of 1833, after the Reform Bill had become law. He feared that power would now pass from the gentlemen of the Church of England to the non-conformist shopkeepers, even to people who were atheists, and to electors who obliged candidates 'to pledge themselves to certain measures'. All these things considered, 'you will see reason to be astonished that we should even now exist as a nation'. (The soldier Charles Napier who had served under Wellington and deeply admired him in the field, thought that politically he was like some magnificent old oak that could not bend before the wind.)

Croker, sharing the Duke's apprehensions, saw a chance two months later to turn a strange event to political advantage. He told Hertford on 6 May:

> A thing has occurred which by giving the Lords an opportunity of doing something, may postpone the necessity of coming in direct collision with the Commons at present. A strange, wild, Navy Captain, half-mad, of the name of Charles Napier, became a Radical in the hopes of being returned for Portsmouth. Failing there, he has turned his energies towards Portugal, has engaged with Pedro to take Sartorius's place, and has collected and sailed with a large steamer, a couple of transports, and 1,000 men. . .

On the following Monday the Duke of Wellington gave notice of a motion in the Lords of 'an address to the King to maintain a bona fide neutrality'. And thus to unship Charles. This King William IV would not be altogether loath to do. He had no love for Black Charlie who had been his captain when he first went to sea, and who had treated him as he treated all midshipmen – brusquely, kindly and without fear or favour, and the then Prince William had not forgotten the rough edge of the Napier tongue on occasions when he had been careless or undisciplined. Now, in 1833, he was King, and was far from pleased to hear of Charlie's escapade, when 'this unprincipled firebrand', as he called Charlie, was offered and accepted the command of a Portuguese fleet whose object was to drive out the usurping Prince of Portugal, Dom Miguel, in favour of his very young niece, Maria da Gloria, the legitimate Queen. Black Charlie, when in command of the *Galatea* at the Azores, had impressed the constitutional leaders, the little Queen's guardians, by his handling of some trouble that arose from Dom Miguel's ships in the islands. Finding Black Charlie at home and unemployed, they enlisted his services.

It was an enterprise nicely calculated to appeal to Black Charlie. In the eyes of most Englishmen Dom Miguel was a tyrant and an oppressor who had abolished the last King's reforms and the parliamentary government of the country. He was reputed to be holding 40,000 political prisoners. Charlie was convinced that the people of Portugal were groaning under Miguel's exactions and injustices; although not all of them were so sure of this themselves. The Queen was pitifully young, said to be beautiful, and her cause was reported to be hopeless. To crown all, the Pope was on the other side, and had given Dom Miguel, a man in his mid-fifties, a dispensation to marry Queen Maria da Gloria, his thirteen-year-old niece. To a man of Black Charlie's sympathies the whole thing breathed corruption and reaction and the doing down of the young. It appealed also to his sense of the dramatic – to avoid disgrace by ignoring the terms of the Foreign Enlistment Act of 1819, Charlie and the four naval assistants who went with him had to assume Portuguese names, and he became, for the duration, Carlos da Ponza, named after the promontory in Italy on which he had landed as a young lieutenant in command of the *Thames*.

Taking it all in all, an Edinburgh Scot could ask for no better cause; but Charlie was not an Edinburgh Scot for nothing. His predecessor in command of the Portuguese Navy, Captain Sartorius, RN, was relinquishing command because neither he nor his officers and men had had any pay for the best part of a year. Dom Pedro, Emperor of Brazil and father of Maria da Gloria, had landed at Oporto in 1832 with a force brought from Brazil to assert his daughter's rights to the throne. Here he was blockaded by Dom Miguel's ships, and from here he summoned Black Charlie to the rescue. But Carlos da Ponza insisted before he left London that the Portuguese constitutionalists should make up all arrears of pay to the fleet, insure his life for £10,000 and give him and the four other naval officers he had with him six months' pay in advance. Upon this the project was very nearly wrecked, until some London city merchants put up the money on the strength of Charlie's naval reputation.

He arrived off Oporto early in June 1833, to be met with gloom by Captain Sartorius. 'By all I could collect from him, the prospect before me was by no means brilliant. The Miguelite fleet was fitting out in great force, and shortly expected to sail. Our force was very inferior in numbers and material, and no dependence was to be placed on the men who had the direction of the war.'

However, ashore they were all received most cordially by General Saldanha, who had served with distinction under Beresford in the Peninsular War, and who cheered them with an excellent dinner, after which 'we mounted our mules and proceeded into the town'. Charlie's spirits, fortified no doubt by his good dinner, rose sharply.

> The weather was fine, the country beautiful, and the scenery enlivening to a degree. On the left were the enemy's batteries, with their flags flying, sufficiently close to observe their sentinels; on the right, at a little distance, the river with its high rising banks, well wooded, and the opposite heights crowned with the Miguelite batteries, occasionally sending their shot and shell from either side into the Queen's lines, distinguished by the blue and white constitutional flag.
>
> Nearly twenty years had passed since I had seen an enemy; the sight of flags, the sound of drums and bugles soon awoke me to a recollection of the scenes of early life, and conveyed a sensation which will be well understood by those accustomed to the bustle of war and camp. The road was tolerably well covered, being dangerous in only a few places, and we passed without molestation. At six we entered the besieged and heroic city of Oporto.

A warm welcome from the Duque de Terceira and some days of delay and frustration followed. Dom Pedro had been told by a French marshal, Solignac, in charge of his army, that the British had landed in order to displace him; he accordingly received Charlie angrily and dismissed him abruptly. Persuaded by next day that this was not so, he received Charlie again, who told him, with his customary plainness, that he had no choice but to lay down his arms or take some decisive step. He should force the Tagus, land close to Lisbon and make a quick march on the capital. As embarkation was bound to take some time, Charlie recommended him to start on it at once, meanwhile contracting his lines and concentrating all defence upon Oporto (Dom Pedro's lack of enthusiasm for Charlie was hardly surprising: the image of the conquering hero was considerably blurred by a badly inflamed and bandaged face – 'my head being wrapped up in flannel like a respectable old lady'.)

No definite answer came to his suggestions; Dom Pedro and Solignac said they would consider the matter. 'All the principal officers agreed with me,' Charlie told his wife, 'but Solignac is doing all he can to prevent anything going on, for fear of losing what he calls "la gloire".' Interview and counter-interview followed each other, but Charlie was in no doubt of the upshot, although impatient at the delay. There were nearby shell-bursts, and 'the town dreadfully cut up... It is a beautiful country and a pity it should be so destroyed. The business cannot last two months more, for want of funds, and nothing but my determination to go home if nothing is done, has an effect on them. The fleet is in tolerable order, and I shall get on well enough when once on board.'

By the evening of 10 May he had his way, and embarked at Foz, with batteries opening up on his boat from both banks of the river – 'between two fires, which to a person in safety would have been very beautiful, but to one in danger very unpleasant. I managed to get safe through the surf, with a boat's crew half of whom did not know how to pull their oars and could not have been worse had they been selected by Dom Miguel himself.'

The 500 men who followed also came through unhurt, 'though peppered most confoundedly'. The force, according to Lieutenant Bingham Hutchinson, consisted of '1500 troops, French and Portuguese, with 50 English lancers... The expedition left the bar of Oporto in four steamboats, three frigates, a small corvette, and a small brig... Some opposition was shewn at the embarkation; but was soon silenced by the fire of the frigate.'

By dint of constantly threatening to throw up the whole thing and take his steamships back to London, Charlie had at length found himself safely on board the *Rainha de Portugal,* commissioned as admiral and commander-in-chief, and permitted to carry out his plan. Captain Sartorius, with a sigh of relief, sailed for home, carrying a letter to Admiral Dundas from Charlie: 'Sartorius is a fine honourable fellow and has behaved nobly. He has been treated infamously, and I think it was impossible for a man to do more than he did. I hope you will reinstate him immediately.'

The *Rainha* was not a very impressive flagship, being merely a 46-gun frigate, but this did not prevent Charlie from issuing an impressive general order:

> On taking command of the squadron of Her Most Faithful Majesty, I feel proud in associating myself with so many gallant officers and men who have already so nobly distinguished themselves in the cause of freedom and the Queen. . .
>
> Should the enemy put to sea, you will know what to do with them. Should they remain in port, attacks will be made on various parts of the coast, and a general rising of the people against usurpation and tyranny is anticipated. My lads! We have battles to fight and great exertions to make. Preserve discipline and look up to your officers and we shall succeed. The eyes of every free man in Europe are on you. . .

But his command, as he wrote, was 'not a bed of roses'. He found his small squadron 'badly furnished in every species of store, with hardly a boat that could swim, not even two anchors and cables per ship, the men almost naked, and no means of clothing them'.

His first job was to escort, with his few frigates, the task force, under the Duque de Terceira, from Oporto to the Algarve, from whence they were to march slowly on Lisbon gathering support. A crowded party set forth, Charlie sharing his cabin with the two dukes, the fore cabin divided by a sail for the rest of the staff, while 'a party of students, serving as volunteers, had no other accommodation than a sail under the half-deck, and ship's provisions, and yet I never heard a grumble from them, they were all devoted to the cause they served and ready to put up with any hardship to advance it.' 'I really like the people,' he reported to his wife a week later. 'We sit down twenty to dinner every day', and he thought some of those on board 'the finest young men I ever saw'.

Euphoria prevailed as the ships proceeded south with a fair breeze. The task force was safely landed at Cacellas on 14 June, a few miles west of the mouth of the Guadiana, and began its advance on Lisbon, while the squadron kept pace along the coast with the slow but triumphant march on the capital. Anchored off Lagos on the 30th, Charlie wrote to his wife:

I go off to Lisbon and if the people will rise, I shall go right in and finish the business. [He was sending her home a hogshead of Madeira, and a monkey for his daughter, Fanny.] I have got rid of all my passengers, and we are getting into order rapidly. I like much better being an Admiral than a Captain. I interfere very little; though sometimes I break out; I hope to correct that. God Almighty bless you all.

Where, meanwhile, was the Miguelite squadron? It was reported off Cascaes – was this truth or rumour? On the morning of 30 July the officer of the watch reported two sails, then three, then four, finally nine. 'I was surprised and delighted,' Charlie wrote, 'but the delight was accompanied by a disagreeable sort of feeling, resembling the sensation of your heart coming up into your mouth and requiring a tolerable gulp to keep it down.'

Brought to bay off Cape St Vincent, the Miguelite fleet consisted of two line-of-battle ships, two frigates, three big corvettes and a brig, to Charlie's two frigates, one corvette, two brigs and a schooner – mounting between them 372 guns to Charlie's 176. 'They were a majestic sight, and although delighted at the prospect before me, I could not but feel appalled at their great superiority and the magnitude of the enterprise I was about to undertake.' As the steamers moved in to join him, Charlie tacked and stood towards the enemy, to prevent the steamers being cut off from him. The breeze this day and the next was too strong, and the sea too rough for him to attempt to board Dom Miguel's fleet, in which plan lay his only hope of success. All day on the 4th the sea ran high, and neither squadron fired a shot. At last, at daybreak on 5 June, the wind began to drop; by nine o'clock there was a dead calm which seemed likely to last, and Charlie resolved to engage.

At this point the steamers upon whom Charlie had counted to take his ships in tow entirely declined to draw the becalmed ships nearer the enemy 'unless two thousand pounds were laid down on the capstan head for each engineer. This being impossible, they were dismissed with hearty curses of officers and men.' Black Charlie longed for his *Galatea* paddles – 'never did I see before an occasion when they could have been more triumphantly employed.' And why not steam warships? Two miles apart, motionless in the calm, the two squadrons regarded each other impotently.

Charlie's luck held. By noon there were cat's-paws here and there over the blue expanse, the swell had subsided, and at one o'clock a steady breeze sprang up from the northward, with smooth water and a clear blue sky. He wrote to his wife:

> We shall very soon be at work. I can fancy your anxiety at Pulbrook, when you hear the fleet is out; and I know you would be delighted if you could see the beautiful sight I have now to leeward of me. I am very comfortable, and firm as a rock... Officers and ship's company staunch to the backbone.
>
> Your own, NAPIER

When the steamers failed him, Charlie had had to abandon his plan of laying alongside the *Dom John* with his *Rainha*, leaving the other line-of-battle ship to his frigate *Dom Pedro*, whilst the corvette *Donna Maria* took on the frigate *Princess Real*. He now hoped to separate the two line-of-battle ships and carry one before the other could come up.

> We were pretty certain of holding our prize, and I felt quite satisfied that Captain Peak in the *Donna Maria* would carry the *Princess Real*; while the Portuguese *Villa Flor* and *Fara* schooner should make the most they could of the *Martin Freitas*, leaving the enemy's three corvettes and two brigs in the hand of Providence, Who was sure to be on the side of the good cause.

He noted sardonically that the steamers took their station to windward, 'ready for a bolt should the day be lost'.

At lunchtime all his captains came on board to be re-briefed and cheer prevailed. Writing from the account of a surviving officer, Williams reported:

> They discussed the approaching action with the utmost confidence, little thinking that in half an hour three of the party would have ceased to live or be mortally wounded. They felt that they were Britons, engaged in a good cause, and about to fight in the same waters where their countrymen had won honour before, and that, great as were the odds against them, victory would assuredly be theirs.

Lieutenant Bingham Hutchinson, who later served under Black Charlie in 'Her Most Faithful Majesty's ship *Dom Joao* (76), ...

bearing the flag of His Excellency Dom Carlos da Ponza', whom he described as 'a taut hand', estimated the opposing forces as: Portuguese, 362 guns and 3,410 men, Charlie's squadron, 172 guns and 965 men. (This did not count the four steamers who had declined to take part.) 'When a breeze struck up in the afternoon, the Admiral immediately resolved to run alongside the enemy and board them. The *Rainha* led the Van.'

7

'We Rushed Aft with a Loud Cheer'

At two o'clock the captains returned to their ships, and the squadron, led by Charlie's *Rainha,* slowly edged away under their courses and top-gallant sails.

> The enemy looked well and firm, and they were plainly seen training their guns as we approached. It was a trying and awful sight, one accompanied with a considerable degree of dread (at least, I can answer for myself). Officers and men were calm and determined, though aware of the danger of the enterprise, the success of which mainly depended on the state we should be in after the first broadside.

All hinged upon them and their ships; the little army in the Algarve would peter out without support, and Oporto might not hold out much longer.

Ninety-eight guns opened up on Charlie's flagship as she drew into range, and the sea round the frigate boiled like a cauldron. 'Very much cut up by the fire of the whole line,' reported Lieutenant Bingham Hutchinson. Few of the gun's crews on the quarterdeck survived, the lieutenant of marines was killed, and so many sailors knocked out that Charlie himself was handling the ropes as them drew under the enemy flagship's stern. The other Miguelite line-of-battle ship, confusingly also called *Rainha,* luffed to, in order the letter to bring her starboard guns to bear on her namesake, but Charlie dodged under the greater *Rainha*'s stern, just as the *Dom John* bore up across her bows, hoping to sandwich the daring frigate between himself and his consort. This was what Charlie hoped too, and when the *Dom John* had gone too far to leeward to recover the weather position, Charlie changed tack, and pouring a full broadside into the enemy's *Rainha* in passing, ran alongside and made fast to her under a heavy musketry fire.

'The Admiral, dressed as a common sailor, followed by his officers and a few men, jumped on board,' wrote Hutchinson. 'I had not intended to board, but the excitement was too great, and I found myself on the enemy's forecastle,' Charlie told his wife, The ship's master was in like case, though it had been settled beforehand that neither was to do any such thing. But the ships had separated forward, after very few men had boarded, and the fighting was desperate, until the Master of the Fleet, running forward along the port gangway, 'from the fore-rigging threw the bight of a rope over the fluke of the *Rainha*'s waist anchor. This checked the ship alongside again, and the remainder of the men then scrambled on board, no easy matter from a low frigate to a high line-of-battle ship.'

'We rushed aft with a loud cheer,' Charlie wrote. They drove back a party drawn up on the break of the quarterdeck. At this point he was knocked out by a blow from a crowbar, but was up again and engaged with Barredas, captain of the Miguelite ship, 'wounded in the face and fighting like a tiger. He was a brave man.' Disarmed, Barredas was spared, but managed to re-arm and was subsequently killed fighting in his cabin. 'The second captain came next, and made so good-natured a cut at me that I had not the heart to hurt him; he also was spared.' The quarterdeck was now gained, and after further fighting on the main and lower decks, the remaining crew surrendered, having fought well and killed many of Charlie's men.

The little *Rainha*, with tottering masts, sails in shreds and one third of her complement either dead, wounded or manning the captured Miguelite line-of-battle ship, and with only Charlie, a midshipman and one wounded officer left in charge, now found herself alone with the line-of-battle ship *Dom John*. Hasty repairs were effected and, joined by the *Dom Pedro*, the frigate *Rainha* set forth in pursuit of the *Dom John*, which – mercifully for all concerned – decided to strike her colours. The *Donna Maria* had meanwhile carried the *Princess Real*, but the *Marin Freitas* had been too strong for the brigs, and was now rapidly making for Lisbon. But the brigs had succeeded in knocking away her fore topmast, and Charlie, leaving the *Dom Pedro* to accept the *Dom John*'s surrender, pursued and took the *Martin Freitas* at sunset. Two brigs and two corvettes escaped, but one of these joined Charlie's fleet next day. Altogether it was as complete a victory as he could have hoped for; by midnight the prizes – two ships of the line, a frigate and a corvette – were manned, their crews secured and the whole party in full sail for Lagos, almost the whole of whose population followed next day the funerals of the fallen, and loudly expressed their relief from 'the most unheard-of tyranny that ever oppressed a nation'.

Wild acclamations from the population were one thing, but Charlie baulked at the morrow's gesture, when a deputation of civic dignitaries in long gowns attempted to place a large laurel wreath around his neck. Having listened with admirable patience and dignity to a very long speech of congratulation in Portuguese, Charlie drew the line at the wreath. Becoming altogether obdurate, he refused to be talked over, 'shaking his head like a bull in a halter', and informing his benefactors 'that we were all heroes, and they were to put the wreath on the table and we would each have our share'. He pulled out a sprig and put it in his buttonhole, the rest doing likewise, 'and the beautiful wreath soon became a complete wreck,' an officer recorded. More acceptable was the reaction from home, where the capture in the cause of popular liberty of an 86-gun line-of-battle ship by a 46-gun frigate was certain to appeal.

Encouraged by the defeat of the threatening Miguelite fleet, Terceira, who had gradually taken hold of the Algarve, now made a bold push to Lisbon, crossing the Sierra Monchique and advancing on the capital through the Alemtejo. At Lagos, where he was harboured and repairing his ships, Black Charlie was greeted on the 12th by letters from a delighted Dom Pedro, telling him that he was now a full admiral in the Portuguese Navy, and making him Viscount Cape St Vincent. 'Very gratifying,' Charlie commented, but added ungraciously that he could have done without the latter honour.

From the badly damaged frigate *Rainha* Charlie had transferred his flag to the 80-gun *Dom John,* in which on the unlucky 13th, the newly made admiral was confronted by a more lethal enemy than any Dom Miguel – the dreaded scourge of cholera, 'owing to the extremely filthy state of the ship' wrote Hutchinson. So virulent was its form that seven men died that first night. 'A gloom came over the crew,' Black Charlie reported, and men who a fortnight earlier had fought like tigers in the action 'were now unmanned and unfit for any exertion'. In a week fifty had died, Black Charlie refusing to leave the stricken *Dom John* for a safer ship in spite of all pleas from his officers. He worried considerably over what might be happening at Lisbon in the week before the west winds seemingly blew the cholera clear. The ships had now to battle against contrary winds; it was the 24th before the *Dom John* made the mouth of the Tagus, where

Charlie learned to his relief that their failure to assist in the assault on Lisbon had not been fatal. Lisbon had capitulated to Terceira on the previous evening.

Amongst the lucky survivors the fun now became fast and furious. Every vessel in the harbour cheered Charlie's ships as they passed and 'at the Arsenal a huge crowd was assembled – the whole population drunk with joy. 'I was hailed as the Liberator of Portugal, cheered, kissed, and embraced by everybody,' Charlie told his wife. After five years of Miguel's tyranny, the liberated city went slightly mad. 'Lisbon does nothing but eat and drink and rejoice;' but if the Miguelites were to make the least push, thought Charlie, they could win back the city. Climax was reached on the return of Dom Pedro to his capital, from Oporto:

> before the steamer with the royal standard had passed Belem, the now peaceful waters of the Tagus bore on their surface all the beauty and fashion of Lisbon, hastening to meet and welcome the Emperor. . . and what with rockets, fireworks, and salutes from the batteries and ships, there was more powder burnt than would have fought a general action.

Dom Pedro seized upon Charlie, embracing him warmly and repeatedly in a series of hugs, put him on his right hand when they sang the Te Deum at the Largo Palace, and did likewise at the celebration dinner. From time to time Charlie urged on his hosts the need to put Lisbon in a state of defence, but no one stopped cheering to listen.

He wrote to his wife to stand by to join him, 'the moment I see there is no chance of our being driven out of Lisbon. I have got into an excellent house, and have also a box at the Opera. I am getting everything ready for you.' Her youngest son Charley's wounds were entirely healed up, and he was now captain of a splendid corvette. She was to let their cottage or keep it, as she pleased. There was no use bringing out a carriage, but he did want his horse, Sancho, to be of the party. On the 29th he wrote to Admiral Dundas explaining why he had not been able to appear at the Admiralty as requested on 5 July (the day of his action); 'so I suppose you have unshipped me.'

They had. Charlie had been struck off the Navy List; and a letter, addressed to Charles Napier, Esquire, told him that they had also removed his Greenwich pension, for services rendered and wounds received when fighting for his own country. Charlie, of course, protested at this latter, without avail; but letters from friends delighted with his action cheered him. From Paris, the generous Sartorius warmly congratulated Charlie on 'your noble and gallant action. . . To say that I do not envy you would be hypocrisy on my part. . . but upon an honester and better fellow such splendid good fortune never could have fallen. . . The cause of humanity has triumphed at last, thank God!'

'Well have you maintained your long and established character, as well as that of the British Navy,' wrote another friend. You have saved Portugal and immortalized yourself.' 'Yesterday we had a famous dinner here in celebration of your action,' William Grant, the banker, wrote from Portsmouth. 'Upwards of 100 dined. It went off very well. Your old friends are not a little proud, I assure you.' A lot of money had already been subscribed towards presenting Charlie with a testimonial, 'in commemoration of British valour. A large sum will be raised, and petitions to the King are being forwarded to restore so fair a name to the Navy List.' In the warmth of all this the cold douche from the Admiralty could almost be forgotten.

Meanwhile Dom Miguel's armies still occupied most of Portugal. Unopposed, they had reconquered the Algarve, while the fireworks of Lisbon were soaring high into the August sky above the capital. In the first week of September the Miguelist army, some 15,000 strong to the Constitutionalists 9,000, appeared before Lisbon, occupying the surrounding heights. Early on the morning of the 5th the Miguelite General Bourmont attacked the St Sebastian redoubts.

Black Charlie was by no means alone in his assessment of the situation. His cousin and namesake, Colonel Charles Napier, wrote:

> The struggle for freedom all over Europe seems to be brought into one small focus – Lisbon. It is not Pedro and Miguel, but Russia, Austria and Prussia against liberty; for if Pedro gains the cause is won; his people will hold him to his promises; if Miguel gains the cause is not lost but a long night of priestcraft will keep the Peninsula in chains . . . Has Pedro any man able to meet Bourmont? Bourmont is not a great general but he seems better than those opposed to him, for who have the Portuguese? Villa Flor brave, but no officer they say. Saldanha tolerable but he cannot be at Lisbon and Oporto too.

Colonel Charles was writing to his brother Henry; he himself had also been invited to help in the fighting in Portugal. Only the fact that he had recently been left a widower with two small daughters held him back, though he had written to Black Charlie for his advice:

> I might do much good, I might even turn the scale against Bourmont. Clouet I am not much afraid of. . . This is vanity, but then the offer came from the Constitutionalists in the first place, so it is they, not I, that overrate my military knowledge. I am not able to judge at a distance but I own I can trace no talent in their system of defence. [Charles went on to describe to his brother how he would defend Lisbon, which would be by attack and sortie and not sitting in the town.] I think they want science and enterprise . . . and that I have enough of both, for what is opposed to me, and therefore I could do good.

Colonel Charles had been in trouble with the home authorities by backing the Greeks and indeed helping them in their War of Independence, but his military reputation had spread, and he was known to be game to fight for freedom anywhere. 'Be assured,' he told Henry, the most peaceful of his brothers and one who looked deeply askance at war for war's sake, 'it is as much the cause of freedom as the Poles, the Portuguese are as brave a people.' (He had long fought alongside them in the Peninsular War.) Recently at war with Russia, the Poles had less good a cause, Charles thought, than the Portuguese. 'The Poles fought for feudalism, and had they gained were resolved not to free their peasants.'

Henry, travelling to Florence this autumn, in search of health for his delicate wife and children, found that Black Charlie's exploits had hit the European headlines and considerably sped him on his way – 'The French from respect, the Italians from fear'. Instead of the usual three or four hours of delay, the Italians had whistled him through the customs at Genoa as though he were a packet of high explosive. Tall and very fair and handsome, he could hardly have been less like Black Charlie in looks, but the fact of his being a naval captain and a Napier had been too much for their nervous systems, he reckoned.

Black Charlie, meanwhile, was concentrating on the job he had been given in Lisbon, that of reorganizing the Portuguese Navy, and trying very hard not to interfere in the land fighting. Not wholly successfully; he had been quite unable to resist visiting parts of Lisbon's outskirts where the fighting was hottest. Like a really good war correspondent, he remained permanently interested. Ever optimistic, he believed that as major-general of the naval arsenal at Lisbon he would soon remedy its lamentable condition – docks silted up with mud, half-finished ships rotting on the stocks, its workmen 'proverbial for their inefficiency and indolence. . . It was a receptacle for the blind, the lame, the lazy . . . they were sleeping about in all directions . . . anything like fatigue being quite out of the question.' However, he assured Dundas, he 'would soon put it to rights, and get up a small navy, ready to leather the Spaniards, should they be saucy'.

All might be sleepy in Lisbon, but things were happening elsewhere. Donna Maria da Gloria, the very young queen, had been recognized by the British government, Lord William Russell had been appointed Minister to her court, and she herself arrived from England on 22 September, to be greeted with more fireworks and trumpets, while her delighted father, Dom Pedro, summoned the Cortes to meet and greet her in October. 'I should not be surprised if they yet lost Lisbon,' Charlie grumbled to his wife; 'if they do, it will be by their own folly, and I will stay with them no longer if it happens.' But Charlie, with his usual luck, or common sense, had plumped for the right side. That it was the winning one was largely due to his personal exertions.

Fortunately for Black Charlie, Palmerston was afraid of French influence in Spain and knew that Talleyrand wanted an Anglo-French military alliance. He also knew that British opinion would not support such a thing. But it was prudent, he considered, to work with France, and so he formed an alliance between Britain, France, Spain and Portugal, which, although not worth as much as his hoped for 'powerful counterpoise' to the three absolute monarchies of eastern Europe, would prevent separate action by France in Spain. He rushed this treaty through the Cabinet somewhat on Black Charlie's lines – 'by a *coup-de-main*, taking them by surprise. . . a capital hit, all my own doing,' Palmerston reported. Great Britain was thus brought in, and Dom Miguel in the end was to be forced to leave. His followers stayed quiet, and in 1836 Queen Maria Gloria was to marry a Saxe-Coburg.

Meanwhile the Miguelite assault on Lisbon failed, and Dom Miguel, still in command of a considerable army and occupying most of Portugal, settled down to blockade on either side of the Tagus as well as on the landward side of the city. Guerrilla bands acting mainly on the part of Dom Miguel continued to ravage the Algarve and places north, committing the usual atrocities, and Black Charlie had to content himself with the despatch of fifty British marines backed by a frigate to save Lagos, which the guerrillas were besieging. As winter came on many of the Miguelite troops deserted, sneaking off home in the darkness; and though Saldanha was able to push the remainder back as far as Santarem, he did not follow up the victory.

On 23 February 1834 the other Charles wrote to his brother Henry:

> Like you I cannot believe Black Charles is inactive with his own goodwill. All I fear for him is his quitting his own element. Sailors do not get on well in their soldiering I think. Only for my girls I would run over for a few days and see what they are doing, and without listing I might find out what is the cause of this check. I hardly know anything for I never see a paper.

But this did not prevent the other Charles from deciding that Jerome ought to be disposed of, though he conceded that 'Count Bourbell seems to be a gentleman'. Colonel Charles was still mourning his wife, lost seven months earlier – 'I always knew it would be terrible to me, but I did not know *how* terrible. . . I hope I shall go on with the children's education, but I have not much genius for it. . .'

He was wrong in thinking that Black Charlie would never make a soldier. By March this impetuous character had lost patience. In the first flush of his arrival in Lisbon, Dom Pedro had urged Charlie always to speak his mind to him. By December Charlie could no longer resist doing just this, very freely; telling the Emperor 'that there was much discontent, that he was losing his popularity, that there would be a reaction and that his Minister of Marine was a blockhead [letter to Colonel Hodges, 20 December 1833]'. Dom Pedro may have listened, but he did not respond. Charlie described him to Hodges as 'a good man, but ill-advised and obstinate'.

The coming of spring made for no military stir at Lisbon. By March, Black Charlie had won a reluctant consent to his making an attempt on the northern ports, still in Miguelite hands. He was doing what he had told his wife he would not do – 'putting his head where he had no business'. On 16 March he sailed for Setubal with 120 British marines and 40 seamen, where he hoped to pick up the Portuguese marines garrisoning the place, with a view to an attack on Figueras. But at Setubal a nasty surprise awaited him – 'It is his Imperial Majesty's orders that the Admiral return immediately to

Lisbon in the *City of Edinburgh*.' 'My return will have a bad effect,' Charlie countered. 'I shall proceed to my destination.'

'This war was unlike all other,' he was to write, excusing himself; 'so much intriguing and vacillation constantly at work that it was necessary for officers to take much on themselves, or give up altogether.'

It was not an easy enterprise. From the Tagus north to the Minho the Portuguese coast is a difficult place for a landing, owing to the Atlantic swell that breaks upon it at all seasons. On 18 March Charlie found that the high surf at Setubal made a landing impracticable. So it was on to the mouth of the Minho, where he landed with sailors, marines and two field guns, and captured Caminha. He was flushed with this success:

> I beat to arms and marched on Fifo, leaving a garrison of one hundred men in Caminha, with orders to patrol on the Velanca Road and organise a force in the town. Here, then, I started, mounted on my charger, a wicked pony that had belonged to the governor, my staff on mules and donkeys or whatever they could find, opening my first campaign at the head of five hundred Portuguese and English marines and sailors, as well pleased as the Duke of Wellington at the head of his army.

Not exactly like Wellington, as they proceeded along the shore with the guns of the *Dom Pedro* and *City of Edinburgh* in support to keep attackers at bay. Capturing Lima, Charlie proclaimed the constitution in the town square and had the appropriate hymn played; adjuring the inhabitants in a proclamation to live together peaceably and not to pay off old scores. Encouraged by his presence, there was now a sortie from Oporto, two more towns were taken, and Charlie felt strong enough to take the considerable fortress of Valença, which he acquired by landing guns and mortars from the *Dom Pedro,* and by a time-honoured *ruse de guerre;* deceiving its garrison into thinking he had more men than he really had. 'I have much enjoyed my campaign,' he wrote delightedly to his wife, 'and we have done wonders with a handful of sailors and marines.'

Portugal continued to entrance him − 'this is one of the finest countries I ever beheld.' The Portuguese general from Oporto scored an equal success; in three weeks he and Charlie had taken all the country between the Douro and the northern boundary. In a box at the opera in Oporto Charlie received further acclamations, and more trouble with laurel wreaths; and 'To my utter astonishment and dismay, two little children came into the box and clapped a naval crown on my head, which of course I took off.'

Returning to Lisbon, and a further brush with the Minister of Marine, he was off again campaigning by the first week in May, landing at Figuerada da Foz, which capitulated, though Charlie experienced considerable difficulty in getting his men ashore. From there he marched to the old Moorish fortified town of Ourem, defiant and well-garrisoned; but by now news of the treaty between the powers had arrived and Charlie summoned the governor to surrender:

> If you uselessly defend the place and spill Portuguese blood, you will be held personally responsible. There is now no point of honour, because there is not the least possibility of being of service to Dom Miguel. I have with me the same men who took the fleet of 5 July; they are ready to receive you as friends, but you will find them devilish unpleasant enemies.

Things got as far as scaling ladders next morning; but these produced the flag of truce. By Ourem Charlie advanced to Galega on the Tagus, where he joined the Liberal army.

The advance party, led by himself, was perhaps a little less impressive than he hoped. Observed by the Marques da Frontera (quoted by Jorge de Oliveria in his memoirs), 'the brave Admiral cantered up upon a farmer's big mare, on his head a plumed cocked hat, a Portuguese Admiral's old coat, the trousers pushed up to the calves, very dusty, unshaven and unwashed, with a big cutlass hanging from his belt'. To an unusual degree Charlie combined a love of the picturesque with a total disregard of what he himself looked like. 'He was accompanied by 2 Aides-de-Camp, one English and one Portuguese, both naval officers astride mules.' (Da Frontera thought they looked like two pilots, navigating inland.) 'The escort was very extraordinary: four English sailors, a little the worse for brandy, and very badly mounted.' They were strung around with cutlasses and had carbines slung across their pack saddles. Charlie at any rate seemed as happy as a king, and da Frontera thought that the whole party was much disappointed to hear that the fighting was over. Retreating from Santarem, Dom Miguel had been finally defeated at Asseiceva by the Duke of Terceira, forced to resign his claim to the throne and leave Portugal forever. This was the only really decisive battle of the civil war, and Black Charlie was very sorry to miss it.

Singular-looking or not, Black Charlie had endeared himself to his colleagues in the Liberal army, and had already been made a Grand Commander of the Order of the Town and Sword. The little Queen of Portugal, 'fair and small and plump', proceeded to make him Visconde de Sao Vicente, and later Conde Napier de Sao Vicente. In England Charlie made no attempt to use this title, but in her old age his daughter Fanny Jodrell proudly called herself Lady St Vincent, despite the prior claim of the great John Jervis.

Peace had come, but Charlie found it impossible to introduce any permanent order into a service so rotted with intrigue and corruption as the Portuguese Navy; his major task was done and he resigned and went home. He had been foolish, he told Dundas, to suppose that single-handed reform of a corruption so well entrenched would be possible. But the Portuguese as a whole treated him and his family with much warmth and kindness. He paid them a visit a few years later, partly to collect debts still owing to his men and to himself, partly to' renew old friendships. He found himself swept into the near-public *accouchement* of Queen Maria, who had now married her Saxe-Coburg (that ever useful house with its supply of royal bridegrooms both Protestant and Catholic).

The entire government and *corps diplomatique* were assembled outside Queen Maria's bedroom with the door open; here they remained from eight o'clock until eleven thirty, when the birth of a son and heir was announced. 'We were all ushered into the bedroom, about forty in number, where, lo and behold! seated in a chair was the Queen of Portugal, looking as if nothing had happened!' Charlie felt moved to kiss her hand; and 'I could not help shedding tears,' he admitted. They then sat down to 'a very excellent dinner', and went home through a blaze of illuminations. 'She conducted herself like a Trojan throughout,' Charlie thought admiringly, and well deserving of the throne he had helped her to win.

8

Frustration

From Portugal Black Charlie had told his wife of his intention of 'buying a place and resting in quiet for the remainder of my life'. Buy an estate he did, with a Regency house at Catherington that had previously been known as Cherry Grove; nostalgically he re-named it Merchiston after the family stronghold that his forebears had built in the 1400s. The rest of the improbable programme never stood a chance. Charlie was at once involved in another fight for one of the Portsmouth Parliamentary seats, helped by his cousin and namesake.

'The Whigs are trying to get the Duke assassinated by their power of the press,' the soldier Charles wrote to his brother Henry on 14 December 1834. 'Cobbett in his letter to Hume says "You are all very Furious at the Duke and say he cannot execute the Reform Bill because he opposed it before it was law."' They were very much mistaken in their man, Charles thought.

> I am delighted at the Whigs being upset. Happen what may, that is an immortal act in the Duke, far beyond the battle of Waterloo. The rage they are in is delightful. We are working on two Whig members in Portsmouth like hell. I trust that Black Charles and Admiral Rowley will upset them; the people are sure to gain for the Whigs will be obliged to be radicals to get in again; and if the Duke will not be so, to stay in, he will be upset. I am sadly afraid he is damned savage about Ireland and will play hell there; however, let us see. He has done more to reform in deeds than all the infamous Whigs put together; still we must have an eye upon him for his rascally companions will scrim him if he lets them. Peel's declaration is humbug; the country won't stand it; it is worthy of a Whig, all general declaration.
>
> Altogether we are in a ticklish way for the Whigs and Tories but a certain progressive one for the people.

Was there a chance that Black Charlie would get in for Portsmouth and be able to press his naval reforms from the vantage point of a seat in the Commons?

Down the centuries of British history a clash of swords on the forecastle had never failed to appeal to the public; and if Black Charlie could not in the 1830s leap from a British quarterdeck onto the poop of an enemy ship, he did himself no harm by leaping from a Portuguese one in the interests of popular government. His boarding and carrying in action of the *Rainha,* 86 guns, by a frigate of 46 guns had had a strong national appeal. It gave him a good press – 'the victory of the forces of liberalism over reaction and tyranny' – and there had been cheers and civic receptions when he landed at Portsmouth. Lord Grey defended him in the House, and though his cause with the limited Portsmouth electorate still seemed unlikely to win, his naval action won him more votes than had his offers to reform local abuses. But they were still not enough to take him to Westminster.

Admiration for him was far from unanimous. Lord Londonderry, who had been backing Dom Miguel on the grounds that his opponents were as bad as the Chartists, had Black Charlie struck out of the Navy List for his victory over that Dom; while Lord Eldon, the crustiest Tory in a House not startlingly liberal, declared that this fate was far too good for him; hanging would have been a preferable solution. Generous Captain Sartorius, whom Charlie had relieved in Portugal, admired his victory greatly, and Black Charlie's family stood firmly by him. 'I now think you an abler fellow than ever before, and I did not think small beer of you then,' wrote William Napier, the Peninsular historian, and Charles senior echoed his praise.

One figure, influential if no longer powerful, remained implacably against Charles the Black. Publicity over Portugal reminded his sovereign of Charlie's shortcomings and abrupt manners to him in his midshipman days. Alive as the captain was to the wrongs and, hardships of seamen, he had very little patience with young officers who lorded it needlessly over experienced men when they themselves scarcely knew one rope from another. From time to time Prince William had been sharply reprimanded, and he never forgot or forgave it. This summer the President of the Royal Academy was so rash as to urge the visiting King William to take a look at a recent portrait of Black Charlie. Thomas Raikes recorded in his journal the royal response to this suggestion: 'Captain Napier may be damned, Sir! And you may be damned, Sir!' And although Palmerston had written that 'to defeat the Holy Alliance in the arena which they themselves have chosen would be no common victory', Black Charlie's association with the enterprise damned it in the eyes of King William.

Philip Ziegler writes:

> It was Charles Napier, late of the Royal Navy and now Pedro's admiral, who routed the Miguelites and restored his new master's position. His feats were a credit to the service in which he had been trained, but the King, somewhat surprisingly, took the achievements of this 'unprincipled Firebrand and Adventurer of the most dangerous description' as a personal affront. The fact that Pedro owed his survival to Napier did much to disenchant the King with his cause.

Royal strictures, freely uttered, did little to burnish Black Charlie's public image, or to help him on his thorny pathway towards the accomplishment of reforms in the Navy. He had always suffered from the delusion that if you are doing right it matters not how tactlessly you go about it. He had his friends and admirers within the Navy, but also his detractors and ill-wishers in the ranks of power. Impotent frustration seemed his likely lot; his passion to reform the administration of the Navy remained unsatisfied and seemed likely to stay that way.

Aside from a considerable difference in mental calibre, Black Charlie in the mid-1830s was not unlike Winston Churchill in the mid-1930s – a forceful figure unwillingly debarred from the activity he craved, writing the history of his Portugal campaign, vigorously and incessantly pursuing policies with which few others agreed, cheered and soothed by a charming and beloved wife and by the delights of painting and country living. Like Churchill he uttered dire and unheeded warnings of coming peril. Like him, Charlie allowed no time for repining. He wrestled with litigation ensuing upon his capture of vessels during the war in Portugal, drove a four-in-hand with gusto all over the Hampshire roads, broke two ribs in a hunting accident and regularly assaulted the Admiralty with his unheeded letters.

Charlie's book, *Account of the War in Portugal,* came out to muted enthusiasm from the press, who told him that he was 'too late in the field', he should have realized that 'as far as the public were concerned, the subject was exhausted'. The *Athenaeum* dismissed the book in six lines; the *Quarterly* and the *Edinburgh Review* didn't bother with it. Charles's unceasing efforts and those of his friends to have his name replaced on the Navy List met with no success. But his two first cousins, Charles and William, both wrote admiringly of his book and of the deeds it recorded. Charles said that he had at first thought that Charlie should have given the book to William to write, 'because he could have given more just praise to you than you do yourself', but had changed his mind on reading it; Charlie's account was stamped with an authority and originality that no other man could give it. . . Your works ashore appear to me to have been done with as much ability as your works at sea, and were much more difficult.'

Family loyalty from men whose opinion Charlie valued was cheering and supportive, but it was not enough. He managed to publish two papers, one on 'Impressment', which he described as 'an un-English and tyrannical custom', and another on 'Manning the Navy'. In the summer he travelled to Scotland, not just to mourn over the ruin of his old home but to seek out his father's old servants and particularly his still surviving nanny, Mary Miller, and to buy annuities for them. The Portuguese adventure had at least made generosity possible.

Things looked up in 1836. 16 March saw Charlie's reinstatement 'on the list of Captains of the Royal Navy, with your original seniority, and that your half-pay shall commence from the date of the said Order in Council'. So far, so good. In July came an invitation to stand for Parliament at Greenwich, against Mr Barnard, and the Conservative, Mr Attwood, chairman of the General Steam Navigation Company. Barnard was a certainty; 'and the contest was in fact, between the gallant captain, in the Liberal interest, and Mr Attwood, the new Conservative candidate,' wrote Earp in his *Life and Exploits of Commodore Napier*.

> At the nomination a scene of most tremendous uproar and confusion took place. A large party of persons employed by the General Steam Navigation Company crowded round the hustings, and by their vociferations and shouts prevented anybody but their candidate from being heard. Captain Napier, when he presently appeared, endured the storm with great good humour

and patience. His pithy and characteristic declaration of principle was audible only to the friends immediately surrounding him; but even this was too great a privilege to be enjoyed, for first came a lump of mud, and then a sort of independent firing of stones, till at length a general volley was given, which cleared the hustings.

Charlie was not one to put up with this one-sided business. 'On the second day Captain Napier ... brought over from the *Medea* steam frigate a party of seventy or eighty seamen under the boatswain, who soon procured for the gallant captain a fair field in his favour.' A hearing secured, Black Charlie embarked once again on his peroration, though attention was a little distracted by one of his sailors 'seated on the top of the penthouse which covered the hustings, waving one of the colours taken from Dom Miguel's fleet in the action off Cape St Vincent. Three sturdy bargemen climbed up the supporters, for the purpose of dislodging this venturesome Napierite'; one by one they went tumbling to the ground, which 'excited much amusement, and was considered an omen of the gallant officer's success'. To no avail; for a third time Charlie remained the defeated candidate.

Warned perhaps by his earlier experience of flying mud, Charlie's appearance on polling day was very far from smart. He wore an old blue frock coat with naval brass buttons and trousers which frequent washings had turned grey rather than white. His large buckled shoes were well-patched, his white socks darned and, right on the back of his head, was a round hat with a bent brim. 'On his left breast dangled a profusion of orders blazing in their brilliancy,' the eyewitness recorded; but these served only to underline his general indescribably unsmart appearance, despite his lively looks, bright eyes, bold features and general aspect of toughness and courage.

And there stood, pelted by the bargemen of Greenwich, the man on whose cool head, ready hand, and unflinching heart had depended the destinies of a nation; one who had gained more victories, and made more captures, with less loss of life, than any man had ever done before; a man quick to plan, prompt to execute – whose very rashness was a carefulness of consequences, and who, when he struck a blow, always weighed how much depended upon that blow being at once decisive.

The shouting died down, the bargemen went home to their teas, the grey river rolled on past the magnificent buildings that Wren had erected for King Charles, to house his ancient sailors. The lights on the Isle of Dogs began to prick out through the misty dusk. For Black Charlie, driving home through the gathering darkness with the powerful river smell of the Thames still in his nostrils, it was just another failure.

All the same, the Government decided that something was due to Black Charlie for fighting such a hopeless election on their behalf; and forgiving him his curious earlier aberrations about ironclads and steam vessels, they offered him command of the *Hercules*. This, with characteristic contrariness, he refused, on the grounds that all his applications for a job and promotion for his stepson, who had done extremely well in the Portuguese affair, besides having other recommendations, had been turned down. Lord Minto was to be told 'that I wanted Charley Elers Napier to be made up, in preference to giving me anything at present'. This and a subsequent fuss he made when, on his award of a good service pension, an inadequate account of his services was printed in the Naval Estimates, was one of those unlucky occasions when his quirkiness over matters not really of immense moment overlaid his truly urgent causes and made authority far less ready to consider these.

Lord Minto, 'to whom he gave his sentiments in the most decided manner, ... declined to make him reparation'; a bored but kindly Melbourne assured him that it was all a mistake, and no slight was intended; Palmerston 'was very civil, but said it was out of his department'. With injudicious persistence, Black Charlie hung on. His honour, in his view, had been impugned. 'Who steals my purse steals trash, but whoso filches from me my good name' etc: the preoccupation of Victorian gentlemen with their personal honour was obsessive, and not without virtue or value. Friends in the Commons took up Charlie's cause; and on 6 March 1838 he wrote joyfully to his wife from London:

I have gained a complete triumph, as you will see by your papers. Sir Charles Adam and Troubridge got up and said it was quite a mistake, and that my services stood higher than that of any officer in the service. William Gordon however would not let them off, and said they ought to have stated them fully.

Wemyss, Codrington, Captain Jones and Deans Dundas also spoke in my favour, so that on the whole, I have come off with flying colours.

The authorities might be increasingly bored with this peppery naval character, but in general his fellow officers approved of Charlie's stand.

Having settled this matter, Black Charlie let fly a few more verbal broadsides. Joseph Hume, MP, was getting up a fuss in the Commons about the promotion of titled officers. Charlie thought the protest snobbish and ridiculous; what did it matter, if they were good and efficient officers ? More sensibly, Hume was also in protest against the huge numbers of admirals and captains; but, Charlie pointed out, 'of 161 admirals only 12 were under 60, and of 702 captains, 160 were over sixty, and many more over 50'. As far as the active Navy was concerned, these were a dead loss. Let no one in the Commons imagine that these ages mattered as little at sea as in Parliament.

There is a great difference between the command of a Fleet and a seat in the House of Commons; a man of sixty may talk to the House for two or three hours, though exposed to the wit, the sarcasm, and the yawns of his opponents, and still preserve the nerve and power of oratory much beyond that age; but an Admiral in command of a Fleet has not only his enemy to look after, but he has charge of that fleet against rocks, shoals, leeshores, storms and tempest, and it requires youth and health to support him in all his difficulties. [As to aristocracy] Why, Sir, there are only six aristocratic names in the whole naval promotion, and God knows, the present Ministry have no great reason to support that body. . .

Already a long shadow seemed to Charlie to be spreading across Europe. Mr Hume was all for economies, and rightly so; but did Mr Hume suppose that we had no enemies?

Are you aware that the Russians had 28 sail of the line in the Baltic the summer before last, ready for sea, and a squadron of 8 sail, with a proportion of frigates and smaller vessels constantly cruising, and we had not one frigate on the home station? . . . Be assured, all sides are tired of your pounds shillings and pence, when they tend to impair the efficient force of the country.

Nothing had yet been done about the manning of the fleet. In March of 1837 Charlie had addressed a long letter on the subject to Lord Minto. Quoting Andrew Jackson's farewell speech to Congress which, apart from its reference to 'our overflowing revenue', applied word for word to Britain, he asked Minto 'Whether we have, during a long peace, done one single act for the better encouragement of our naval officers and seamen', and assured him that we had not. Charlie went on to repeat his earlier and unheeded points, adding that, apart from Graham's Registration Bill, nothing had been done about the manning of a fleet in the event of war. Things were as ever: 'Recourse must be had to that infamous, oppressive, and most abominable of all measures – impressment. Your Lordship is not aware, nor is the country aware, of the extent of the evil, or it never would be tolerated for a moment.'

Charlie's counter-suggestion, that all seamen should be obliged to serve three years in a ship of war before they could become able-bodied seamen in the merchant navy, 'I have no doubt would be objected to as encroaching on the liberty of the subject; but it bears no comparison to impressment.' And not without passion, Charlie launched into an indictment of this hated system:

> Should war take place tomorrow, and press-warrants be issued, the whole of the seamen would instantly disappear, and an im-mediate stop be put to trade. Captains and officers, naturally anxious to man their ships, would be seen prowling about in the sea-ports at night to entrap any unfortunate fellow who might venture abroad. Houses where seamen were supposed to be con-cealed would be broken open in the most violent manner; resis-tance would be made on the part of crimps and seamen; and scenes of riot and bloodshed would take place, disgraceful to a free country. Men would be torn from their wives and families whether they were seamen or not, and secured on board the tender, and would no longer be heard of, unless they were found useless.
>
> The worst characters are generally employed as press-gangs, and care little about either law or justice.
>
> One would suppose, since such cruel measures are adopted to force men into the service, rewards would be given to induce them to remain. Not at all. Last war many men never set their foot on shore; their pay was bad, and even when advanced to

petty officer, the augmentation was so trifling that many men preferred remaining as ABs. When they came into port, instead of finding relaxation, they had harder work to perform. If abroad, they got no pay: if at home, they had the pay in one hand and the topsail sheet in the other. The Jews and vagabonds of all descriptions were alone benefited by it. Situations in the dockyards were rarely given to good men; their only hope was Greenwich Hospital when no longer fit for service... after twenty-two years of deliberation at the Admiralty nothing has been done, by any Board, for the permanent manning of the Navy.

Black Charlie himself, given a free hand, would offer bounties on enlistment, freedom to depart after ten years' service and a good pension after fifteen years. Surplus naval men, passed-over lieutenants, pursers, clerks, midshipmen to be retired and offered jobs as clerks in all naval establishments; not at once, but when these became vacant – 'They should be filled by men who had actively served the king, and who certainly have a greater right to a comfort-able berth than civilians who know nothing about the service.' Ten years service in any of the king's ships should exempt men from any further call.

Should these regulations be adopted, the Admiralty would have abundance of opportunities of rewarding old and meritorious officers whom they could not promote; and our seamen, instead of going to America, would stay at home, and having completed their time in a ship of war, would man our merchant ships, and teach the young apprentices that there was nothing dreadful in the naval service, and that if they conducted themselves well they were sure to be rewarded.

Outside, the March winds blew round the house at Catherington, and Black Charlie waited in vain for a command to be offered him. But all that was offered him was occasion for a further assault on the sensibilities of the authorities, when in 1838 a commission was ap-pointed, with the Duke of Wellington at its head, to enquire into the state of the Army and Navy. Its pens and ink were hardly collected, its sheets of paper barely laid out, before Charlie weighed in with his habitual emphasis. How great a nuisance and busybody he appeared to the authorities at this time is not clear, nor would it have seriously

influenced Charlie, hoping with his constant dripping of water to
wear away a stone, and undeterred by the rebuffs and indifference
that were his invariable answers.

'It may be thought great presumption in so humble an individual
as myself. . . but I do it from a conviction, that if things are allowed
to continue in their present state, a great catastrophe will befall this
country.' He pleaded once more for a reform of the Board of Admiralty; 'I trust a strenuous effort will now be made to rescue the
Navy from political thraldom. . . The Navy should be governed by
a naval officer' – and not by a Cabinet minister who, in his possibly brief term of office, was too busy appointing and promoting his
friends and relations to have much time for anything else.

He pleaded also for the neglected individual:

> A naval officer has no person to whom he can speak officially.
> The junior Lords shelter themselves under the First Lord, and he
> again under the Board. . . I know at present many gallant of-
> ficers who have been severely wounded in the service, and who
> have been constant in their application for employment, receiv-
> ing the dry unfeeling letter that their applications are noted for
> consideration at a favourable opportunity.

And Black Charlie pictured them, as he had so often known them, in
poor little seaport lodgings, breaking the seals and opening the Admiralty letter with so much hope and longing, only to discover hope's
sickening deferment. 'And when they come to the top of the list they
are superannuated, because they have never served.'

Charlie admitted that naval gunnery at least had improved, 'but in
everything else we have gone back. . . Lord Collingwood (and he was
no bad authority) complained in his letters of line-of-battle ships not
having more than two or three officers who knew their duty; if that
was the case in war, how much more must it be now in peace.' There
was a lack of zeal in the younger officers, and 'as for seamanship,
they know nothing about it. . . the discipline, the zeal, the energy,
created by war are gone by.' Of course there were exceptions, but
'in general, there were now nothing but lackadaisical young officers
who obtained promotion through powerful interest. . . and old officers broken-hearted and disappointed and almost without hope of
promotion', a combination that did not make for an effective fighting
force.

He seemed never to lose heart; or the confidence that because what

he advocated was right and fair it would all in due course be put into
execution. In April he was writing to Melbourne – 'and I trust you
will give it a patient perusal. Other nations are making such exertions to improve their navies, and to establish a systematic plan for
manning them, that it appears to me absolutely necessary that this
country should do something. . .' He outlined his plans for recruit-
ment and training once again. In August Palmerston was his target: 'I
observe the French are greatly strengthening their squadron in the
Gulf of Mexico, and from the nature of their armament, there cannot
be a doubt but they intend attacking St John de Ulloa', and if everybody thought that fortress was impregnable, they had another think
coming. 'I know the Admiral – he is young and enterprising; if he
takes St John de Ulloa, Vera Cruz will be at his mercy, and they may
probably make a second Algiers of it.'

The editor of the *Sun* was the next to catch it; in September he had
published a letter from an anonymous character called 'Stoker' who
held that if Russia showed signs of sending her armada to Leith
or London, Britain could have 200 armed steamers at sea within a
week who would tow into our harbours 'every ship of the enemy'.
He was duly chewed up by Black Charlie. What made Stoker think
that armadas announced their forthcoming appearance? They just
appeared. Was Stoker 'really serious in believing that in one week we
could collect two hundred steamers, strengthen them for guns, make
magazines, provision them, store them, and man them with between
20,000 and 30,000 men, and then train them to fire shot and shells in
one week?' Silence fell upon the September musings of Stoker.

The French would always be with us – difficult, touchy, secre-
tive, tricky, up to no good, concerned wholly with France and her
gloire; the idea of them as the everlasting enemy died hard. But Black
Charlie was all the same aware of them as members of the same club;
he thought Russia the real enemy of Western civilization. They were
the Scythians, whom Greek and Romans had feared and hated, the
outsiders, the bully of Eastern Europe and its peoples and now expanding beyond their own Eastern frontiers as fast as they could go,
and certainly up to no good in the Levant.

By the end of 1838 there was a smell of danger in the air. Whether
in order to shut him up, or whether they felt in need of all the Black
Charlies they could lay their hands on, at the end of the year Black
Charlie was given command by the Admiralty of the 84-gun *Powerful*. He was ecstatic. *Powerful* was commissioned on the first day of

1839. Two months later she was ready for sea, though still considerably under-manned. The four horses of Black Charlie's four-in-hand were put out to grass as he himself put out to sea, butting down-Channel against the equinoctial gales, happy as only a long-grounded sailor in such circumstances could be.

9
Lebanon

In the 1830s the situation in the eastern Mediterranean was, as so often, menacing and obscure. The Turks were failing, Egypt was rising, and Britain and France, still potent in the region, were dominated by their fear of Russia, and of the steely Czar, Tennyson's 'Icy Muscovite', who seemed as terrifying in his day as Stalin was to seem in his. Russian arms held Poland in a death-clamp and were about to embrace Tartary; her heavy shadow lay over Persia, even over India – hence over British minds. The forepaws of the bear stretched from the North Cape to Ararat, from Lvov to Samarkand. To save the Levant from Russia's clutch, the Western powers had all but sacrificed Greece; to prop up the tottering Ottoman Turkish Empire was felt to be a prime necessity. It was a dyke whose collapse would drown every land between the Black Sea and the Indian Ocean, between the Dardanelles and the source of the Nile.

The writings of Pushkin, Turgenev and Tolstoy had yet to teach the West that Russia was not all barbarism. The Czar's total power over his brave voiceless millions made his country seem terrible. To William Napier, then writing, Russia was 'the most formidable and brutal, the most swinish tyranny that has ever menaced and disgraced European Civilization', and the whole of his generation remembered how the Russians in the Napoleonic wars had cut off their prisoners' heads, and peed all over everyone's drawing room at the time of the peace conferences. The Russians who came into the political or educated worlds of the West were few, and those that did spoke French, repudiated the tongue of their homeland and loudly deplored its barbarities. Russia was the land of the serf and the *knout;* her immense centralized power made her 'the cornerstone of despotism in the world'. Ambassadors told stories of the fun and glitter of St Petersburg, the wide streets with their stately buildings, and of the gleaming and mysterious beauty of the Orthodox rite; but travellers into the interior of this unknown country brought back other tales.

'Inept for everything,' announced one Frenchman, 'except for the conquest of the world.' And only too apt, it was felt, for that.

The troubled waters of the Levant afforded splendid fishing grounds for anyone with imperial ambitions. Mohammed Ali, the brilliant and ambitious Albanian who had become master of Turkish-held Egypt, threatened Syria and was thought to have designs on the Ottoman throne at Constantinople. He was backed by Czar Nicholas. The French, with their usual refreshing single-mindedness and moral nakedness, were secretly aiding both Mohammed Ali *and* the Turks, hoping to win out in the Eastern Mediterranean whatever happened, since nothing could conceivably be more beneficial for any people than to come under French sway and adopt the French way of life. The British, whose opportunism was laced with a genuine desire to help other countries to be themselves, invited charges of hypocrisy and confused everyone else.

Hesitant, cagey, and often at odds with each other, Britain, France and Austria decided in 1839 that the sustaining of Turkey was still their best bet (despite their Christian disapproval of Turkish harems, and the deprecation by other ruling monarchs of the Sultan's habit of sewing up unfaithful wives in sacks and dumping them in the Bosphorus overnight). With this general end in view, it seemed wise in the early months of this year to dispatch a few three-deckers in the direction of the troubled Levant.

They found a dangerous situation. Advancing into Palestine in November 1831, the Egyptian army under Ibrahim Pasha (who was Mohammed Ali's adopted son), assisted by an Egyptian fleet commanded by one of Napoleon's ex-officers, had taken Acre, and from thence gone on to conquer Jaffa, Gaza, Jerusalem and Damascus. In July 1832 Ibrahim's army inflicted resounding defeats on the Turkish forces at Homs and at Hammah; he entered Aleppo on the 17th, won a further victory over the Turks at Alexandretta and pushed forward into Asia Minor as far as Adana. The Ottoman throne had scarcely ever been more seriously threatened.

At this point the Russians offered Turkey their help, which the suspicious Sultan refused. A similar offer from the French, who had not endeared themselves to Moslems by their recent conquest of Algiers, received a similarly dusty answer. The British, for once, hesitated to go it alone.. A summer somnolence settled over the eastern Mediterranean's stony hills and brilliant blue waters, the armies enjoying a kind of four-month-long siesta. But by the end of the year Ibrahim of Egypt had defeated yet another Turkish army and was within a hundred miles of the Sea of Marmora.

The Sultan's nerve broke at this point: he accepted Russian help, and on 20 February 1833 a Russian squadron of nine ships entered the Bosphorus and anchored within sight of long-desired Constantinople.

To their credit Britain and France struggled hard over the next years to bring Turks and Egyptians to terms; and Mohammed Ali, whose official position, however rebellious, was still Viceroy of Egypt under the Sultan, was at length persuaded to be content with Syria, Aleppo and Adana. The Russians meanwhile slipped another two squadrons and 5,000 soldiers into their fleet in the Bosphorus.

Britain and France now strove more or less openly to resist Russian designs, and Turkey and Egypt flexed their muscles and built up their fleets. By 1839 Egypt had twelve brand-new battleships and the Turks almost as many. Neither wished to be openly aggressive, but the Egyptians backed rebellions against the Turks in Albania and Crete, and the Turks equally backed rebellions against Egypt in Syria. At one point the Egyptian admiral Osman Pasha defected with the Cretan tribute and hastened to take sides with the Sultan, but this, though bad for morale and pocket, had no great effect on Mohammed Ali of Egypt, and Osman Pasha was quite briskly murdered in Constantinople.

Things hotted up in the spring of 1839, when the Sultan threw caution to the winds and advanced into Syria across the Euphrates. The French persuaded Mohammed Ali to treat, but his orders failed to reach his adopted son in time to stop Ibrahim Pasha gaining another crushing victory over the Turkish army on 24 June at Nazib. Then, on the 30th, the Sultan died, and internal rows accompanied the accession of his sixteen-year-old son. The situation, for Turkey, was one of extreme peril.

By the end of June both Britain and France had told their admirals to concentrate forces in the Levant. The desire to pour oil on the troubled waters was at this point genuine. Their orders were to prevent, if possible, a collision between the Turkish and Egyptian fleets and to urge both military commanders to an armistice. But they were to waylay whichever should refuse. (There is something very pacific and safe about the word 'waylay'.)

Now a still more dramatic event altered the whole picture. Ahmet Pasha, in command of the Turkish fleet, becoming convinced that

Khosrev, Grand Vizier to the new young Sultan, was in Russian pay, set sail for Alexandria with the entire Turkish fleet. Here, on 15 July, he was warmly received by Mohammed Ali.

It is to the credit of the Russians that they did not take advantage of this golden chance to occupy Constantinople, which had been their steady aim for centuries. Perhaps they were occupied elsewhere; perhaps they respected the British, French and Austrian fleets, now assembled in force at the mouth of the Dardanelles. For a year there was a lull, while everyone argued. By the time Mohammed Ali, under pressure from the allies, offered to send back the Turkish fleet, the young Sultan, feeling sufficiently secure of British and French support, declined to treat. Outbursts of unrest in Syria made Mohammed Ali send 12,000 troops, who landed in Beirut in late June 1840. By 1 July the *Powerful* 84, under the command of Black Charlie and accompanied by the *Edinburgh* 72. and *Castor* 36, were off Beirut 'to protect British interests'. They had orders not to interfere with the Egyptian fleet. For a month Black Charlie sat powerless in the *Powerful* whilst the Egyptians under their French-born general easily suppressed the revolt (mainly Maronite), and the smoke of the burning Christian villages rose up from the Brumana hills.

Black Charlie had been at Cork when Admiralty orders arrived to send him east. He had put up a notice in Portsmouth –

> Wanted, Active Seamen for the *Powerful*, Captain Napier. The *Powerful* is a fine ship, and in the event of war will be able to take her own part

which attracted some response; the jollities in the Cove of Cork attracted still more. Captain Pearn, the master, reported:

> men, women and children – gentle and simple, frieze and fustian, poplin, silk, satin. As many were admitted as could be received; but frequently whole boatloads were obliged to wait until some of those already on board had left. The band occasionally played, the dancing among the better classes took place on the poop, much to the enjoyment of the Irish lassies, who became our partners for the nonce, and the captain enjoyed and entered into the fun as much as any of us.

Hearing that *Ganges* and *Implacable* were already ahead of him, Charlie induced Pearn to get *Powerful* with her 2,400 tons and her 84

guns under sail in an hour. At Gibraltar on 12 July they learned that
Implacable and *Ganges* were three days ahead, but by hugging the
African shore (and a fig for the Dey of Algiers) they made such good
use of the land breezes that when, twelve days later, they swanked
into the Grand Harbour at Malta with every inch of sail set and the
band playing the latest number, they found themselves a day ahead.
The squadron proceeded to the Dardanelles, practising gunnery all
the way – 'You are killed! Why the deuce don't you fall down?' –
and spent an idle winter at Smyrna while negotiations went on. The
sailors held donkey races and 'Captain Napier, a bit of a fox-hunter,
rode his own horse in the steeplechase, and won the race in pretty
style'.

Bored, frustrated and convinced that the powers were making a
mess of things, Charlie grumbled to his wife in November: 'I would
much sooner live in a garret on bread and cheese than be here.'
He thought the wisest thing we could do was to acknowledge
Mohammed Ali – 'you would thus give the Turks a powerful ally,
instead of a discontented Pasha, a much better way of keeping Russia
in check than the present.'

The Pasha in question was unmoved by his suzerain's sentence of
deposition, announcing that 'such declarations are not new, this is
the fourth'; he hoped to get over it well as he had the other three,
'with the help of God and the Prophet'.

The Prophet certainly seemed to be doing well by Mohammed Ali.
His adopted son, Ibrahim Pasha, had overrun Syria; he still held the
Turkish fleet; and in France the Chief Minister, Thiers, was making
fiery noises on his behalf, insisting that the Viceroy be given the
Pashalik of Syria as well as of Egypt.

Through Ponsonby, ambassador in Constantinople, Palmerston
urged the Sultan to withdraw the sentence of deposition and confirm
Mohammed Ali in the Hereditary Pashalik of Egypt. For a moment
all the Great Powers, fearful of war, concurred. Black Charlie,
irritated and suspicious, wrote from the Levant to Palmerston in
January, urging him not to trust Russia – 'to Constantinople he will
get, sooner or later, unless we play a vigorous game... All that
Russia wants is time; and to see us embroiled with the French; they
will then pounce on Turkey.'

The plans of the Great Powers, as so often happened, were over-
set by the passions of those actually involved. Early in the summer of 1840 the mountain people of the Lebanon rose against the

oppressions of their Egyptian conquerors; Mohammed Ali sent his
squadron from Alexandria with 15,000 troops; these set to with a
right good will and when the allied ships arrived off Beirut the whole
coast was smoking from its destroyed villages. Heavy columns rose
from the convents, churches and houses on the heights of Brumana.

The powers now finally decided that Mohammed Ali must be, as
gently as possible, pushed back into Egypt. At this point Black
Charlie, to his indignation, had been ordered back to Malta, to do an
exchange with the dockyard admiral. Halfway there, he met the
Ganges with orders for him to reverse course and return to Beirut.
Now in command of six warships, he sent a letter to the Egyptian
admiral telling him to stop burning villages, to which he received a
polite compliance; but whether because the Egyptian admiral was
in fact a Frenchman, with no real stomach for burning Christian villages, or whether because of the strength of Black Charlie's
squadron, we shall never know. Momentarily, an uneasy peace
prevailed.

The situation was further complicated by the extreme touchiness
of those involved. The Sultan sat immovably at Constantinople;
Mohammed Ali sat obdurate at Alexandria. The French were very
much on their toes, considering that their honour had been impugned
during the negotiations, and Black Charlie was in no mean pique
because of the Admiralty's attempt to replace him by the dockyard
admiral just when things were getting interesting. Russia hovered,
enigmatic and menacing. Only the slightest spark was needed to set
off a European conflagration.

The London Convention which had been concluded on 15 July had
immediately sent its terms to Mohammed Ali, and he was given until 5 September to accede to them. Admiral Stopford, commander-
in-chief, was at Alexandria in *Princess Charlotte* with *Bellerophon*
and two Austrian ships. On 31 August he visited Mohammed Ali,
as did the Austrian admiral; to both of them the Egyptian Viceroy
made quite clear his refusal to ratify the London Convention. Neither
power could afford to allow the probable dissolution of the Ottoman
Empire at the hand of the enterprising Viceroy, knowing full well
that if they did, the power who would actually move into Constantinople would be the Russian Czar.

By 7 September the ultimatum had expired and open war
began. Leaving the newly-joined *Asia* and *Implacable* to cruise off

Alexandria and protect British interests, Stopford joined Black Charlie at Beirut, with HM Ships *Benbow, Revenge* and *Hastings,* the frigate *Pique* with engineers and artillery, three corvettes and a brig. When intercepted and told to reverse course on his way to Malta, Charlie had added *Thunderer, Ganges* and *Gorgon* to his original force of *Powerful, Edinburgh* and *Castor*. He had meanwhile tried to achieve something without anticipating the end of Mohammed Ali's period of grace by anchoring *Powerful* and *Edinburgh* close to Beirut's fortifications, and *Ganges, Thunderer* and *Castor* opposite the Egyptian camp.

As this had no effect upon Suleiman Pasha (the French officer in command, previously known as Colonel Sève), Black Charlie had withdrawn his ships and settled down to blockade. It might be a long business, since he had learned from the capture of an Egyptian cutter that Mohammed Ali was in full expectation of help from France; and this prospect had been confirmed in a dispatch from the British ambassador in Constantinople. On 9 September the British force off Beirut was reinforced by four Turkish frigates and their flagship; with the Austrians, this added up to a total of thirty-one warships. If the French did weigh in on the side of Egypt, there would be plenty to oppose them. But the French were luckily too canny for this.

General Sir Charles Smith, sent out in command of the British land forces, succumbed at this point to a local fever and was sent to recuperate in the healthier surroundings of the embassy on the Golden Horn. Thus the projected landing at Junieh, ten miles north of Beirut, was put under the command of Black Charlie who, ever since Busaco, had ' longed to show what he could do as a soldier and suffered no qualms whatever at his scant military experience and total want of training.

Though Mohammed Ali had been given twenty days' grace by the allies to decide whether to retire to Egypt, his army in Syria, which had successfully put down the revolt before the allies arrived, was in no mood to depart, whatever the Pasha told it. It was 7,000 strong and under the command of Abbas Pasha, an immensely stout individual with, according to Lieutenant Elliot of the *Powerful,* 'an expression veering rapidly between extreme rage and inanimate stupor'. Concerting his considerable skills at procrastination with those of the Governor of Beirut, 'an old gentleman dressed in a rich embroidered blue jacket and petticoat trousers and slippers' (Elliot), Abbas managed to do nothing at all to fall in with Charlie's demands that he should allow the departure of 4,000 Turkish prisoners, and stop sending his stores to safety inland and repairing his fortifications. Charlie could only threaten him with the bombardment of Beirut, but from his intercessions on behalf of the refugees and the persecuted from the Christian villages, Abbas Pasha knew well that Black Charlie was too humane to attempt anything of the kind.

'It will be very difficult to keep clear of the French,' Charlie wrote gloomily. Mohammed Ali would pretty certainly send up his reinforcements under the French flag; and what then? 'We must search French vessels, which they will not allow; I will not do it without orders.' Diplomacy rather than action seemed to be the order of the day; meanwhile Charlie contented himself with reconnoitring the entire area. Lieutenant Elliot wrote in his journal:

> Only think of the Commodore's energy and activity. He went on board the *Gorgon* steamer, as we thought only to look along the coast for a mile or two, and was missing for two days. On his return we found he had run over to Cyprus, reviewed the expedition there, to see what he had to trust to, hurried their motions and set all the troops a-drilling; then started off to St Jean d'Acre, examined its fortifications and weak points, and returned without almost anyone but ourselves knowing he was out of the ship.

6,000 Turks, 1,500 British and Austrian marines and 200 engineers and artillerymen were to be landed. Lieutenant Elliot reported:

> All that night we were hard at work with the boats conveying the troops on board the four steamers, which we crammed till there was not room for another man upon their decks, and what was left we took on board here. Not a soul but the Admiral and Commodore had any idea where we should land, and all was kept a strict secret. The Admiral it appears had so much confidence in the judgement and discretion of his gallant second-in-command that he allowed him to make his own arrangements, with regard to the when and where and how the attack was to be made; and well has his confidence been placed, for no one on earth could have managed better.
>
> At daylight the steamers, with all the boats of the fleet in tow, the *Powerful, Revenge* and *Thunderer,* and all the smaller ships were under sail; but a dead calm obliged us to anchor again. A

breeze however sprang up in the forenoon, when we all stood away to the southward of the town, in which direction we soon saw many of the Egyptians marching in double quick time. This feint to draw the enemy away answered admirably; for as soon as the breeze freshened we all bore up and ran helter-skelter for the north, leaving the Egyptians in a few minutes many miles astern, who, in turning about after us, got well peppered by the ships at anchor, who all opened their fire upon them as they passed.

The *Powerful,* with her flock, soon ran down to the little bay and village of D'jounie, about ten or twelve miles to the northward; and, ordering the small ships to anchor at certain distances along the shore, we pushed right in, till we all but touched the ground, with the steamer alongside of us. The *Revenge* and *Thunderer* kept a little out, to act when required. In three hours every man of the troops was landed, without a casualty or a shot fired, and ere night, had taken up, for safety, commanding positions; the few of the enemy's troops making a precipitate retreat before us.

All the night we were hard at work, forming entrenchments and arranging our field pieces, twelve in number, on the all but inaccessible heights. . . Morning found us pretty well prepared and ready to drop with the fatigue of two nights of the heaviest exertion I ever underwent. All, however, seemed in excellent spirits, working like tigers and longing to have a shot; even our brother Turks, who are no means given to breaking their backs at work, assisted cheerfully in carrying stores and sandbags; and the activity of our Commodore was beyond belief – working, bellowing and running about everywhere; one moment rapping a lazy fellow over the head and the next working away himself.

Established above the direct road from Beirut to Tripoli, they cut off all communications between these Egyptian-held towns. Ibrahim Pasha, at Baalbek, made no move; so that Black Charlie occupied Gezira, capital of the province, and stormed and took the castle of Djebail, thus encouraging the local Lebanese to descend from their hills and seize eagerly on the muskets and ammunition brought for them, in such large numbers that *Cyclops* had to be sent for a fresh supply.

Black Charlie reported to Lord Minto:

Ibrahim Pasha has been reconnoitring my flanks and front but
he cannot get at me with any hope of success, and I think it
probable that he will fall back. The peasantry are coming in
from all quarters for arms, and I think they will make the mountains too hot for him. I get on wonderfully well with the Turks,
who are very slow coaches; but I think we shall improve.

I wish your lordship, however, to be quite aware that it is not
with 6,000 Turks, though occasionally assisted by the Marines,
that Syria is to be conquered. I wish you would send out as many
marines as could be spared – they are worth an army of Turks. . .

It was not only the young lieutenants who felt excited; the commodore shared their elation. He wrote home delightedly:

Fancy me, commanding a mixed force of 7,000 men in the
mountains of Lebanon!. . . I expected to be attacked immediately; but now I don't care if they send 20,000 men against me.
The country are flocking in for arms, and I hope ere long to be
able to drive the Egyptians out of Lebanon, and from the
coast. . . I never saw such a beautiful mountainous country as
this; it is cultivated to the top of the highest hills. I visit all the
posts every morning; am up at four o'clock and on horseback,
and go through an enormous deal of fatigue.

When I am sure what my opponent, with his 20,000 men,
intends doing, or if he intends nothing, I shall take 1,000
marines and a couple of steamboats and attack every place on
the coast and arm the mountaineers. . .

God bless you all! My quarters are in a church, with a gun in
it, and a magazine of powder alongside of me. I am in excellent
health.

As it seemed clear that Ibrahim contemplated no instant move,
Black Charlie suggested to Stopford that there should be an attack on
Sidon, depot for the southern division of the Egyptian Army. Stopford was not keen on this idea. He demurred, hesitated and finally
agreed on 23 September, but with a condition that at once aroused
Charlie's stubborn opposition. Stopford had matured into a kindly,
undecided man, who longed to keep everybody happy. He wrote:

Your name, my dear Commodore, is too well established, and

your liberality and kindness too well known upon points of
service, to allow me to suspect for a moment that you would
wish to deprive a brother officer of a few sprigs of laurel, with
which you are so well covered. The good of the service upon
which we are employed is your first wish, [and the Admiral felt
sure that] Captain Berkeley would be most happy to attend to
all your suggestions.

Not so, Charlie replied crisply.

My dear Admiral, there is nothing in the whole world that I
would not do to please you, or forward the service, but I do not
see how I can put myself under a junior officer, when we shall
have 500 English marines and 500 Turks. You must know that
as yet I have had all the fag, and surely I ought to reap the
advantage of it.

Pending the agreement that Charlie felt sure that the admiral
would give, he exercised his men in a sortie in force across the Dog
River, Nahr el Kelb, encountered and scattered a body of Albanians
and took 400 of them prisoner. Stopford's agreement arrived next
day; Charlie was to meet Berkeley in the *Thunderer* off Damour on
the 25th. This was swiftly followed by a message to the effect that the
proposed attack on Sidon was off.

Nothing for it but to tackle the admiral in his own flagship, and
after what was probably another excellent dinner, Charlie received
the go-ahead, promising Stopford that he would be back in forty-
eight hours, plus the garrison of Sidon.

Off Damour next morning he duly met *Thunderer,* and also the
Austrian *Guerriera,* commanded by the Archduke Charles Frederick,
plus a Turkish corvette, the *Gul Sufide,* the 18-gun *Wasp,* and the
Hydra and *Stromboli* steamers, the last most opportunely newly arrived from home with nearly 200 marines on board. The landing
party consisted of 750 marines, 100 Austrians and 500 Turks. Off
Sidon the wind died, the large ships were towed in by the steamers,
and a boat was sent in under a flag of truce to request the governor of
the city to surrender. This he refused to do. The Turks were landed
for a flank attack, and the warships opened up with broadsides on the
entrenchments thrown up to oppose the landings. After half an hour
of this Charlie ordered a cease-fire, to see if the enemy would take the
chance to retreat into the town. They did not; the bombardment was

renewed; the marines were landed on the beach to the north of the town and advanced for an assault on the walls. Pattison Hunter, an eyewitness, reported:

> While the sailors were engaged in the perilous task of landing the troops, Commodore Napier, in one of the *Gorgon*'s boats, had got under the breach. When my attention was first called to this point, he was nearly up to his armpits in water, making a scaling ladder of the shoulders of his boat's crew. He succeeded in mounting, but had hardly time to look in before a discharge of musketry from an opposite building obliged him to abandon the attempt.

Thwarted at one breach, Charlie made for the next. At the head of the marines he broke into the barracks, skirted the eastern wall to the upper gate of the town, burst it open, and took the citadel. By this time completely carried away, Charlie rushed up one of the turrets of the citadel and signalled success to the ships in case they should mistakenly renew the bombardment. 'He raised aloft his cap on the point of his sword,' wrote Hunter; a piece of panache which sent the cheers echoing back to him from the crews of the warships in the bay.

Sidon had been taken with the loss of only four marines killed, a dozen Turks and another twelve marines wounded. It was crammed with stores, arms and ammunition. A letter was found from Suleiman Bey to the governor of the town, who died fighting bravely. 'For the love of Allah and the Prophet,' the governor was adjured, 'stand up and drive the English into the sea.' The idea had become prevalent among the Egyptian troops that the English were invincible. For all Charlie could do, there were some outrages – the Lebanese, who had suffered much, quickly appearing and taking it out on the luckless Egyptians. The house of Suleiman Pasha was sacked, and Charlie hastened to write him a letter of apology: 'I assure you I beheld with great regret that your house at Sidon suffered so much. A detachment of Egyptian soldiers had opened fire from your house, which rendered its occupation necessary. . .' Charlie prided himself on the scant loss of blood in taking this considerable stronghold, and that 'the disorder had been quickly put an end to'.

He embarked half the garrison as prisoners and with a fair wind the *Powerful* was off Beirut that evening. Having promised to be back victorious in forty-eight hours, he was back in twenty-four.

Giaour Napier

The Grand Prince of the Lebanon, Emir Beschir Cassim, an elderly chief of the mountain people, had all this while been cautiously sitting on the fence, sending equally polite messages expressing his friendly intentions both to Ibrahim Pasha and to Admiral Stopford. Earlier in the month, when Charlie was at Junieh, Stopford had ill-advisedly bombarded the luckless city of Beirut, and then withdrawn his ships and scattered them down the coast which, as Charlie considered, gave him the worst of both worlds. He had incurred the odium of bombarding the city without the necessary follow-up of landing to take it. Also 'it gave Suleiman Pasha the opportunity of telling the mountaineers that he had beaten off the British squadron', which settled the Grand Prince more firmly on the fence.

At home the bombardment of Beirut was frowned upon by many. The other Charles Napier thought it 'sad work to destroy Beirut. It is great cruelty beating down a town full of women and children and bedridden old people and sick; it is very dreadful to fire on any but troops.' Stopford's excuse was that his flag of truce had been fired upon; many thought that this was not good enough.

By now the inactivity of the Grand Prince had been noted in Constantinople, and his nephew and heir, known as the Little Prince, was sent a firman telling him to take over command. The news of Charlie's capture of Sidon had encouraged the Little Prince to launch an attack on the Egyptians, the success of which moved him to concert a plan with Black Charlie whereby they should attack Beirut from the landward side while a simultaneous attack on the town should be made from the sea.

By the end of September large reinforcements had arrived from Egypt, including 40,000 men under the hitherto unbeaten Ibrahim Pasha. Admiral Stopford accordingly called on Black Charlie to leave his established positions above the Dog River; to attack would be 'pregnant with risk and uncertainty'. But to retreat, as Black Charlie pointed out, was to ditch Emir Cassim, the Little Prince, now advancing from inland to join him. He wrote:

> You do not seem to be at all aware of my present position. I am strongly posted. The enemy is within musket shot of me, strongly posted also. The Emir Beschir is marching on his rear, and I have two battalions ready to cross the Dog River higher up to support him, so that . . . we shall probably destroy the enemy. . . The steam boats, if you can spare them, should be kept in the Bay, for if we defeat this army, we ought to fall instantly on Suleiman.

At this point Charlie received a note from Sir Charles Smith at Tyre, now recovered and in command, telling him to retire. 'If I were to retire, the Emir Beschir and all his men would be cut to pieces,' Black Charlie concluded categorically.

Stopford was temperamentally disinclined to the instant falling upon of anyone: 'I have only to repeat the orders of Sir Charles Smith, now commanding the troops, that you either fall back upon Junieh, or come down to where the steamers are. You will, of course, apprise the Emir of your intended retreat. . .'

Black Charlie had not the slightest intention of retreating. While he had been away taking Sidon, the Egyptians had established themselves on the heights of Boharsef, to his north east, burning the houses of the mountain people in revenge for their having joined the allies, and had driven their wives and families across the Dog River. Charlie wrote: 'It was heart-rending to see the unfortunate women and children encamped under trees in the Mountain, without the means of subsistence, and on our part, without being able to afford them much relief.' He did what he could, however, in the way of both shelter and food; the fame of his kindness spread, and the fame of his deeds, considerably exaggerated, spread also; he was known amongst the mountain people as Commodore el Kebir, and as 'Giaour Napier', an appellation to which Byron's poem had given an inordinately romantic ring.

This *réclame* had probably gone a little to Charlie's head. The sufferings of the Lebanese women and children had affected him more; and like most men of his generation, his religion was to him an integral part of life – these were Christians, warred upon by Moslems. The whole situation was one to call up the crusading element buried not very deeply in the Western European soul. All of which combined to make Charlie very ready to risk court-martial, disgrace and dismissal from the Navy in a cause in which he deeply believed and in a battle which he felt he had a good hope of winning.

Not that there was much to choose between either side in the matter of cruelty. Charlie had been horrified to find his road strewn with dead and dying Egyptians after a local skirmish in the hills, the wounded stripped by the mountain men and left to die of hunger and exposure. With the utmost difficulty he persuaded some local peasants to drag the wounded under cover in a roadside cottage and to give them water.

All the same, his spirits remained high. This was the land as the Bible had led him to expect it would be – the cedars of Lebanon, the stony hills, the harshly cold nights, the daytime of blazing sun and unremitting heat, the small fields, short commons, poverty. It seemed to make the substance of the Bible ring even more true than before. He told his wife: 'I have been eleven hours on horseback over most dreadful roads, but through a beautiful country. I have five horses, three of them very fine. I took them all. . . I never was in better health or better fit for work than I am now.'

At daylight on 9 October Charlie sent an Arab battalion to join Jochmus, his Turkish second-in-command, who had previously occupied Kornet Sherouan, a village on the crest of the hill which led, along a considerable hog's back, to the heights of Boharsef, on which the Egyptians had dug themselves in. Charlie's spies had assured him that the Egyptians were not present in any considerable force; so that he was startled to be told at breakfast that in fact Ibrahim Pasha himself was present, having joined Suleiman with sizeable reinforcements. This being so, Black Charlie, in consultation with his officers, decided that it would be better to await the arrival of the Little Prince, reported a day's march away, before launching his attack.

From his position on the hill overlooking St George's Bay and the town of Beirut, Black Charlie was encouraged next morning to observe that the Egyptians were evacuating the town – this left him with only the armies in the open field to deal with. Less encouraging was yet another letter from Admiral Stopford with a formal order that he should 'return without a moment's loss of time and with due security to his troops, which seemed in some degree of insecurity'. Hearing that his advance posts had been driven in, Charlie counter-attacked and obliged the Egyptians to retreat. By noon on the 10th, to his relief, the Little Prince and his forces had joined him. Charlie ordered the advance along the two miles of hog's back ridge, leading to the Egyptians' first position, up a steep hill of zig-zag tracks, built up terraces and large upright rocks affording maximum protection to the waiting Egyptians. A detachment of mountain men under Lieutenant Duncan of the *Powerful* were to turn the enemy's left, and to allow the others to go forward under cover of their fire.

Two Turkish battalions advanced boldly, finding good cover amongst the rocks; another, advancing along the road in column under Jochmus, received such sharp fire that they broke into skirmishing order, and advanced so rapidly – 'with the exception of some few whom I was obliged to stir up with my stick' – that Charlie decided to keep his last battalion in reserve to cover their retreat, which seemed not improbable. It was an anxious moment; would the Turks break in face of the concentrated fire they would come under at the top of the hill? But the Turks ran in upon the Egyptians with their bayonets and the first position was taken.

The second enemy position appeared more formidable. Although a hundred yards of level plateau stretched ahead, beyond that was precipitous broken ground, with trees and high-walled terraces affording protection to the defenders. This half mile was succeeded by a slightly longer stretch, of broken but tolerably level ground, commanded by the heights of Boharsef, on which were Ibrahim and his main force.

The Turkish battalions, not unreasonably, had decided enough was enough and that they had done their day's work; they sank into positions of comfortable repose in the shade of the stone walls they had so gallantly stormed. At this point all Charlie's powers of persuasion failed, and the image of Giaour Napier was slightly dented by the shower of stones and even the use of the flat of his sword, with which he aroused his allies from their wonted siesta. After which, through heavy Egyptian fire, Black Charlie, lame leg or no, led his combined force of British marines and Turkish soldiers at a brisk double across the open ground towards the final assault, accompanied by Jochmus, Selim Pasha and Lieutenant Bradley of the *Powerful*. After half an hour of sharp action they stood in triumph on the heights of Boharsef. Ibrahim fled, his troops scattered, leaving all baggage, ammunition and stores to the victors. Casualties on Charlie's side amounted to no more than fifty killed or wounded; 700 Egyptians had been taken prisoner; the dead seem not to have been counted.

Still out of breath, Charlie was handed a letter, written that morning by Stopford – 'Return forthwith to your position at Junieh with the troops under your command, with all due caution and circumspection.' He replied:

My dear Admiral,
    I, this afternoon, attacked Ibrahim Pasha and totally defeated him. He was driven from position to position, and Selim Pasha is still after him. I do not know how many prisoners we have made. The Turks behaved nobly.

Yours faithfully,
CHARLES NAPIER

Now 2,000 of Suleiman Pasha's army deserted, leaving all their artillery behind them, and Beirut was evacuated without further loss of life; but Black Charlie was unable to persuade Stopford, or General Smith, to pursue the Egyptians, or to attack their remaining strongholds at Tripoli and Acre before they had time to rally.

At home in Chester his namesake applauded:

Would that another Charles Napier were there also with a strong brigade, we might give the name another shove... Charles Napier will probably open the ball, he is taking decided steps apparently, and no doubt by order of government; no man more likely to win. He has at least checked the horrors which that ruffian Ibrahim was perpetrating.

From the *Queen Charlotte*, Stopford reacted generously, telling Charlie that no words of his 'could do justice to his splendid operations at Boharsef'; and he was 'fully sensible of the benefit which I, and the whole expedition, have received from your indefatigable services...'

Even the Admiralty approved, a novel sensation for Charlie; Lord Minto congratulated him on 'the signal services you have rendered, the energy, activity, skill and gallantry you have displayed, the indefatigable zeal and exertion which have enabled you to triumph over all difficulties'. The enthusiastic Lieutenant Elliot, of the *Powerful*, really let rip:

There is not, or cannot be, a man here who does not give the highest praise to our Commodore for his tact, discretion and valour. The Turks have taken a great fancy for him, and almost adore him. Proud as they are towards Christians, the soldiers flock round him, kiss his hands, or even the tails of his coat; and the war-cry among them to the last battle was 'For God, the Prophet, and the Giaour Commodore!' whom they say they would follow to the world's end. Such is the effect of true bravery, conducted with discretion and ultimate victory among even such barbarians as these are.

Not altogether surprisingly, next month's taking of St Jean d'Acre was accompanied by further argument and more indignant letters between hesitant Stopford and impetuous Charlie. By the end of October Tortosa had fallen and Tripoli had been evacuated by the Egyptians; Acre was now their only strong position on the Syrian coast. On the evening of the last day of October, the expedition sailed from Beirut, laden with 3,000 Turkish soldiers and 2,000 Royal Marines forming the landing force. Eight sail of the line, five frigates, four steamers and two brigs, after a forty-eight-hour passage due to the contrary winds, confronted the famous fortress late on the evening of 2 November. Acre had defied Napoleon, and cost Ibrahim Pasha a six-month siege before its water ran out. Its angled fortress presented two faces to the sea, walled and bristling with cannon, in one place a double tier of them.

Soundings, taken under cover of darkness, showed that the ships could hardly come near enough to effect a breach in those formidable walls, and it was decided to try and blast the way through them with a preliminary bombardment, from as close in as the depth would allow. Stopford proposed that the steamers should tow in three battleships and then return to tow in three more, until all were in position. This, Black Charlie pointed out, would be 'dangerous and impracticable'. For a full two hours the first three ships would be exposed to the concentrated fire of the batteries, and would probably be disabled long before their consorts could arrive to help them. Captain Boxer, of the *Pique,* which had been reconnoitring Acre and its surrounding seas, cut Charlie short while he was still in full stream. 'We have settled the whole of the matter and the positions to be taken up, and, Commodore, it is no use your interfering.'

Charlie brusquely seized up his hat and went back to his ship; but in the morning, in calmer frame, he was back on board the flagship informing the admiral that he felt it was his duty, as second-in-command, to tell him that his plan was doomed to utter failure. He had his way; the ships were to go in on the usual Mediterranean breeze of afternoon, in two divisions – Black Charlie leading in *Powerful*, and followed by *Princess Charlotte, Thunderer* and *Bellerophon* with *Revenge* in reserve. Though under sail, these were to tackle the western face of the fortifications; the Turkish admiral (possessing the rather occidental name of Walker Bey) was to lead in to attack the south-eastern angle, followed by *Benbow, Edinburgh, Pique, Castor, Hazard, Carysfort, Talbot* and *Wasp*, with three Austrian and Turkish frigates. *Powerful* was to go in from the south, the other ships to take up their positions in succession to the northward of him.

At the last moment the wind changed, starting to blow from the north, so that Charlie had to make a lightning decision:

I could not anchor on the south western face of the fortress . . . had I done so, the ships following could not have got ahead of me. . . I passed a small battery and anchored alongside the strongest part of the walls of Acre, on the north west front.

After I let go my anchor, the whole thing having been reversed, I naturally expected that the following ships would pass outside of me, and, by anchoring in succession ahead of me, occupy the ground between the south western and the north western angle of the fortress. . . The thing was so well known in naval tactics, while, at the same time, it was so consonant with common sense, that everyone knew about it.

In fact they had anchored behind him, line astern, leaving a gap in the line of fire. Between them Stopford and Charlie had made a muddle of it. Charlie asked defensively:

What did Lord Nelson say? Why, that no ship could do wrong which anchored alongside the enemy. I anchored alongside the enemy at the strongest portion in the face of the fortress . . . as close to the batteries as the depth of the water would allow me. . . The ships following me did not take up their proper positions . . . they thought I had got into shoal water, but I made no signal of shoal water.

All I can say is, I took up my proper position, and the other ships did not. I do not mean to say that it was for want of skill that they did not do so, as I believe they were under the impression that they were to keep always to the north of me.

This error, whoever's it was, made no kind of difference; the fire of

the line-of-battle ships anchored within 500 yards of the fortifications
was overwhelming. The Egyptians fought bravely, but had raised
their guns too high, so that they were unable to lower them in time.
After three hours their powder magazine blew up, killing more than
1,000 men; and Acre surrendered.

Under cover of night the Egytians evacuated the town, and British
troops landed next day to take possession. But the misunderstanding did not sweeten Black Charlie's relationship with Stopford.
Going on board *Phoenix* next morning to congratulate the admiral,
Charlie had received a somewhat crisp comment on his previous
day's manoeuvres, at which he instantly took offence. His long
explanatory letter followed. Stopford was a charming, easy-going
man who disliked disputes as much as he disliked taking decisions; he
apologized, and they made it up two days later. The soldier Charles
Napier commented:

> Black Charlie is doing his work in Syria like a good fellow and
> trying to prevent horrors. Her Majesty would not be the worse
> for a dozen such black gentlemen as he. Glorious news of the
> taking of Acre. What will not boldness do? A strong fortress
> which has stood siege after siege taken in three hours by ships!
> The poor Egyptian slaves have been slaughtered by thousands
> for the obstinacy of that rascal Mohammed Ali. Poor fellows,
> their fate is hard, to fall for a tyrant they detest. What a life mine
> is [he thought in rain-swept Lancashire] drivelled away in read-
> ing courts martial!

In January he reported:

> Black Charles and Stopford at loggerheads. So it will always
> be when government gives power to mediocrity and age, when
> an active vigorous man known to be all enterprise is second-
> in-command; but the Admiralty never yet acted with sense or
> judgement, or common justice; what board ever did?

Doubtless not without a sigh of relief, Stopford was able, after
Acre, to send Black Charlie to Alexandria with a detached squadron.
But Giaour Napier had by this time really taken the bit between his
teeth. At Beirut, watering his ships, he wrote to Palmerston in a quite
unorthodox and by-passing manner:

> I believe the best thing to settle this affair would be at once to

say to Mohammed Ali: 'Withdraw from Syria and give up the Turkish fleet, and you shall keep Egypt.' If your lordship and the Allies have any notion of that, try me as a negotiator, with six sail of the line which I am to have, and I daresay I should succeed. I believe Egypt would be just as well governed by him as it would be by one of the Turkish Pashas; he is an old man, and it is hardly worth risking a European war to turn him out.

And, as everybody well knew, the French would never allow it. Mohammed Ali besides was very far from being beaten; he still had 60,000 men in Syria, and the British fleet could not operate in support of the Turkish forces off this coast in winter, with its open coastline and absence of harbours. Palmerston, persuaded by the less aggressive Melbourne, had now told Ponsonby that if Mohammed Ali would withdraw from Palestine and the Holy Places, restore the Turkish fleet and submit to Turkish suzerainty, he should be confirmed and recognized as hereditary pasha of Egypt. At Beirut Black Charlie was shown this dispatch, but he had been some while at Constantinople and he knew the pace of deliberation around the Golden Horn. He felt certain that Ponsonby and the Turks would never negotiate quickly enough; there would be morning calls and afternoon waits, and all the old Byzantine legacy of frustration and delay, while winter came on, the winds rose, and the British fleet was driven into shelter at Smyrna once again; and then what?

Acting on his own initiative, he went ahead in the *Medea* to Alexandria and saw Mohammed Ali, a cheerful rogue who immediately took Black Charlie's fancy. He was allowed to visit the naval establishments, which he thought wonderful. 'In twenty years he has created an army and a navy and a dockyard that would do credit to any nation.'

Walking about the town, Charlie noted how pleased the inhabitants were at not being bombarded by his squadron: 'much satisfaction in the countenances of the inhabitants of all nations and religions at being released from the apprehension they entertained of having their town knocked about their ears.' He had found Mohammed Ali

a man of low stature, a good deal marked with the smallpox, his complexion sallow, his eyes quick and penetrating. He wears a fine white beard, and when in good humour, has the most fascinating manner; but when out of temper his eyes sparkle, he

raises himself up in his corner, and soon convinces you he is
much easier led than driven.

But Charlie had no intention of driving him; and in fact no need.
Lieutenant Bradley of the *Powerful,* who accompanied Charlie,
reported that the Pasha had been 'delighted with him, said that he
had many times heard of the Commodore . . . and would at any time
prefer being the friend than the foe of such a man'.

On a second visit to the Pasha, Charlie was able, in spite of
indignant mutterings from the affronted French ambassador, to persuade him to agree to Palmerston's terms. Asked his credentials,
Black Charlie answered that they were the known desire of the four
great powers for peace. What of his personal credentials? the Pasha
asked. 'My credentials are the double-shotted guns of the *Powerful*
and the honour of an Englishman,' Bradley heard Charlie say.
Mohammed Ali was fortunately pleased by this reply, Black Charlie
continued to persuade, and that night sat down in his cabin to write
to Minto, First Lord. 'I do not know whether I have done right in
settling the eastern question. . . If I have done wrong I must bear the
whole blame.'

Everyone was furious. Angry messages shot round the Levant like
rockets. Ponsonby wrote to Mohammed Ali, repudiating the Convention. Stopford wrote to Minto, repudiating Black Charlie. The Sultan protested against the Convention, the assembled ambassadors at
Constantinople declared it null and void. Ponsonby thundered to
Charlie, 'I call upon you to abstain from any attempt to carry your
Convention into execution.' Charlie thundered back at him, 'I know
my duty to Her Majesty full as well as your lordship, and I have
always done it.' But to his wife he wrote, 'I shall either be hung by the
government or made a bishop. God bless you all.'

In the event he was all but made a bishop. The Convention
was signed on 27 November for Mohammed Ali by a gentleman
ominously named Boghus; it was honoured by the powers and
Charlie's action was officially approved. To Minto's commenda-
tion for his gallantry in the campaign, Palmerston added his con-
gratulations on his negotiating powers. He received decorations from
Austria, Russia and Prussia – 'all humbug,' he commented. The Duke
of Sussex, in a letter beginning 'My Dear Old Friend Charley Napier',
forwarded him the order for a KCB, and asked him to bring back a
Turkish scimitar.

'The French are in a rage, and Boghus Bey quite delighted that everything is settled without their intervention,' Charlie told Lord Minto. To his wife he wrote in triumph: 'The French have done all they could to prevent Mohammed Ali agreeing to my terms, but I have beat them all. . .'

Signed on 27 November, the Convention was only just in time. On the 29th a violent gale caused the Royal Navy's blockading squadron the leave the Syrian coast and take refuge in Marmorice Bay. Even so, *Bellerophon* had missed being driven ashore at Latakia by a whisker. Thus left unguarded, all the places taken by the allies could easily have been recaptured by Ibrahim Pasha who still had a considerable army in Palestine.

Black Charlie returned to Alexandria to make sure that the Turkish fleet really was returned to Turkey under the terms of the treaty. At the behest of the Alexandria merchants, he went on to persuade Mohammed Ali to fix the price of cotton and to carry into effect the 1839 trading treaty with Britain.

'This finishes a question that has well-nigh set Europe in a blaze,' Charlie reported in January 1841 to his friend William Grant. Not quite; there were a few hiccups before the Treaty of London, to which France also adhered, was signed in that city this 13 July.

Lieutenant Elliot of the *Powerful,* in a letter to a friend describing the Commodore's eccentricity of dress and bearing – 'his black bushy eyebrows, large round face, and his trousers far too short' – concludes:

Mind, you are not to laugh at him, for he is one of the greatest characters of the day. . . He is by no means always a pleasant officer to serve under, but one must forgive much for the honour of being commanded by such a character. His high honourable principles and gentlemanly feelings are beyond dispute; yet he is snappy and irritable at times; but shines particularly at the head of his own table, which is always well found, and no want of wine. . . Some of his enemies would have him hanged, drawn, and quartered for meddling in the treaty. What a complete victory he has gained over them! Lord Ponsonby to boot! He cares not a straw for any superior as long as he conceives he is doing the best for his country – and no one knows better than himself when he is right or wrong. He is a fine fellow and I will stick up for him against all the world.

11

'Now Monsieur's Beat'

In February Charlie had received the thanks of both Houses of Parliament for his scrviccs in Syria; on returning home he found himself a popular hero, with cheering crowds, civic dinners, the freedom of the City of London, and invitations from Liberals to stand for Parliament at Falmouth and at Marylebone. Exception to all this was taken in some quarters. Justin McCarthy (*History of Our Own Times*) wrote: 'The bravery of Charles Napier, the hot-headed self-conceited commodore, was enthusiastically extolled and his acts of successful audacity were glorified as though they had shown the genius of Nelson or the clever resource of a Cochrane.'

In the main, admiration prevailed; but no one in the administration was eager to see so persistent a critic of the Admiralty let loose in the Commons, and Black Charlie was obliged to go on half-pay. In the general election of the summer he was returned for Marylebone, having first informed its voters that he meant to retain his independence of action. He took his seat on 19 August and made his maiden speech on the 25th. 'When I got up, I forgot the second part of it, and was, as you may suppose, in a funk,' he told his wife. His flag could brave a thousand years the battle and the breeze, but he was thrown into confusion by having to confront politicians of his own breed.

> The thread gone, I was discouraged, and left out a great part I intended to say; . . . Berkeley, who was patting me on the back, I thought was pulling me down. . . But still, it went off very well, and I was much cheered. . .
>
> Since then I hear so many ridiculous speeches, so little to the purpose, that I shall soon acquire confidence. I shall, however, take care never to speak on what I do not thoroughly understand.

As there was plenty that he did understand, he would have no lack of subjects. The previous winter at Smyrna, apart from winning steeplechases, he had had leisure take a good close look at the French squadron, anchored close by in the harbour, and had confided his thoughts to Lord Minto:

Powerful, Voula Bay, December 1, 1839

I am now lying alongside a French eighty-four, manned with 890 men, looking, both inside and out, as well as a British man-of-war, exercising their guns, and firing at a mark with as much precision as an English ship, and exercising their sails quite as well, even to shifting their top-sail-yards and sails; better found than our own ships are, with the exception of sails, and better armed in every respect; every gun fitted with detonating locks that never miss, good muskets, good cartouch boxes, and good pistols; men sufficient to work their guns, leaving a large proportion to small arms, and to attend to the sails, and a reserve of nearly 100 men below, to replace casualties, exercising and improving every day, with a system of promotion which encourages officers to excel each other to obtain it.

Now, my Lord, . . . I will endeavour to make a comparison between this ship and the *Powerful:* the latter mounts eighty-four guns, and is manned by 645 men, including sixty boys; when the guns are even imperfectly manned, there is not a single marine left to small arms, not sufficient men for the passage of powder, very few to attend the rigging, and the guns fitted with locks not to be compared to the detonating ones.

Now, my Lord, I go into action with this ship; and with the precision both ships fire, and the addition of 100 muskets playing upon me from all quarters, I cannot expect to lose less than 100 men killed and wounded, the first five minutes; admitting the enemy have double, which is not likely, I am reduced to 545 men and boys, the other to 690; my fire must slacken, while his, from replacing the casualties from his reserve, and from the musketry, will be as lively as ever. Let me ask your Lordship what chance should I have of taking my opponent?

Is it because we speak English and they speak French? for I know of no other reason. We all know the French are brave men; we know that though we took them last war, they never did surrender till after great loss; and in the last year of the war several actions were undecided; and at that time their experience was nothing in comparison to what it is now: every exertion is made by the French Government to improve their navy, and it is wonderful to what point they have arrived, and are still advancing.

France had more ships in the Mediterranean than we had; if need arose, how were we to man the reinforcement of ships, or get them there in time?

We might be defeated, before they arrived. What a state would England be in then, and how would we regain the superiority? Perhaps never. I am no alarmist, my Lord, but I cannot shut my eyes, and I think it is my duty to convey to you my opinions

For the rest of his life Black Charlie would continue to do just this, and to persuade his country's government not to rest forever comfortably on the country's laurels, remaining impervious to the need to reform. And not, if possible, to start every war armed for the war before last.

By now Black Charlie's large build had settled into a considerable bulk. He weighed fourteen stone, and halted more than ever in his confident walk. Bred in Georgian days, he drank rather more whisky and smoked more cigars than many of his Victorian contemporaries thought right or fitting. If he suffered pain from his many old wounds he never mentioned it or made it an excuse for outbursts of irritability. Stalwart and shabby, he would stump in and out of the Commons, urging his views on the need for naval reform in and out of season; pressing above all for the abolition of impressment and of the dreaded gangs that dragged men forcibly from merchant ship or home port, and for the discouragement of flogging, a punishment which he thought not only abominably cruel but self-defeating. He met with little response. These things had always been; must always be. And the tactful approach had never been Black Charlie's strong suit.

In the mornings he pressed on with writing his *History of the Syrian War*. The other Charles thought he had better have left the writing to William, historian of the Peninsular War, because William could have stressed his personal bravery as Charlie himself could not; but when he came to read it, he decided that the immediacy of Black Charlie's first-hand account made it right that he should have written it. Some critics considered that the book took too long to come out, appearing when the public had lost interest; others disagreed. 'It was a curious distinction of the 'fighting Napiers', one contemporary wrote, 'that they wrote almost as ardently and ably as they fought.'

Charlie had been disappointed by the recommendations of the Naval and Military Commission. He told Admiral Sir William Parker:

> I cannot say they have done much for the naval service. Aged naval officers were still in command. Look at the age of the French Admirals and ours; be assured some mischief will happen some day or other. At the beginning of the Revolutionary War, you may remember how the young French generals beat all the old Austrian ones; and we had better take care the young French Admirals do not serve us the same.

To the Secretary of the Commission he made this point at length and with a wealth of practical illustrations:

> Lord Rodney became a Rear-Admiral at forty-seven, and fought his action at sixty-four; he was the first British Admiral who broke the enemy's line; and. . . there appears to have been great want of decision on the part of Lord Rodney who was suffering at the time from gout; and it is very well known that Lord Hood was displeased at the result of the action, and urged Lord Rodney to renew it.
>
> Lord Howe was commander of a squadron at thirty-three, and Rear-Admiral at forty-five; he fought the Battle of the 1st June at sixty-eight; his second-in-command, Lord Graves, was the same age, and Lord Bridport sixty; he took six sail of the line, and allowed six or eight to escape under their spritsails. A man of his time of life was not equal to three days' fatigue of mind and body; had he been between thirty and forty, the greater part of the enemy's fleet would have been captured.
>
> Lord St Vincent became a Rear-Admiral at forty-three, and attacked the Spanish fleet, of very superior force, at sixty-three; but it was the youthful Nelson who won the battle, by disobeying signals; in this case the superiority of the enemy was so great, that any man of any age would have been justified in declining a battle.
>
> Lord Duncan was a Rear-Admiral at fifty, and fought the Camperdown action at sixty-six; he was certainly no common man; had he been fifty he could not have borne down on an enemy's fleet on a lee shore with more nerve and decision.

Lord Nelson fought the Battle of the Nile at thirty-nine, Copenhagen at forty-one, and Trafalgar at forty-seven; many men of his age would have done the same thing; but I doubt whether Lord Nelson himself, between sixty and seventy, would have attempted either the Nile or Copenhagen; and most certainly, at that time of life he would not have fought the Battle of Trafalgar in the way he did... He captured twenty-three sail out of thirty-three; had he fought the action at a distance from the land, not one ship would have returned to tell the story... His example will never be followed by one man in a hundred, unless he has youth on his side.

Sir James Saumarez was defeated at forty-four, in a brilliant action on a French squadron off Algeçiras, and in less than a week refitted his shattered squadron, attacked and defeated double his force, blew up two three-deckers and captured a 74. Had he been sixty-four instead of forty-four, it is more probable that neither action would have been fought.

Besides the actions I have enumerated, we lost many opportunities for want of decision; look at Lord Hotham's bungling actions in the Mediterranean, and Sir Robert Calder's foggy action; they were both too old, and quite incapable of fighting decisive battles.

The great error in most of our naval battles has been in not following them up; a victory once gained, our commanders were quite satisfied with themselves, and I don't wonder at it; nothing is more agreeable than to find a battle won, and one's head still on one's shoulders; and nothing more disagreeable than to renew a battle with impaired energies.

What was to happen now, with late promotions and a list of ageing captains and admirals? Black Charlie demanded to know; and he urged a detailed programme for better promotion and retirement jobs for those too old to fight effectively. No one took the slightest notice.

Sir Robert Peel was hardly in office before Black Charlie was at it again, repeating his arguments for reform. And why must the entire Board of Admiralty be moved with every change of government?

Just as they begin to know their business they are replaced by a fresh set, who have their lessons to learn, and invariably entertain different notions from their predecessors; hence arise the constant changes that take place, ruinous to the discipline and well-being of the service, and expensive to the country.

Black Charlie had the grace to apologize for his 'presumption in writing to a Prime Minister about to form an administration', but if things went on as they were 'a great catastrophe will befall this country'. And Peel had such a large majority that 'you may almost do as you please'.

Peel was to do as he pleased in other respects, notably in the repeal of the Corn Laws. As for Black Charlie, when his hour struck he was to forget instantly, in the twinkling of an eye, all that he had previously argued upon the folly of employing aged admirals upon enterprises of great pith and moment. When it's ourselves, it's different.

Through the fogs of indifference, an occasional ray of sunlight came to cheer him. In 1843 his beloved daughter, Fanny, married the Revd Henry Jodrell; and Lyndhurst, Lord Chancellor, on appointing his son-in-law to the living of Gisleham in Suffolk, wrote to Black Charlie: 'It is true that you are a violent party politician, but your claims on every well-wisher of his country, and on every admirer of gallantry and talent, are irresistible.'

The Administration, however, continued very successfully to resist them; and, in particular, all Charlie's efforts to have the position and pay of seamen regularized. He started again on Lord Ellenborough:

> It was twenty-five years before I could get the least attention paid to the Registration Bill [to register all seamen]. Your Lordship must be quite well aware that I have no other object than the public good. It is certainly not in my interest to say anything unpleasant to the Admiralty; had I held my tongue last year, I should certainly have commanded the Experimental Squadron.

The tenacious Charlie went on, perfectly aware that he was doing himself no good. The fact that he was constantly proved to be right did not endear him to anyone.

Nor would they make any use of the invaluable experience that Black Charlie had gained in the construction and sailing of his own six steamships. The turn over to steam went on haltingly; and to Charlie's critical gaze the Admiralty seemed even to have lost the skill of building satisfactory sailing ships. Sticking rigidly to sail as they did, and to the good old wooden walls, those in charge of construction should at least see that the Navy's ships were seaworthy. To Charlie it sometimes seemed as if a kind of lethal paralysis had seized on those in charge of his country.

The British public simultaneously gloried in its Navy and neglected it. The relationship remained static for several hundred years – much praise, small reward. 'Why should the State be troubled with this needless charge of keeping so great a navy in such exquisite perfection and readiness, the times being peaceable?' the Elizabethans had asked Sir Walter Raleigh. He thought this 'a pretty superficial argument to bleare our eyes'. Let the Navy go, and from the Continent 'those proud mastering spirits would be more ready and willing to shake us by the eares as enemies than to take us by the hand as friends'. 'Our condition is dark and sad,' Robert Blake, General at sea, wrote to the home authorities in 1655, 'our ships extremely foul, winter drawing on, our victuals expiring, all stores failing, our men falling sick through the badness of drink . . . the coming of supply uncertain . . . our mariners apt to fall into discontents through their long keeping abroad. Our only comfort is that we have God to lean upon.'

Times changed; official parsimony was pursued with unswerving fidelity. Men were expendable; money was not. When Black Charlie later complained of the state of some of his ships he was officially told to 'put them in the front' – they would 'serve to be knocked to pieces in place of better ships'.

After the Battle of Quiberon Bay in 1759 some wag from the lower deck summed it up:

> Ere Hawke did bang
> Monsieur Conflang
> You gave us beef and beer;
> Now Monsieur's beat
> We've nought to eat
> Since you have nought to fear.

Substitute, in due course, Boney, Kaiser and Hitler for 'Monsieur', and there is the complete history, one of extraordinary meanness. Up until 1918, some sailors regularly starved after the signing of the peace treaty, as did the wives and children of those killed. Even in 1940 the widow of a destroyer captain was given £180 per annum to live on, plus £36 per annum for each child, and had to subsist on grants from funds bequeathed by generous and farsighted admirals. Not until the Falklands War were these wrongs righted.

In 1846 Charlie was writing with increasing passion to yet another First Lord of the Admiralty, in this case Lord Ellenborough, about the faulty construction of new warships.

> If your Lordship will look at the return of the Experimental Squadron, you will see that the *Albion* rolled over 45 degrees, the *Superb* and *Vanguard* 40 and 42. [*Rodney* and *Canopus* were not much better.] They are absolutely unsafe, for if they fall into the trough of a sea at a time another rises to windward, I verily believe they would go over... As to the steamers, they are still worse. [Nothing has been done] to secure their boilers and machinery from shot... Seventeen years ago I wrote to the Lord High Admiral, pointing out what a steamship ought to be, and I have repeated it often without effect... I did not write from theory, several years before I had built six steamers, and my experience cost me upwards of £10,000.

As to the cruisers, *Terrible, Retribution* and *Avenger*, all had serious errors in construction; and whenever Charlie had moved for an inquiry in the House he had been told he was exaggerating. No one at the Admiralty took any notice of the opinions of officers, who had, after all, to sail and fight in the ships. It seemed to Black Charlie that he was able to do no more good to the Navy in Parliament than he could out of it. All the while many of the reforms he had suggested were, slowly, very slowly, being effected. But there seemed to some of the exasperated members of the Administration to be no holding Black Charlie; no sooner had they put one matter right than he was on at them about another, with the same unabashed and tactless energy.

It must have been with a sigh of relief to all concerned that the commodore was made rear-admiral in November 1846, and in May of 1847 Commander-in-Chief of the Channel Squadron, hoisting his flag in HMS *St Vincent*. This, at least, would keep him absent from the Commons for a while.

12

A Want of Discretion

The squadron was sent to Lisbon, where trouble was said to be on the brew. As a compliment to the Portuguese, Black Charlie asked to be allowed to use his Portuguese title. Palmerston refused in a slightly mocking vein – 'We cannot be parties to the de-nationalizing of one of the brightest ornaments of the British Navy.' So Black Charlie remained plain Admiral Sir Charles Napier.

He was not long out of hot water. An article in *The Times* accused him of using his position to press for his arrears of Portuguese pension. But here the British Minister to Portugal, Sir Hamilton Seymour, came to his rescue; and when questions were asked in the House, a letter from Seymour was read out, demonstrating how untrue the accusations were. The Portuguese Finance Minister had opened the question by saying he was sorry that the pension was so much in arrears and offering to pay as soon as possible. To which Black Charlie had replied that he had no wish to be paid first, he 'must take his chance with the rest'. Seymour added that the services the Admiral was rendering were of great value to the country. 'That', Lord Auckland wrote, 'is probably an end to this exaggerated and misrepresented affair. I believe that all are satisfied.' But of course they were not; and the many toes upon which Black Charlie had trodden continued to itch for the return kick.

The end of the year was saddened by the loss in a terrible storm of the *Avenger*, whose seaworthiness Charlie had doubted. She was one of the steamships in his squadron at Lisbon; out of control, she had run on the Sorelle rocks off Sicily with a loss of all but three men. Among the dead was Charlie's much-loved stepson, Captain Charles Elers-Napier, long since adopted as his son.

In the new year disturbances in Ireland sent the squadron to the Cove of Cork. The row died down as suddenly as it had arisen and Charlie, as usual, had a good time in Ireland, in between landing parties of seamen and marines and organizing field days around this lovely bay. Everyone had supposed that he would do well with the fleet, but Palmerston noted with surprise that Charlie seemed well able to work peaceably with the Minister at Lisbon: 'Seymour's letters and despatches show that Napier has been cooperating most cordially and successfully with him.'

Had the years, and a spell in Parliament, brought discretion? When sent to Mogador on the Barbary Coast to punish some Riff tribesmen who had attempted to capture a becalmed British merchantman, Black Charlie even refrained from pursuing several thousand tribesmen into the depths of Morocco with a party of fifty marines. What could have come over him? Friends were less surprised to hear of his efficiency in handling the fleet and his energy in practising gunnery and landings.

Palmerston wrote to him:

> We hear that nothing was ever more brilliant than the state of your squadron and that it is animated by a spirit that makes it worthy of its commander. While our ships are in such good order and we have enough of them at sea, our neighbours across the Channel will take care to keep quiet. Diplomats and protocols are very good things [he added, in a famous confession of faith] but there are no better peace-keepers than well-appointed three-deckers.

When Admiral da Costa Cabral, a radical turned royalist, happened to be on board Charlie's flagship when Queen Adelaide visited on her way to Madeira, a cry was set up at home that Charlie was interfering in a party spirit in the political differences at Lisbon. Black Charlie amazingly refrained from blowing his top.

Lord Auckland asked the Admiral:

> I beg you to forget what is passed; to hold the natural tenor of your way; to bear in mind – as you have done – your instructions; and to be on terms of hospitality and good fellowship with all parties. . . I can only assure you that I look with pride and satisfaction at the manner in which you have fulfilled the objects of your command.

This happy state of affairs soon ended. On New Year's Day 1849 Lord Auckland died, to be succeeded as First Lord of the Admiralty by Sir Francis Baring, who had been Black Charlie's Conservative opponent in the 1833 Portsmouth election. Friendly letters followed –

'. . to do nothing proves often the greater judgement and prudence than to run risks for little good,' Baring magisterially told Charlie when expressing his satisfaction over the business of the Riff tribesmen. But on 5 April, when the Channel Squadron returned to Spithead, Charlie found orders to haul down his flag. He was to be replaced, after about half the usual length of the appointment, by his second-in-command.

The last to take this lying down, Charlie immediately protested; writing to ministers in the bluntest of terms:

> Bad as the naval administration was before the Navy and Victualling Boards were abolished, it is ten times worse now. . . There is no responsiblity whatever, for the responsibility of the six gentlemen comprising the Board of Admiralty is not worth a straw. . .
>
> Who is responsible for the many millions of money thrown away in building an inefficient fleet that the Admiralty do not know what to do with? . . . had the First Lord been a naval officer the country would have fixed responsibility on him – he could not escape. How can a civilian know whether a butcher's tray or a washing tub is the best form for a man-of-war?. . . The Admiralty cost £36,303. £4,503 goes to the First Lord, who knows nothing. . . Our dockyard people have no idea of the waste of time and materials in their work: all naval officers are aware of it, but we are told we are no judges.

He was, of course, immediately at odds with the Administration, and when he applied for the Mediterranean Fleet, Lord John Russell not surprisingly gave it to an easier officer, a member of the board, Admiral James Dundas. He explained, mildly: 'It is necessary to choose an officer who will possess the full confidence of the government, an officer in whose secrecy and discretion the Queen's Ministers can rely.'

Black Charlie came back at him pugnaciously: 'I don't dispute, my Lord, your right to appoint whom you please, I dispute your right to damn my professional reputation. This is not the time to affront an officer who has rendered some service to his Queen and country when France with an army of 40,000 men is in a blaze.'

Still nursing a wounded honour, still determined to be vindicated, Black Charlie sent the whole correspondence to *The Times*, who took his side:

The government held an officer guilty of misdemeanour in disclosing administrative malpractices which were reckoned among secrets of state. . . Why [Delane, the editor, asked] should he be bound by professional consideration to connive at robbery of the public? The government assigns to professional incapacity a slight which was in reality due to political offences. Lord John Russell identifies the secrecy and discretion exacted from an officer in high command with the secrecy and discretion expected from an accomplice in a job.

Black Charlie's indignant rumblings did not exactly sweeten the intractable Napier image already existing in high places.

Baulked of the coveted naval command in the Mediterranean, Charlie was now past caring how he offended. The latest scare had 'left us with not one full-manned line-of-battle ship in England . . . We have Russia on our left flank, with a large fleet in the Baltic, and France with a harbour capable of holding a large fleet in our front, waiting only a railroad from Paris to make it complete.' Gone were the days when fleets and armies took months to collect; steam and the railroad had made appalling surprises possible. What would happen if France and Russia were to gang up against us? 'I do not think they will pay much attention to Cobden's Peace Congress. One wants to go to Constantinople, the other wants to go to the Rhine, and we want to prevent both. . .'
Why could we never learn?

During the latter years of a long peace influential imbecility was in charge of promotion, so that we started every war with a large proportion of the high command unfit for their duties. While democratic clamour starves down the establishment to a ruinously low standard in point of amount, aristocratic cupidity paralyses the direction and nullifies the exertions of that part which is allowed to exist. The disasters at the commencement of the war of 1756, during the whole of the American contest, during the first years of the Revolutionary contest, and in the dreadful campaign of Afghanistan in 1840, may be all traced to the combined operations of these causes.

In 1848 the eruption of half Europe into revolution had stirred Charlie into fresh effort. He conceded to Lord John Russell:

It may be argued that the French are quarrelling among themselves. What, my Lord, would unite them so soon as a war cry?
It appears the Government have got the better of the Red
Republicans. The people of France are told by their President
they have an army of 450,000 men, a sailing Navy nearly equal
to our own, and a steam Navy far superior... Were Louis
Napoleon to hold up his fingers, and pronounce the name of
England, I verily believe the whole army, Red Republicans and
all, would throw up their caps, and rush to the sea coast, just as
the gold diggers do to California. [Then] it would be Hey, for
England! and what, my Lord, have we to prevent them? Let Mr
Cobden and his party arbitrate as they will ... and no man
will be happier than I shall be to see all our establishments
reduced... But until he has got his arbitration into play, let us,
for God's sake, take care of ourselves...

He proceeded to outline a plan.

Why, he asked, did he feel called upon to write to the Prime
Minister?

For six years that I sat in the House of Commons, I endeavoured
to draw the attention of Government and of Parliament and,
through them, of the country, to the enormous waste of money in
the Naval Department, and more especially in the construction
of steam ships of war; the then Board of Admiralty, and their
predecessors, being equally culpable, successfully resisted all en-
quiry; and on one occasion, when I warned them of the folly of
building five or six iron steamers without trying one, I was met by
the Secretary exultantly proclaiming 'We're building forty!'

Never had the authorities taken the elementary precaution of
getting together the constructor, engineer and seaman, to solve the
vital problem of ensuring protection for a warship's boilers and
ammunition.

Although I had more experience in the construction of steam
vessels than most naval officers, I had not the presumption to
suppose that all my views were correct; all I asked at different
times, in and out of Parliament, was the appointment of a committee of naval officers and engineers, to weigh well all the difficulties and come to some system, instead of groping in the
dark, and wasting the public money.

We seemed to learn nothing. During his time in command of the Channel Squadron, twenty-nine steamships had come under Charlie's consideration. He had sent detailed reports on their shortcomings to the Admiralty with nil results: '... we are still working in the dark, and the four or five steamers now on the stocks will be little more efficient than those already in the water. . .'
Money might be short, the remedy was clear.

Search closely into all your departments; ransack the dockyards, and you will find the means of saving thousands and thousands of pounds, appoint a committee of experienced steam officers to decide her future steam vessels shall be built; give up cutting and carving and changing ship's bows and sterns; give up converting good sailing ships into bad steamers at an enormous expense; and you will have no occasion to go to Parliament for your money...

No reply, and a fortnight later Charlie was at it again. The whole trouble lay in the constitution of the Board of Admiralty, involving as it did 'delays, blunders, confusion and waste'. It never seemed clear who was responsible for what.

Who is responsible for all the bad ships that have been built and broken up? How comes it that the best two-decked ships we have are copies from the French? Who is responsible for allowing so many ships to be built after the plan of the late Surveyor, which is now abandoned?
   There is no want of talent in the country; a better man cannot be found for the Surveyor's department than Sir Baldwin Walker. Give him rope enough, and – I will answer for it – hundreds of pounds will be saved and there will be no more bungling... I feel quite certain the country will get tired of giving money to the Navy to be expended without doing good. Thousands of pounds might be saved in your dockyards. That is where you ought to economize – not in paying off your seamen, whom you have encouraged to come into the service, and whom you may want when least expected.
   I remain, your Lordship's obedient servant,

Charlie concluded inaccurately. Disobedient or not, would anyone ever listen to him? He went on firmly believing that in time they would.

After his chagrin over the Mediterranean command being given to Dundas 'who hardly ever saw a shot fired', and had not been actually at sea for thirty years, Charlie grumbled, he had effected a further burning of his boats by enlisting the press on his side. 'I owe my position to my sword alone,' Charlie had declared proudly, pointing out his absence of 'interest with any party', but he was now to stick his neck out a long way in owing it partly to the press. For twenty years he had tried to bring reforms to his beloved Navy by a continuous private correspondence and by speeches in the Commons; now he was going public in a thorough manner. Not only, aided by William Napier (now a general and a KCB), did he publish his earlier letters to the authorities; far worse, he started writing to *The Times*. The odium thus acquired fell upon Charlie, and not upon its editor, John Delane, for his forthright support. 'We shall not be expected to acquiesce in this view of public duty,' *The Times* leader had declared. It was not 'laudable discretion to keep the country in the dark . . . over the hundreds and thousands a year unnecessarily squandered in our naval establishments'. Delane did not sweeten the pill by pointing out of Charlie that: 'Many of his recommendations were actually adopted, and savings of consequence effected. This proves that his suggestions were both sound and practicable.' Charlie was not 'bound by any professional considerations to connive at the robbery of the public'.

Were all officers expected to be lickspittles, *The Times* inquired (only rather more politely). 'Failing this obsequiousness, his professional qualities will be called into question, and he will be told that "no confidence can be placed" in his ability to command a garrison or a squadron.'

The row rumbled on. After a passage of arms in the press with the Duke of Portland about the fighting qualities of *Retribution* and *Terrible,* and the sailing qualities of the brigs *Helena, Pilot* and *Frolic,* at all of whose trials Charlie had been present and His Grace had not, Portland carried the battle into the midst of the foe. He wrote in *The Times:* 'I join you most cordially in professing the highest respect for, and admiration of Sir C. Napier, the General. What I know of the Admiral does not incline me to make the same profession as to him.'

The shades of evening appeared to be closing round Black Charlie. Written off in many quarters as just another irascible old windbag, he had to content himself with the pleasures of home, augmented when the other Sir Charles Napier bought a house in his near neighbourhood. 'I have had fun with Black Charles,' the General wrote. They had mocked each other about their plantations and their fishponds 'full of queer fish' Black Charlie had teased; and the General had 'offered to put him in it as the queerest fish of all'. But the older Sir Charles, conqueror of Sind, had come home from India only to die; in August of 1853 his painful disease had finally overcome him.

Black Charlie told his wife:

The General was buried yesterday and all Portsmouth were at his funeral. It was not an official one [the other Charles had also fallen foul of the Government] but all the soldiers and officers and the Navy attended; it was a pleasing thing to see such respect shown to so good and great a man. He had suffered much and long before he died; he fought a battle with the Enemy with as much courage as he always did, but was beaten at last.

Charlie himself may have felt a bit beaten. His first cousin and namesake, his lifelong friend and supporter and sharer of jokes from childhood onwards, had gone. Although his brother Tom was now general, KCB and Governor of Edinburgh Castle his brother Francis had died in India. Charlie's naval stepson, whom he loved, and upon whom he had counted as a staff for old age, had also gone. Professionally he was shelved and of no account, and the naval establishment was still chaotic – 'We are blundering as much as before we did. . . What is doing in one dockyard is undone in another; nay, more what we are doing in one part of the same dockyard we are undoing in another part.' If he felt that he had spent a lifetime whistling down the wind, he could hardly have been blamed.

But Black Charlie had always been one of the Never-Say-Die Brigade. His resuscitation came from an unexpected quarter. In May 1854 Czar Nicholas of Russia ordered his troops into Roumania, en route to enforce his demands upon Turkey. In answer to a letter from the new First Lord, Sir James Graham, awarding him a vice-admiral's good service pension for 'gallant conduct on active service', Black Charlie wrote: 'I see the Russians have crossed the Pruth; if my services are wanted, I am quite ready for work, both in body and mind.'

13

'Gallant Charley'

The Administration were in a fix. Someone must take the fleet into the Baltic, to bottle up the Russian ships, and if given a chance, destroy them; but who? Sir James Graham of Netherby, precise, black frock-coated, conscious rectitude up to the eyebrows, considered the alternatives. The great Cochrane, now Lord Dundonald, was seventy-nine, and stipulated that if he were given command of the fleet against Russia he must be allowed to destroy the great stone fortress of Kronstadt by a chemical process he had recently invented. (Dundonald worked continuously in the laboratory he had built behind his London house; had he split the atom? We shall never know.) This condition shook the Admiralty. Sir William Parker was known to be in failing health; Sir George Seymour was not much fitter and in any case was in Bermuda. Dundas was in command in the Mediterranean. There remained Black Charlie.

Graham wrote to Queen Victoria:

Sir Charles Napier is an excellent seaman, and combines boldness with discretion. He has served in large squadrons, and he has commanded them. As a second-in-command he may not have been submissive, as a chief he has been successful in command. The appointment will give confidence to both officers and men, and his name is not unknown, both to enemies and allies.

If he has the faults of his family he is not without their virtues [Sir James continued, on a patronizing note that would have profoundly irritated Charlie, had he known of it]. Courage, genius, love of country are not wanting, and the weighty responsibility of a high command, without depressing him, would give steadiness to his demeanour.

The one consideration which seemed to strike no one, least of all Charlie, was that in March of this year he would be sixty-eight.

On shore he has given just cause for complaint. But at sea and in command he is a different person, and Lord John Russell in the Cabinet yesterday, regardless of all former displeasure, pronounced an opinion favourable to the appointment. The entire Cabinet came to the same conclusion.

It was a conclusion which they took some weeks to communicate to Black Charles. He tried three times to see Graham, and was refused. He pointed out: 'The time to organize a fleet is short, we have a powerful enemy to meet, we may have to fight a great battle in a few weeks at sea.'

'The command is a very serious affair and cannot be decided in a hurry,' Graham told him some weeks after the decision had been taken. Charlie's major concern was over the manning of the fleet. 'It would be very difficult to keep clear of France in her excited mood,' he had thought in 1848; and ever since then, with thunders from his native oak, he agitated constantly in the press about the shortage of trained seamen; why did the public imagine men could be trained overnight in sail and in gunnery? Now, in his old age, he was to fall victim to the maladministration that would be responsible for the miseries of the Crimea, and against which he had so long, so bravely and so tactlessly contended.

The fleet was still scattered hither and yon, unorganized, not yet manned. All the seamen of long standing were with Admiral Dundas's fleet in the Mediterranean. In the seaports a Russian war made little appeal. France was the time-honoured foe and no one felt themselves in danger from Russian attack. The Merchant Navy's new iron steamers, and the far more beautiful and swift new clippers, exerted a powerful attraction upon young seamen. Largely as a result of Black Charlie's incessant pressure, impressment had been abolished, and a bill passed by which a bounty could, in the event of war, be offered to all experienced seamen who volunteered promptly. This offer Graham declined to make; there were not the funds to do it.

By the end of 1853 the Crimean War loomed with dreadful inevitability; but few people took it very seriously. Defeating the Russians would offer no major problems; it should be a Home by Christmas affair. As the year ended, Black Charlie mourned to Sir James Graham: 'Had I been in the Mediterranean now I could have rendered good service. I should have had considerable influence with

Turks, as having led them to victory, and they have not forgotten me.'

On the whole euphoria prevailed; except amongst Cassandra-like characters such as William Napier, who knew the state of disorganization in the army, and was accurately predicting the disasters that were to follow, advising remedies and being snubbed for his pains.

A cautionary note was also sounded by Captain B. J. Sulivan of the Navy writing to *The Times* in December, and warning the public over the absurd expectations aroused by the popular press, which assured them that the British and French fleets would quickly destroy Sebastopol and the Russian fleet of equal size anchored under its harbour fortifications. Sulivan pointed out that neither Nelson, Collingwood nor Exmouth ever thought of attacking a French fleet at Toulon, however great their own superiority in ships; and ships, as the Duke of Wellington had recently said, could not contend successfully with stone walls. Recent improvements in guns and ammunition favoured batteries rather than ships. Sulivan ended by assuring the public that the admirals would attempt as much as any men in their situation would be justified in doing. This note of sanity was drowned in the press chorus.

By January war was imminent, and Black Charlie, in Norfolk with his daughter, was hemmed in by thick snow and 'no carriage way open in two miles of our house'. Undeterred, Charlie set out for London through the drifts, stumping steadily in the snow with a lad to carry his carpet bag, keeping under the lee of the hedges till he gained the highroad where he had ordered a fly to await him and take him to Lowestoft. Small joy awaited him in London.

> I am told by the different Lords of the Admiralty and indeed by everybody, that I am to command the Baltic Fleet; but the Government are not taking any vigorous measures to man the fleet, and it will be quite impossible to get it ready for action by the time the Baltic is open.

Once the ice melted to free their fleet. the Russians could slip through into the North Sea and do goodness knew what damage before anyone was there to stop them. Charlie was kept in great suspense, he told his daughter a few days later:

> ... not so much on my own account, as on account of the

short time there is to organize the fleet. [He found the Cabinet] quite insensible to our danger, and too parsimonious to offer a bounty, and very few efficient men are entered.

The brunt would fall on me, if I went. They [The Cabinet] are perfectly ignorant and Graham will not listen to the Board. I told Lord Clarendon that if the fleet were not properly manned, no man of character would take the command. He said I was always finding fault. I replied that my finding fault was the cause of us so far having a Navy, and if they would give me a ten pound note in one hand and grog in the other, I would man the fleet for them.

Charlie's forthrightness came near to queering his pitch. 'Under these circumstances, I should not be at all surprised if I was not appointed.'

Appointed he was, but on 24 February Sir James Graham refused to issue the bounty. He told a protesting Charlie, 'It would be a sign of distress, impolitic and unnecessary.' He could not sanction it. Nor were the sailors to be equipped with warm clothing. They must either buy it themselves, or go without. And Napier, 'if dissatisfied with the preparation . . . had better say so at once, and decline to accept the command.'

The furious old Admiral came back at him from 18 Albemarle Street on the 24th:

I never refuse duty. I never made difficulties when service was required, and after a life spent in honour, I am not going to make them now . . . with the means at my disposal I will do all I can for the honour and glory of my Queen and country which shall not be tarnished in my hands . . .

But to his daughter he had admitted on 23 February: 'I yesterday was nearly pitching the whole concern to the Devil. I urged Sir James Graham to give a bounty, which he refused, and then wrote me an improper letter.' (Improper was a word still without salacious undertones.) But the prospects for smooth cooperation between Commander-in-Chief and Civil Lord seemed dim.

When the first division was ready for sea, Black Charlie was to proceed to Wingo Sound, on the coast of Sweden, and there wait for the rest of his ships, at present still making their way home from Lisbon, Bermuda, the Indies, and other still more distant stations. His flagship was the *Duke of Wellington,* a large three-decker with 113 guns. His captain was George Gordon and the Captain of the Fleet was Sir Michael Seymour (the 2nd). The battleships to follow him in the line were *Royal George, St Jean d'Acre, Princess Royal, Hogue, Ajax, Blenheim,* with *Edinburgh* (flag of Rear-Admiral Chads). His screw frigates were *Impérieuse, Arrogant, Amphion* and *Tribune;* in addition were the paddle steamers *Leopard* (flag of Rear-Admiral Plumridge), *Dragon* and *Valorous.*

There were no gunboats, essential in the shoals and narrows of the Gulf of Finland and the Baltic shores; 'it may be possible for you to hire some small vessels of the sort and size required,' Graham hazarded on 12 March. As to the absence of skilled seamen, he could pick some up in Scandinavia. There was also a shortage of stores, clothing, shot and shell and small arms ammunition.

Whatever the seamen thought, popular enthusiasm was great. 'Despotic Nick' deserved defeat, sang the music halls. The Czar was a tyrant, and broadsheets showered forth like snow. 'Bold Napier!' they cried, and 'Give it to him, Charley!' and 'Hurrah for England and Charlie Napier!' In one popular song he was 'England's bluff old Charley'–

> I'll tell how British seamen brave
> Of Russian foes will clear the wave
> Old England's credit for to save
> Led on by gallant Charley. . .
> No Russian foe can e'er withstand
> So brave a man as Charley. . .

and including the truly appalling couplet:

> Our gallant tars led by Napier
> May bid defiance to the Bear. . .

'It is the deuce of a job', Charlie told a friend. His discomfort was piled high by the country's overweening confidence. Diners at a Reform Club banquet were in the same wildly bombastic frame of mind. Lord Palmerston and others eulogized Charlie, and gave such appallingly free rein to the frantic boast and the foolish word as made the Admiral's hair stand on end. These who were lauding him up to the skies had never seen a shot fired in anger and appeared to have no notion of what war could or couldn't do, at sea or on land; and would be the first to howl at him and his men for failure. Charlie, afterwards accused of bombast, remained surprisingly calm, talked about the lambing season, and made a sober estimate of his chances. He praised his ships, but:

> I do not mean to say that our fleet is yet in order, but I believe that, considering the officers that have been appointed to it, it very soon will be. With the force that we have, although it is not equal to the Russian force, I believe that by the assistance of the screw we shall be able to attack a very superior force.

Should this chance come their way, Charlie felt sure that 'every sailor and every officer in our fleet will remember the words of Lord Nelson, that England expects'.

At Portsmouth Charlie could hardly have been more closely mobbed by cheering crowds had he been Nelson himself; and there was a further flow of guff at the Guildhall from the Mayor, Alderman Styant. Charlie was 'one of the greatest men of his age'. This was followed by another outpouring of adulation from the municipality. In vain did Charlie, in a sober speech, implore them to dampen expectation. After thirty years of peace there were few present to recall the actual horrors of war. Enthusiasm had taken hold, and as he spoke, cheer followed cheer.

Charlie told them in a brief speech of thanks:

> I will do the best I can. But gentlemen, you must not expect too much. We are going to meet no common enemy; we are going to meet an enemy well-prepared. I am sure every officer and man in the fleet will do his duty gloriously, but at the same time, I warn you again that you must not expect too much The fleet is a new one, the system of warfare is new; great consideration is required to ascertain how it is best to manage a fleet urged by steam. The system of warfare is entirely different now to what it was formerly; but we will do our best – and I am sure I shall remember to the last day of my life the kindness of the people of Portsmouth.

Loud cheers. But one reporter, doggedly sticking to his party guns, described the speech as 'one of complacent self-assurance'.

Black Charlie hoisted his flag in the *Duke of Wellington*, and the ships put out from Spithead on 4 March 1854, standing up Channel

with a fair wind and all sails set. To the young and the unknowing
there was an air of regatta about it all; an atmosphere of innocence
and picnic. 'Gloriously they bore along, followed by the prayers and
good wishes of us all,' wrote Queen Victoria, who led the fleet out
to sea in the Royal Yacht, *Fairy*, her eyes filling with tears as the
crews of each warship cheered her from the rigging as they passed.

The hearts of its commanders were heavy. It was a fleet under-
manned and ill-equipped: a sprinkling of coast-guards were the only
experienced seamen on board. Some of the sailors were cabmen, the
majority had never been to sea at all. The men sent into these icy seas
were short of clothing; the fleet was short of stores, of every kind of
equipment, of shot and shell. Sent to operate in a shallow sea, they
lacked pilots and charts, and were without gunboats or mortars. The
Monarch had, Charlie reported, 'hardly a man in her who knows a
rope, she could barely sail, let alone fight'; Captain Codrington of the
Royal George was issued on the day of departure with 200 rifles, but
no cartridges; his repeated demand for them went unanswered. It was
the same old sad story – the peace-loving nation forever assuming
that unreadiness is a safeguard, and that war is to be avoided simply
by hating it and hoping it will never happen. And what harm had
Russia ever done Britain, apart from switching sides during the last
long war and fighting alongside Napoleon instead of against him for
three years? Russia to many clearly came into the category of 'a far
away country of which we know little'. The Czar was a tyrant but
seemed as far distant as the Oxus. Any personal peril could therefore
be discounted.

Black Charlie's earlier activities no doubt remained in official
memories. Given half a chance, he would land with a party of 500
marines and attempt to encircle St Petersburg. His orders were
distinctly laid down. He was to contain the Russian fleet and if
possible bring it to action. He was to blockade the great waterway of
the Baltic and 'cut up' Russian trade. He was by no means to
contemplate the possibility of an attack on Sveaborg or Kronstadt, or
'to risk the fleet in any desperate enterprise'. In May Graham again
cautioned Black Charlie against impetuosity:

> I by no means contemplate an attack on Sveaborg or Kronstadt;
> I have a great respect for stone walls, and have no fancy for
> running even screw line-of-battle ships against them because the
> public here may be impatient.

But by autumn the public impatience had got the rectitudinous Sir James Graham in its grip.

14

'You Must Grope Your Way'

Enthusiasm for this Russian expedition was minimal amongst the seamen. Henry Seymour, of the *Cumberland,* reported very gloomily to his father, Admiral Sir George Seymour, in Bermuda, of 'the insubordination and ill feeling in your old ship's company who have been behaving atrociously'. Admiral Berkeley had been on board, he had reported from Spithead on 7 April, 'and had made the sailors an excellent speech on our arrival', but his only response had been a general murmur of 'Leave! Leave!' They had sulked all the next day, Seymour complained, and done little work,

> ... tho' three ringleaders were given 4 dozen lashes each for agitation meetings [and, though contrarily,] they had cheered cordially enough when turned out to see off the 95th regiment to Constantinople, that night Ordinary Seaman Kirby had thrown a knife at the boatswain and had been supported by several men when the boatswain collared him.

Henry Seymour, who evidently was no sharer of Black Charlie's dislike of the lash, ordered that the recalcitrant Kirby should be given three dozen:

> I was afraid of going further than I did for fear of killing him. At the beginning of the second dozen I reprimanded Freeman for not punishing properly and immediately a murmur in the back-ground of 'Shame' arose, and a considerable movement among the men took place, enough to cause all the officers and myself to draw their swords. I went close to the men and endeavoured to find somebody to pitch upon. But all was quiet again, though an uncertain sort of quiet ... I cannot say how friendly and energetic Adl Berkely has been in my support.

None of which seemed to bode well for the campaign, though by the time the *Cumberland* had taken on 'shot, shell and powder for the squadron' at the Downs on the 10th and was proceeding towards

Kioge Bay ('we go through the Great Belt as we are very deep now'), he was able to report:

> everything now is quite right on board and I have not the slightest fear for the future. The men are working cheerily again and our troubles I hope are at an end. We must work to establish a new character. . .
>
> Now my dearest Father believe me you shall have a different account of us if the Russian fleet come out.

But would the Russian fleet oblige? All hinged upon this. B. J. Sulivan, captain of the surveying ship *Lightning,* and arriving to join the fleet this April, shared Black Charlie's gloomy views as to its readiness to make war.

> The newly commissioned ships were very badly manned. The whole state of the fleet proved without doubt that we were utterly without means of fitting out a war fleet in an emergency. [He at once noted the cavalier way in which Charlie was being treated by the home authorities.] He wisely disposed his fleet to prevent Russian ships passing the Belt, and yet in consequence received a reprimand . . . In reply to Napier's request for pilots, he was informed 'You must grope your way in your own survey vessels.'

On 9 April a Swedish naval officer told Sulivan that such was their dread of Russia that 'every Swede was with us in heart'; there was a feeling that their hearts might have directed them towards supplying a local pilot or two. Sulivan was not in favour of this; he considered that a Swedish pilot might well be in Russian pay and tempted to lead ships to their doom.

Sulivan was an unusual man, combining strong religious feeling with a level-headed realism, and a judgement dispassionate and unprejudiced. He was a handsome man, with beautiful deep-set eyes that were extremely useful as well; he could discern the moons of Jupiter without telescope or glasses. He succeeded in stopping swearing amongst officers and men of the *Lightning,* and was careful of the feelings of Finns, Swedes and Russians, paying on the nail for all supplies taken on shore. He had thoughtfully provided himself with a quantity of copies of the Bible, in Swedish, Finnish and Russian, which he was to distribute when occasion arose. He kept a journal and wrote regularly to his wife and to the affectionate son who became his biographer after he died as a full admiral.

Among the ships assembled and assembling at Kioge there were no shallow draught vessels essential for operations in the shoals and narrows of the Gulf of Finland and along the Baltic shores. Graham had thought it possible for Charlie to hire some small vessels from the locals. This turned out not to be so. And, as to the absence of skilled seamen - 'pilots may be obtained at Kiel ... you may perhaps contrive to pick up some Norwegian sailors, but they dislike the Swedes and will not pull together in the same ship.' As Black Charlie had nothing to offer these, apart from the doubtful pleasure of fighting in someone else's war, all attempts to enlist them failed.

Writing from the anchorage at Kioge and listening to the reports of shortages of stores, clothing, shot, shell and small arms ammunition, Charlie insisted that:

> ... a number of small steamers are absolutely necessary, for dispatches, for fire vessels, and also to protect us from fire vessels. . . Though we are now lying in a neutral port, I take it for granted the Russians would not be very particular.

'We are getting on fast with our exercises,' he reported hopefully on the 22nd. 'Admiral Chads (*Edinburgh*) and *Ajax* are very badly manned; pray reinforce them.' 'I hope to hear that you have been able to enter men in the Baltic,' Graham replied coldly to this plea. Reporting to Graham on the 26th that *Neptune*, *Bulldog*, *Monarch* and *Vulture* had joined him, Charlie added that 'the former will do well, but *Monarch* is bad, hardly fit to go to sea, and certainly not fit to fight. It would be better to give them more time, for in the state they join me they are only a nominal force.' As such, they were enough to frighten the Russians into staying in harbour, but not good enough should they come out, which everyone in the British fleet heartily hoped they would.

'I have not been able to get pilots either here or at Elsinore,' Charlie reported; but all the same the fleet were through to the Baltic and anchored off Kiel (at this time still Danish) by 27 March. Captain Lyons in the *Miranda* had been sent scouting up the Baltic, and even after forcing his ship through fifty miles of ice to see what was going on in Reval, reported the Russian fleet still ice-bound at Sveaborg. 'Up at six every morning,' Charlie told his daughter, 'but I am very well. This is a splendid ship, and we are getting on with our exercises.'

He besought Admiral Berkeley: 'Be sure you send us powder and shot. And men! *Ajax* and *Monarch* are badly manned ... The *Monarch* is in a deplorable state ... there is hardly a man in her who knows a rope.'

As to powder and shot, Berkeley answered him:

> You must hold hard in the expenditure of powder and shells for practice ... Like everything else, the shells are on a peace establishment ... the stock is barely sufficient to meet what may be required in action – without expending any for practice.

Sir James Graham urged Charlie not to be 'over nice, and refuse to take on board good seamen' wherever they came from. He imagined an eager crowd of Danes, Norwegians and Swedes, pressing to sign on. None did.

Shortages everywhere; but even by arriving in Kiel before the Baltic ice melted, Black Charlie had already achieved what his Victorian biographer calls 'the kind of silent victory never properly understood or appreciated by the public'. The Russians were now effectively bottled up in the Baltic, and their northern trade was at the mercy of the Royal Navy; but at home this buttered no parsnips. Charlie was cheered by a letter from his old friend Hamilton Seymour, now in London, who had recently been ambassador in St Petersburg and was well aware of the forces that Charlie was up against. He wrote:

> I am doing all I can to make our countrymen more moderate in their expectations, and to explain to them that you cannot sail over the ice and take Kronstadt by the wasp's nest process, and even if Kronstadt is taken, the Winter Palace is too large to be packed up for erection in Trafalgar Square.
>
> Good luck attend you. The closer you clip the wings of the Great Bird of Prey of the North the happier I shall be.

Good luck seemed a fitful fairy. The fleet lay in heavy fog, as the cold air from the melting ice met the warmer layers from the southern seas. 'When the sea opens I shall have thirty in my front,' Charlie told his daughter, 'and unless I am reinforced shall have enough to do.' The Admiralty were still refusing the bounty, 'and the ships that are here are not fit for action. I suppose', he added wistfully, as his ships rolled at anchor in the pervasive fog, 'that everything is beginning to look beautiful at Merchiston ... My love to the children. I shall long to get home again after the turmoil of command.'

The Admiralty now gloomily told Charlie that intelligence

reported that the Russians had mined Sveaborg, Kronstadt and Reval, and had two floating batteries at Kronstadt armed with 98-pounders, plus 128 guns mounted on a fort, and that the Russian plan was to lie close in harbour until these had pounded the British ships into disablement. They would then come forth, summoning the Sveaborg division, and complete the destruction.

Black Charlie, whatever press and public might urge, was too wily an old fox to walk, without gunboats or mortars, into this trap.

Forgetting their orders of 10 March for him to proceed to Kiel, on the 24th the Admiralty had sent Charlie a sharp reprimand for having done so; he should have 'remained in Wingo Sound until further orders'. Charlie countered this in brisk terms:

> Had I waited until the ice broke up, and the Baltic was free, while I was passing the Belt, the Russians might have passed the Sound, and what would the Government then have said to me? Suspended me, to be sure, and serve me right.

'You are a queer set of fellows at the Admiralty,' he told Admiral Berkeley. By 8 April he had a letter from the Board expressing 'entire satisfaction with your proceedings'. Queerer still. The First Lord added a cautionary note. 'I rely on your prudence in not knocking your head against stone walls prematurely, or without the certainty of a great success.'

There was irritation at home with Black Charlie for banging on so constantly about the manning of the fleet. 'Have you been able to pick up any Swedes or Norwegians?' Sir James Graham asked hopefully on 5 April. 'We are coming to a dead stand as to seamen,' Admiral Berkeley had admitted on 30 March. 'Something must be done, and done speedily, or there will be a break-down in our present rickety system.' As Charlie could have told him, there had been a breakdown already. On 6 April Berkeley was telling Charlie that *St George* and *Cumberland* would be joining him, 'but men – men – men are wanting.' He thought the Czar must be mad not to 'try his strength with you, while he musters double your numbers, and whilst your crews are so miserably raw'. There was method in the Czar's madness. The Russians were to prove themselves as effective in exploiting the defence possibilities of their ice, their shallows, and their narrow rocky passages as they were on land of making use of their terrible winters.

Not only crews were raw. Some of the senior officers were not so polished either. It was understandable that *Cressy* and *Princess Royal* should collide in the shifting fogs, but 'though I am doing all I can to keep the captains up to the mark, I meet with little success; they attend to neither signals or guns. . . The fact is, they know nothing about it, and say so.' Nobody attempted to keep station; the fatal lack of training was all too evident to interested observers; and the Prussians, drawing their own conclusions from the lumbering British fleet, quickly placed their port Memel at the service of the Czar. The British government, amazed and shocked, reacted by telling Charlie to capture any British colliers bound for Memel, on the doubtful grounds that the coal *might* be meant for the Russians.

Sulivan shared Charlie's doubts about the fleet. It mustered in all thirty pennants, he wrote early in April:

> . . . but most of the large ships want time to get into anything like order. The admiral and captain of the fleet are not particular enough, they let the ships form a bad line anchoring, and do not make them move again; but they work them hard at the guns.
>
> The *Duke of Wellington* sails beautifully. . . *St Jean d'Acre* running freely nearly comes up to her, *Neptune* is an astonishing ship. Though an old 120 she sails nearly equal with the *Duke*, and having the *Regent*'s old crew, is certainly the crack ship of the fleet. . . *Boscawen* is also one of the fastest. . . *Edinburgh* is in good order and goes well. . . *Euryalus* is the most beautiful ship I ever saw . . . the finest vessel in the world.

Of the rest he did not think much, and '*Hogue* has 2 or 3 times had a desire to run over us', as Sulivan led in his little surveying vessel, the *Lightning*. Even the Admiralty admitted that 'there is want of energy among the superior officers that must be noticed'.

The Swedish government had prudently declined to join in against Russia, and the Danish pilots, who alone knew the Gulf of Finland, were forbidden by their government to serve in British ships. He could get round this, Black Charlie told Graham, if he were authorized to offer the pilots enough money. Permission refused. The French Squadron was clearly not going to arrive until mid-June. 'You must hold hard in the expenditure of shells for practice,' Admiral Berkeley again cautioned Charlie, as April went on.

A more even temper than Charlie's might by now have become a little ruffled. Surprisingly, Charlie's held. He sent *Leopard*,

Impérieuse, Tribune, Dauntless and *Lightning* north under Admiral Plumridge to examine the anchorage and fortifications at Hango Head, and to see how the ice was getting on, and if it still bottled up the Russians at Sveaborg. He was cheered by the arrival at Kioge Bay of *Archer, Boscawen, Caesar, Basilisk, Desperate, Magicienne, Cruiser* and *Driver,* all undermanned, but anyway *there.*

The captain of the *Dauntless,* returning on 18 April, reported the Gulf of Finland free of ice as far up as Sveaborg, in which harbour he had observed seven sail of the line and a frigate. So now, at last, Black Charlie could go north, confident that in the event of the Russians venturing out, he would be able to give a good account of them, notwithstanding that his squadron was still very far from efficient. Causing it to be announced in Berlin, Stockholm, Copenhagen and Hamburg that all Russian ports were under blockade, he addressed a signal to the squadron. Russia's official declaration of war had been made on 27 March, Clarendon informed Charlie on his arrival in Kioge Bay. On 12 April the squadron left Kioge Bay, passing to the northward of Bornholm and eastward of Gottland.

Black Charlie's signal to his fleet had a fine old-fashioned ring:

> Lads, war is declared with a numerous and bold enemy. Should they remain in port, we must try and get at them. Success depends upon quickness and precision of your firing. Also, lads, sharpen your cutlasses, and the day is your own.

But the day of cutlasses, the long day of cutlasses, was done; and Charlie's day perhaps had gone with it.

15

'Pause Long, and Consider Well'

Leaving *Conflict, Cruiser, Archer* and *Desperate* to blockade the Russian coast from the Gulf of Riga down to Libau, and sending *Neptune, Royal George, Boscawen, Hogue, Blenheim, Ajax, Euryalus, Dragon* and *Vulture* to intercept vessels trying to pass between the Russian and Swedish coasts, Charlie himself stood on for the Gulf of Finland in the *Duke of Wellington*. He had with him *Edinburgh, St Jean d'Acre, Princess Royal, Caesar, Cressy, Impérieuse, Amphion, Leopard, Magicienne, Gorgon* and *Driver*.

'No pilots, no buoys, no beacons,' Charlie mourned to Sulivan, when with his squadron near Hango Head. He had intended to run up the Gulf to reconnoitre Sveaborg; yet why, Sulivan wondered, had he not taken his surveying ships with him? He felt that the Admiral's constant demand for pilots was on account of the jealousy of Gordon, his Master of the Fleet, who insistently wanted them, disapproving of the naval surveying ships, who might steal his thunder. Probably informed of the British failure to obtain any local pilots, the Czar 'has taken away all the lights and beacons', in the justifiable hope that the British would run themselves aground in these tricky, uncharted seas.

'A great part of yesterday and all today a north east gale with rain, sleet and snow mixed ... it is just like a very bad winter's day at the Falklands,' Sulivan reported on 29 April. At the mouth of the Gulf of Finland the ships had encountered a gale from the east blowing directly down it; any attempt to approach Sveaborg had had to be postponed. Sulivan wrote:

> We cannot afford to weaken our force either by loss of ships or men, for we have now ships with very reduced crews, through sickness. A Russian fleet so superior in numbers would take advantage of any disablement and come out.

'In the night we tacked every two hours between the shoals off Hango Head and Dager Ort,' Charlie told Graham, 'by no means pleasant cruising ground with a squadron not one of whom, with the exception of Chads and Keppel, knew how to keep their station.' He thought that the Russians at Kronstadt, once free of ice, 'might push out a squadron, if they were bold, and get into the North Sea'. The Czar, however, knew a trick worth two of that. His ships stayed snug, while the British battled through the fog and the gales, with their undermanned ships and underclothed sailors.

Replying to this letter, Sir James Graham sent Charlie further implicit instructions:

> In the first instance you must feel your way and make good your hold on the Gulf of Finland. . . I by no means contemplate an attack on Sveaborg or Kronstadt. I have great respect for stone walls, and have no fancy for running even screw line-of-battle ships against them. Because the public may be impatient, you must not be rash. Because those at a distance from danger are foolhardy, you must not risk the loss of the fleet in an impossible enterprise. I believe both Kronstadt and Sveaborg to be all but impregnable from the sea, Sveaborg especially; and none but a very large army could cooperate by land efficiently, in the presence of such a force as Russia could readily concentrate. If you have no means but naval at your command, you must pause long, and consider well, before you attempt any attack on the Russian squadron in their strongholds. . .
>
> These considerations must not be overlooked by you, lest in the eager desire to achieve a great exploit and to satisfy the wild wishes of an impatient multitude at home, you should yield to some rash impulse, and fail in the discharge of the noblest of duties – which is the moral courage to do what you know to be right, at the risk of being accused of having done wrong. . .
> Reflect on it, and I am certain that your judgement will not err.

So far, confidence all round; but this did not extend to the newspapers. Charlie had been forbidden by the Admiralty to take the *Times* correspondent on board, which was a pity, as he might thereby have avoided much press odium. Other papers had their 'feed men', paid correspondents among the officers of the fleet. Graham told Charles: 'These reporters who misrepresent as well as comment, produce false impressions on the public mind, and render the conduct of warlike operations, whether by sea or by land, infinitely more difficult.' Charlie personally didn't mind their being there, provided that they did not unwittingly give away any information valuable to the foe.

Not only the press and public were impatient. Victor Montagu, a midshipman on board *Princess Royal,* recorded that:

> Throughout the war, Captain Keppel and Lord Clarence Paget . . . were always trying to infuse more spirit into what was done. How the Baltic-Do-Nothing policy affronted those two enterprising minds! Keppel was full of dash and fire, always blessed with an iron constitution. . .

Keppel's dash and fire, two years later, were to cause him to run the *Raleigh* on a rock off Hong Kong and lose her; and he had to be hauled out of the Canton river, in the midst of a battle with numerous hostile junks, by the third Sir Michael Seymour; but he was a charming and much-loved man, and his influence was considerable. He had friends in all walks of life, and many of these dwelt in the seats of power. His opinions carried weight with them.

Twelfth out of the sixteen children of the 4th Lord Albemarle, Harry Keppel was now captain of the *St Jean d'Acre,* known to the seamen as the 'Jenny Daker'. He was the possessor of at least nine lives and well prepared to throw one away in the Baltic. He had started living dangerously at an unusually early age. When in June 1809 a fifth son, seemingly stillborn, was ushered into the Albemarle family, they had said a brief prayer, and put his pale, shrimp-like little body into the fish-kettle, preparing to bury him in the back garden of their London house, a proceeding not yet illegal. As the lid was about to be laid on, the family nanny, hawk-eyed as nannies are where babies are concerned, saw the faintest movement of the baby's left eyelid, as if in an almost imperceptible wink. She fished him out of the fish-kettle, and he lived to be ninety-five.

Keppel had served with Black Charlie before, in the *Galatea,* where he got into some trouble when truanting ashore at a dance in the West Indies. He had been somewhat mocking of Charlie's paddles:

> Old Charlie had a hobby, which was that he could propel a ship with paddle wheels which could be fixed or withdrawn from a ship's sides . . . propelled by iron winch handles attached to stanchions on either side of the main deck . . . They did not succeed against the slightest head wind.

Lord Clarence Paget too, commanding the *Princess Royal,* had

been unimpressed by Charlie's attitude when he met him at the start
of the Baltic campaign:

> Charlie began by lighting his cigar and saying that he had the
> deuce of a job in hand, to go into an enemy's waters and attack
> a foe numerically superior and of greater efficiency than our
> own . . . in fact, he said, with a raw squadron.

To Paget, this seemed defeatism rather than realism, and he was far
from being unique in his opinions, as the blockading ships lay in the
lee of Gottska Sando, a small island in the Baltic midway between the
Swedish coast and the island off the north of the Gulf of Riga in
Russia.

Would the Russian fleet oblige? There were hopeful rumours. On 12
May, off Gottska Sando, Henry Seymour reported:

> A frigate coming in, the signals flying about there being 20 sail
> of Russians ready for sea off Helsingfors, and the fleet were
> weighing in consequence as I thought; I hoisted 'ready' and Sir
> Charles good-naturedly allowed me a steamer to bring me out
> with the others – it was a very thick fog. . .
>
> Since then we have been cruising continually off this small
> island, and disagreeable work it has been, there generally being
> a fog for 8 hours daily out of the 24.

Whenever the weather made it possible, the work of manoeuvring
and exercising was incessant, he reported, and the weather was bitterly cold:

> I can hear nothing whatever being in contemplation, which I fear
> will give rise to dissatisfaction at home, and I wish the Admiral
> would make a move, if not towards the greater fortified places
> which I believe would be useless, yet Hango which is not so very
> strong and would be a good station at the entrance of the Gulf of
> Finland would be a something to keep the spirits of the Fleet up.
> It is I know bad criticizing the conduct of one's chief, and I don't
> know whether Hango would be tenable after taking it, but the
> few officers I saw the day I arrived were impatient and wishing
> much that a move was made in some direction.
>
> The Admiral whom I dined with and who was civil to me
> talked openly about not wanting half the ships they were sending

out to him, that they were useless and he had rather not have them, that no Fleet had ever been sent out here before June and a great deal of similar language, blaming the Admiralty for not having given our men what leave they required and so forth.

(The *Cumberland* had returned from years in the West Indies only to be sent straight to the Baltic.)

We go on pretty much as usual in point of working but we are rather improving, we do I think a little better than any except *Neptune*... We are in the Van squadron under Adl Corry ... which squad is composed of sailing ships and we do not find ourselves so much astern as was expected. We at all events sail better than our second ahead, the *Prince Regent*... The *Boscawen* appears to move quite wonderfully in very light winds when we do not get through the water at all.

Henry Seymour wrote to his father, George:

I never can regret for one instant your not being the Comdr in Chief of this fleet. The cold, the fogs would bring you an extra enemy in the shape of gout and if the Russian Fleet will not come out no credit will be obtained here by anybody. [By 27 May] after all our haste we are still cruising off the island of Gottska Sando... Sir Charles Napier took away most of the screws eight days ago to cruise off Hango... We have just heard that the *Arrogant* and two other vessels not liners were sent to bombard the forts commanding the Hango anchorage.

Perhaps things were going to move at last, but he thought Black Charlie was most unpopular:

... and I hear nothing except regret expressed that you are not in his place, but I do not join in this regret and I am sure there is little honour to be gained without the Russians choosing to come out, and much anxiety and responsibility to be endured, and a Public at home urging impossibilities which to say the least of it must be very annoying to the Comdr in Chief.

I therefore think great allowance ought to be made for Sir Chas. [But had Black Charlie, always a taut hand, become too taut altogether?] His language is much too strong to such officers as Codrington, Cochrane etc., who everyone knows are very zealous men as indeed are all that I have seen out here,

Wodehouse, Egerton and others all have come in for it as well as our friend Jock Ramsay but I hope you will not hear of my being among the black-listed.

Cumberland was at any rate maintaining her high reputation for gunnery, and 'I think your suggestion of having a gun moved to both bow and stern ports before going into action very desirable and certainly shall follow it.' But would there be any action? To the sailing fleet, groping its way through interminable Baltic fogs, it seemed unlikely.

A succession of fogs and heavy gales kept Black Charlie's squadron in harbour at Elgsnaben, below Stockholm, and he seized this chance to make friends with the King of Sweden, known to be the happy possessor of no fewer than 328 gunboats, upon whose cooperation the British Admiralty were counting. Charlie was authorized to offer the King repossession of the Aland Islands, full of Swedes, and latterly a Swedish domain, but occupied by the conquering Russians thirty years previously. He received a dusty answer. King Oscar told him that neither he nor his people desired conquest, even of the Aland Islands, populated almost entirely by his own people. 'His position was delicate and he would remain as he was.'

Charlie told the Foreign Secretary, Clarendon, that he was unused to diplomacy but had done his best to carry out Clarendon's wishes. The Foreign Secretary cheeringly told him that his visit had 'produced an excellent effect'. Clearly Clarendon shared the Administration's concern over Charlie's reputed rashness. He told Charlie:

> We have watched your proceedings with the deepest anxiety and everybody rejoices that you have had the moral courage to resist impossibilities that could only have been attempted to satisfy the home public.

To some extent Black Charlie had become the victim of his own reputation. Few people at home rejoiced in his morally courageous resistance. Why could not Charlie do as he had done in Syria? Why not confront the tyrant of Russia as he had confronted Dom Miguel, the Tyrant of Portugal? Gale succeeded gale, fog drove in on fog, as the ships lay off Elgsnaben, straining at anchor and in constant danger of dragging. Unaware of Baltic conditions, the home public was already shuffling its feet. Surely a younger man would have gone into the attack? Surely Charlie would have, himself, in younger days?

Off Gottska Sando in the *Lightning*, Sulivan had noted the arrival of the first French warship, the *Austerlitz*, on 1 May. He considered her 'a lump of a ship'; but she was at least forerunner of the hoped for better things to come. On the 2nd they were 'still detained by dirty weather', though the frigates were watching Riga and the entrance to the Gulf of Finland, and *Valorous* and *Vulture* had sailed to reconnoitre Bomarsund, principal fortress of the Aland Islands. Sulivan had begged to be allowed to go too, but the Admiral, still influenced by his Master of the Fleet, would not allow him to leave his ship. Since there were no pilots to be had, the ships would have in future to proceed everywhere with the surveying vessels in advance.

Sulivan felt discouraged. 'Bear on, submit, and do so moreover with a good grace and with a smiling face ... bear and forbear,' Admiral Beaufort (of the Beaufort scale) advised him from home. Sulivan did so; and by 14 May felt that Charlie had come to appreciate his value, and took him surveying with him. The weather was such 'that we were half buried keeping alongside *Duke* ... one of these Baltic fogs rolled in from the sea and completely hid the ships from each other, with narrow passages and rocks between islands to find their way through...'

No fleet, thought Sulivan, was ever in a more trying position:

> ... the way every ship was taken care of in such a place in thick fog shows that the officers were much more competent than the Admiral allows. The badly manned *Monarch* was got out of great danger by skill and promptness, Captain Erskine being one of our best officers.

To Sulivan it seemed that Admiral Michael Seymour was not allowed to exercise his proper influence as Captain of the Fleet, while the Master had too much; the latter had advised strenuously against Sulivan's being allowed to reconnoitre Sveaborg. Nargen, the Master insisted, was an unsafe anchorage. Sulivan thought it

> a misfortune for the Admiral and for the whole fleet that he had in such a position an officer such as the Master, who, instead of helping to give him confidence when he was so anxious about the safety of his ships, seemed to delay his movements and to encourage his weakness.

Henry Codrington, captain of the *Royal George*, a thoroughly experienced officer and not a personal friend of Black Charlie, wrote home from the *Royal George* at Elgsnaben, with a bitterness that far exceeded the Admiral's:

> I suppose the warlike public of England, and of course its mouthpiece, are expecting to hear that the squadron has taken Kronstadt, burnt or sunk the Russian Squadron, and is dictating peace at St Petersburg!!! And no doubt when they hear that we have done nothing at all of all this, we shall have them writing us down as cowards – or at least as incapables. Ah, I wish they could come here to the Baltic themselves and see the circumstances and difficulties and then try their hands at them.

Who that had never met them could conceive the conditions – the ceaseless groaning of the ships' timbers around the icy crews, the straining ropes, seas breaking monotonously in freezing foam, stormy headlands appearing and disappearing through the mists? Codrington declared:

> The very least of our difficulties would be finding the Russian fleet coming out to meet us. I would willingly bargain for that. But I should be very sorry indeed, if, urged on by public clamour, our squadron, either here or in the Black Sea, were engaged in a struggle with batteries. I don't see any advantage to be gained by it beyond the attempt to satisfy the cry of the people 'that live at home at ease' for the blood of those who are fighting *their* battles abroad.
>
> But were our squadrons crippled in such a contest with batteries, their fleet might, and probably would, come out and gain a victory over our shattered ships. What a mess that would be! If this squadron fails, England has no reserve ready, and would find some difficulty in beating off from her own coasts a Russian squadron which – under these disastrous circumstances to us – could easily get out of the Baltic, and pay Leith, the Thames and Portsmouth a visit. For us to attack batteries simply as such, simply because they have the Russian flag up, would be insane folly.

It would be another thing if they could come at the ships behind the batteries.

Meanwhile our presence at their doors has stopped their trade and is detaining at the northern end of their empire an immense body of men who would otherwise have been disposable for over-whelming Turkey... A battle lost to us in the Black Sea or in Turkey will be bad enough, but it will not be a tenth part of the disaster that a battle lost here would be to England. If this squadron is crippled by storms, or by the enemy, it will be a sad mess for England.

A week later, still held by the weather at Elgsnaben, Codrington felt no better:

I am now wondering what our chief will decide on doing. No doubt he is feeling the difficulties of his position... You see, he is urged on, on the one hand, by the state of excitement and highwrought expectations into which England has worked herself up about this Baltic squadron and what great things it is to do, and especially about him, Sir C. Napier personally, and what deeds of successful daring he is to accomplish... On the other hand he now finds himself here brought face to face with difficulties which no one in England (not even the Ministry) have any idea of, and which they, not knowing the place, or seeing the circumstances with their own eyes, cannot imagine.

He now sees his own character and the honour of our flag at stake, not to say the safety of the squadron and the protection of the English coasts, if we risk an attack without the certainty of crushing resistance with so little loss to ourselves as to leave all our ships efficient.

And if the English flag, after all this fearful excitement at home, does suffer a reverse, then will come the question 'Who's to be hanged for it?' For in such a case, it will be considered necessary to hang or shoot or morally extinguish SOMEBODY, to appease the indignation of that righteous, ill-used British public, who at their tea and toast, reading *The Times* or *Herald* by the warmth of their comfortable fireside, are sure that it must all be the fault of the admiral, captains or officers; and not at all due to the continual disregard of the earnest warnings given for many years past by our best officers and cleverest heads of the increasing extent and efficiency of Russia's naval and military preparations, and the sad deficiency of ours. [These were false economies.] ... It is well for us that our contest is not against France instead of Russia.

A merciless wind beat upon the wooden walls of the *Royal George*, and her captain's ink surged in its well. Giving his pen a fresh dip, Codrington demanded an answer – 'Who's to be hanged?' Not, he felt certain, the Ministry:

> ... it will become a question of the professional halter being tended to the Baltic Squadron (that is to the survivors), the commander-in-chief or his captains. If the commander-in-chief can't fasten it round the neck of any unlucky or dead captain who, in the latter case, can't speak for himself (which has before now been a great national convenience), in faith he will have to wear it himself; and I think Sir C. Napier is quite clear-sighted enough to have contemplated such a prospect. Now I don't think the *Royal George,* or any other ship here, will let herself be gibbeted for public satisfaction, if human endeavours can prevent it. I am sure all of us would far rather be shot by the Russians than hanged physically or professionally by our countrymen, however unreasonable they may be. But our prospects are not of the pleasantest... As yet we have not got yet from England one pound of powder or one single shot, though all of us have necessarily been expending ammunition largely in the drilling of our men at quarters.

Though Sulivan might consider Black Charlie to lack plan and act upon impulse, he had been explicitly instructed to 'feel' his way, And so, on this By Guess and By God principle, on 5 May, in what proved to be a brief interval of moderate weather, the squadron had weighed anchor and left for Hango Head, under steam.

Charlie wrote:

> Just as we got into the most dangerous part of the channel amongst rocks and shoals, a thick fog came on. Two or three of the leading ships had cleared the rocks, but the rest were enveloped in a thick fog and could see nothing. There was nothing left for it but to proceed and take our chance, and by the blessing of Providence we all escaped.
>
> *Cressy* discovered a rock almost under her bows, and just cleared it. *Caesar* found herself on the wrong side of another, and escaped by a miracle. *Monarch,* who was in tow, broke her hawsers and anchored. *James Watt* went back and succeeded; she was not so much engaged. The *Duke of Wellington* hauled

through another channel, which Mr Biddlecombe (the master) had surveyed. The *Austerlitz* persevered and went on ... the *Boscawen* and *Regent* were detained and did not start. When I see the rest of the Captains I will give you an account of them. I have been fifty-four years in the service, and I never saw a fleet in such a position and no human foresight could have provided against it.

Black Charlie was hoping that his small force of six ships of the line and two frigates might induce the Russians to come out and attack it. Surely, they wouldn't let slip a chance like that? As he well knew, unless they were tempted, he was powerless. Also, he had a shrewd idea of who was the most likely candidate for the hangman's rope so accurately predicted by Captain Henry Codrington, son of Edward, the victor at Navarino.

16

Gulf of Finland

On 22 May half the fleet were at Hango Bay, on the south-western point of Finland, a country then in Russian hands. Here an American ship that had left Kronstadt on the 19th reported that there were twenty-one sail of the line ready for sea there, four more fitting and thirteen steamers, and at Helsingfors were fifteen more ships of the line – in all forty. The Russians had told him, and he told Sulivan, that 'they were not coming out, as they cannot contend with the English ships, unless we first knock our ships to pieces against their batteries, and then they can finish us'. Whether this piece of valuable information confided to Sulivan ever reached the home authorities is uncertain. Sulivan himself was pleased to be sent in by the admiral to buoy the rocks of Hango Sound but less pleased when he hit one himself, 'a hard crack but we glanced off it, heeling over a good deal'. He was glad to hear that Charlie 'had no intention of attacking the batteries, which would involve grave loss and little gain'.

On 20 May Charlie had a letter from the Admiralty urging him to take the fleet into the Gulf of Finland, to which their Lordships received a crisp reply. He thought it more important to try and lure the Russians out with his small force, rather than making a futile demonstration with his whole force inside the Gulf in thick fog.

> I am perfectly aware that steam makes a great difference in naval operations; but steam has no effect on fogs. Their Lordships appear to think I am going too slow. When I passed the Belt, their Lordships thought I was going too fast. . . Their Lordships may depend I shall go to the upper part of the Gulf when I can; but I must leave a sufficient force off Sveaborg, where there are 8 or 9 sail of the line besides frigates and steamers. . . All that can be done I will do.

From Hango Sound on 23 May he told Admiral Berkeley:

This is a good anchorage but entirely exposed to southerly winds.

I am lying within range of their batteries. I long to knock them down, but I shall lose a good many men, and unless I could hold them it would not do any good.

He heard that besides its twenty line-of-battle ships, Kronstadt was garrisoned by 10,000 Russian troops. Despite which the steam frigates *Arrogant* and *Hecla* made a dash up the intricate channel and carried off a large Russian merchant vessel, with the loss of only three men. They reported that the Russians had fought with great bravery and determination; they would not prove a push-over if and when they could be brought to an encounter.

From home, Charlie's first cousin, the historian General Sir William Napier, sent him a word of caution. Handsomest of the family, and cleverest, William had been severely wounded in the Peninsular War, where he had highly distinguished himself; but his habitual war with authority had sharpened his tongue and he never minced matters:

Your situation is just what I expected but the fogs and the shallows are formidable. I am not surprised at your doubting Graham; he has good intentions in the main, but they are only intentions; he is physically and morally a coward, and of course deceitful and not to be trusted; but I believe, if his selfishness does not interfere, means well by you.

Lord John [Russell] and others hate you, and will be glad to have you fail. Aberdeen fears you will hurt his friend Czar Nicholas, and the object of the Whig part of the Cabinet is evidently to keep you down; they will never be able to unmake you in the opinion of the nation. The name [William added proudly] is deep in the hearts of the people. . . If you get plenty of good gunboats you will be able to do something. . .

From the Army point of view, Brigadier-General Jones now reported that gunboats and rockets were essential 'in any operation carried on against the Baltic ports'. But of gunboats there was no sign nor sound.

Thus simultaneously alarmed and reassured, Black Charlie proceeded up the Gulf through the shifting fogs of 2 June. By now he had thoroughly recognized Sulivan's worth, and sent him to take a close reconnaissance of the Aland Islands. Charlie told him to take care – 'he would have no fighting for fighting's sake' – and the islands were full of Swedish families who must on no account be harmed. Sulivan himself said that nothing would induce him to fire

a shot at defenceless houses full of women and children. He
reported that the Russian prisoners captured by *Arrogant* and *Hecla*
were pitiable and terrified, convinced that they would be shot and
constantly prostrating themselves. He reported back to Charlie that
an attack on the fortress Bomarsund with ships alone 'would be
attended by a loss and risk too great to warrant the attempt, unless
aided by a sufficient land force to carry the Tower by assault'. Black
Charlie was to act on this advice.

By 12 June Black Charlie was at anchor off Sveaborg, where a
letter from Graham, now increasingly anxious for results, reached
him urging him to try floating batteries, divers and diving bells
against the Kronstadt and Sveaborg defences, but 'No rash experi-
ments,' he cautioned in the same breath. The situation was tantalizing; from his anchorage Black Charlie could actually see the Russian
masts. The Master of the Fleet had gone in to survey the entrance
passage, Charlie told Graham, and had found

> a three-decker moored head and stern across to block the pas-
> sage . . . intended to be sunk in the passage if an attempt is made
> to force it.
>
> The Emperor might have saved himself much trouble, it is so
> well fortified by rocks and shoals. But it is now unassailable by
> ships, I doubt whether it could be got hold of, even by a large
> army.

And if Sveaborg were seized, how held when the ice returned and cut
its garrison off from reinforcement or supply?

This kind of comment was exactly what the Administration did
not wish to hear – the cold touch of fact descending on the warm
glow of fantasy. The Admiral went on:

> If Kronstadt is as strong as it is represented, it will be impossible
> to touch it. Therefore, all I can do is to offer them battle, and if
> they do not accept it, return and see what mischief I can do
> along the shore.

He must wait till the French admiral, now daily expected, arrived,
before deciding on the next operation. Bomarsund on the Aland Islands, now reconnoitred, seemed the best bet. One great advantage of
such an attack was that it might bring the Russians out in an attempt to save it. Sulivan had reported a strong granite fortress, heavy
guns, and a narrow channel up which only one ship at a time could

proceed. 'If 10,000 men could be spared, I think it might be reduced, but no time should be lost.'

At home political pressure was mounting and Sir James Graham was becoming increasingly irritated both by the Russians and the Swedes. Why could not such people play the game by the rules? They seemed to have no idea of what was cricket and what was not. The Russians were 'skulking within the harbour' and the Swedes were utterly declining to join in, though he had long felt certain that they must. He was, he told Charlie,

> pleased with all your operations and well aware of the impossibility of triumphing over an enemy that will not fight you on fair terms . . . a disgrace to Russia that she dares not show a ship in her own waters; [but] it would be madness to play her game and rush headlong on her granite walls, risking our naval superiority, with all the fatal consequences of defeat, in an unreal contest with wood against stone, which in the long run cannot succeed.
>
> I had reliance on your prudence, which was doubted. Your brilliant courage was proved long ago.

So far, so friendly. Could the Civil First Lord really not mean a word he said?

By mid-June the sails of the French ships were sighted off Baro Sound, and Commodore Michael Seymour and the Master of the Fleet went with an offer that the British steamers should tow Admiral Parseval's ships into this unknown anchorage. The offer was accepted. The command in the Baltic had now become divided, and the French general was also to be independent. 'Mutual confidence and forbearance must be the rule,' Graham pointed out; and it is much to the credit of the not invariably tactful Black Charlie that he and the French admiral became and remained friends. The French ran true to form, always refusing any form of cooperation that might conceivably be thought derogatory of their honour, and fairly frequently running ashore and having to be hauled afloat by the British ships. Even the pacific Sulivan complained of the time and effort too often spent by the British in towing French ships.

Both admirals now decided that the only way to take Sveaborg would be 'by a large military force occupying the islands and throwing shells into it'. Without gunboats and mortar vessels, attack from

the sea was impossible. According to Admiral Chads's detailed survey, the island forts guarding the entrance to the channel mounted
'2,000 guns of the largest calibre; and are of enormous strength'.
By all reports, the same applied to Kronstadt; to be certain of this
Charlie was going up the Gulf to have a closer look at it, whilst the
home authorities were deciding whether or not to mount an attack
on Bomarsund, a plan of which Charlie was strongly in favour and
for which he was slowly winning the approval of the French admiral.

More friendliness from the home powers cheered Charlie, and
the weather had suddenly become summer-like, and indeed balmy.
Several of his ships were still without their full complement of
men, and all attempts to enlist Swedes or Danes were defeated by
the vigilance of their governments and the small pay offered. But
meanwhile, in a quiet way that never managed to hit the headlines,
the detached squadron was doing great harm in capturing or destroying Russian ships, stores, and building yards. On 20 June they were
back at Baro Sound to be revictualled.

Admiral Berkeley had recently become First Sea Lord, and wrote
to Charlie in approval of his proceedings:

> You are giving the Government satisfaction, and the Board. We
> all feel – no one more than myself – that nothing can be done
> against such places as Helsingfors and Kronstadt; and I have the
> most full reliance that had anything been possible, you would
> have attempted it. They won't come out and you can't get in.

Things were no easier in the Black Sea. 'At Sebastopol nothing can
be done by ships.' On 27 June Graham again congratulated Charlie
on being 'restrained by a sense of duty from embarking on any
desperate enterprise. . . Whatever man can do, I am certain will be
done by you.'

Rear-Admiral Chads's detailed report on Sveaborg, dated 14 June,
soon reached the Admiralty and told them that the fortifications
made it 'unassailable but at immense sacrifice of life and loss of ships;
and even then an attack would be of very doubtful success'. The only
possibility was to take the nearby island of Sandhamm and to
bombard from thence the Russian fleet anchored in defence of the
deep water channel approaches to Sveaborg, to do which 'forty guns
of large calibre and a supply of 300 rounds of ammunition per gun'
were needed. The taking of Sandhamm would involve '6,000 troops
and 3 or 4,000 seamen and marines'. But on 27 June Graham wrote

that 'only eight Lancaster guns are ready, and very few of the shells'. The chickens of many years of neglect were come home to roost.

If not Sveaborg, how about Kronstadt, near the heart of the Russian Empire – the fortress guarding the mouth of the Neva and the approach to St Petersburg, the Czar's capital?

On 22 June, leaving nine sail of the line, a frigate and four steamers to continue blockading Sveaborg, the allied fleet weighed for Kronstadt, the British ships under steam, the French under tow, twelve British ships of the line and six French, plus nine steamers. They proceeded very slowly on account of the shifting fogs and the necessity of sending the steamers ahead to mark the shoals, the Russians having removed all beacons even up here, including the lighthouse on Seskar. The gulf narrowed as they went ahead, between the Finnish pine forests and the cultivated fields. Off Seskar Charlie sent a line to Graham, telling him he would offer battle if the Russian fleet came out, and go back if they did not. 'On my return I hope to hear what your intentions are about the Aland Islands.' He gazed shoreward across the calm sea, scarcely stirring above its innumerable rocks and shoals. 'The whole coast is a labyrinth,' he told Graham, 'and not a fit place to knock a fleet about without danger, as we are forced to survey every place we go into.'

There was something strange about the utter stillness and silence, and the dark forests ashore, in which no branch stirred. What lurked within this mysterious, hidden land? The matter that really disturbed Charlie was that four cases of cholera had been reported on board his ship. Otherwise they had been lucky. 'We came here very well,' Charlie told his friend Berkeley, 'for the weather was fine.' Had it not been, 'the Gulf is not fit to be navigated by a fleet, and we steer from rock to rock, but on a dark night that could not be done without lights.' Oh, for the open sea, to blow away the cholera, and with sea-room in which to confront and defeat the Russian fleet! The silent nights, now hardly dark in this northern midsummer, closed round the fleet, and the cholera cases increased.

The fleets crept on until, on 26 June, Kronstadt came in sight, the golden domes of her cathedral gleaming in the misty sunlight behind her massive fortifications. The Russian fleet was seen to consist of twenty-five ships of the line, five frigates, four corvettes and thirty-two lesser war vessels; there were thought to be more vessels of war invisible behind the harbour defences. Scenes of activity were to be observed, and the raising of steam in the steam vessels. But the Russians were safe within their harbour, and though heavily outnumbering the allied fleet and possessing unlimited ammunition, they prudently stayed where they were. Fortunately they did not know that the impressive British ships contained only enough ammunition for a four-hour battle, after which they would have been helpless as far as their guns were concerned. For Charlie it would have been a race against time, after which his small arms and cutlasses would have had to come into action.

It remained to survey the available approach channel for future use. The frustration felt by officers of the fleet had by no means abated, and on the day the ships reached Kronstadt Harry Keppel hazarded another of his nine lives. Lord Lichfield had brought his yacht *Gondola* up the Gulf to see what was going on, rather as if to a regatta, and he took Captain George Elliot of the *James Watt*, Lord Clarence Paget and Harry Keppel for a trip, running in close to the entrance to Kronstadt to take the closest possible look. Here they only just avoided capture by a Russian steamer thanks to two patrolling British frigates that came up in the nick of time to rescue them. Which was as well, as the Russians still had the reputation of executing prisoners of war, although, certainly, aristocratic ones stood a better chance.

Sulivan was also taking advantage of the 'lovely weather, but too warm'. He hoped it would fall to his lot, in his small ship, 'to take the lead in bearding the Bear in his den. I suppose we are come up to try and tempt him out. We have only 18 sail-of-the-line. They have, I believe 24 in Kronstadt and 8 the other side of us at Helsingfors.' He was longing to get on with the attempt on Bomarsund, but realized that both Black Charlie and Parseval had to wait for permission from home, since they could not act in sufficient force without withdrawing ships from the blockade of the Gulf.

> ... and to have taken the marines from twelve or fourteen sailing ships-of-the-line, not very well manned, and to have left them to blockade 26 Russian ships of equal force would have been running a risk no admiral dare venture on.

They had perforce to wait for the French soldiers to arrive, ferried by British ships. Meanwhile there was the pleasant prospect of getting as close as possible in discovering the lie of the land around Kronstadt.

On the 27th Sulivan reported:

It seems strange that we should be quietly lying at anchor within 3 miles of the enemy's fleet, but it is all-important steam that enables us to do so. [They could cut and run at any minute, luring the Russians onto the main body of the fleet.] Their ships look rather slummy in appearance. They are all placed to resist an attack, and evidently think of nothing else. The channel is certainly formidable and quite impregnable. After passing all the heavy forts below, if not destroyed by them, our leading ship would have all those 124 guns and 2 three-deckers' broadsides raking her, besides all those of all the ships at longer distances on her starboard bow. If she could possibly survive all this and pass between the three-deckers, carrying away their bowsprits, she would find the broadsides of three two-deckers close above pouring it into both bows. All their ships are moored head and stern.

Having had his thorough look, Sulivan went about in *Lightning* and returned to the fleet.

Henry Seymour too was telling his father of the remarkably fine, warm and settled weather. On 26 June he and the *Cumberland* were 'outside the Islets forming Baro Sound, anchored on a bank about a mile and a half out'. They were due to move nearer Helsingfors on the morrow and had sent two steamers ahead to find them suitable anchorage, but 'the weather is now so perfectly fine that little protection is required and you may anchor almost anywhere'. He was glad to hear that his father approved of the way he had dealt with the trouble in *Cumberland* at Portsmouth - 'which approval is everything to me.'

Warm weather had its lethal disadvantages. 'The smallpox is I think now checked but it is getting rather near the cabin. My boy died, and the cook caught it and I thought I was in for it too.' His father was always anxious to know how well the different ships sailed, and Henry very willing to oblige. *Cumberland* did best under double-reefed topsails, *Boscawen* in very light winds. *Ajax*, *Hogue* and other ships of that class 'cannot sail at all,' Henry stated flatly, 'and the *Majestic* is always astern . . . they have been christened the War junks.' *Impérieuse* under sail was 'beautiful to look at, *Euryalus* sails and steams very well indeed' and was not far short of

those beautiful ships the *St Jean d'Acre* and the *Princess Royal* who are always under very small sail as well as the *Wellington; I have seen the latter tack with the three topsails double-reefed and fore topmast stay-sails without courses and without any after sail set at all, but the water is very smooth here and *we* have not, yet disgraced ourselves by missing stays which cannot be said for all of us.

Cumberland had had a brush with a Swedish coaster in a thick fog in the Baltic; no great harm done.

The miracle was that none of us ran into each other as when the fog lifted there were eight or ten of us close together standing all sorts of ways, and drums, bugles etc. on all sides of us. Considering the time the ships have been in commission I think they are in very fine fighting order; but complaints are very general against the Coast Guards who are giving themselves all sorts of airs and making all sorts of difficulties.

And who now, off Sveaborg, was booked to lead the Charge of the Light Brigade, were it to be made?

17

Deadlock

For this task Harry Keppel had either been booked or had booked himself, according to Henry Seymour. Telling his father that he was hoping to exchange with Jock Ramsay as captain of *Euryalus*, as *Cumberland* was due for home; and sympathizing with his father's wish to see more ships like the lovely *Euryalus* built for the fleet, Henry Seymour said:

> We shall also want some heavy screw ships as I am convinced a vessel like the *St Jean d'Acre* going 11½ under steam would go over anything if she could catch them fairly amidships. There is a three-decker moored across the narrow channel between Sveaborg and Helsingfors and she lays in 9 fathoms, but if an attack is made H. Keppel is to go for her with his bows barricaded, but he would have to go through her as well as sink her as she would hardly be under water if fairly sunk. He might be trusted to keep the *Acre*'s head straight at it.

Certainly he might; but not even the dash of Harry Keppel would enable his ship to jump a moored three-decker as though she were a high fence in the hunting field. And, luckily for his fleet, Black Charlie was not Lord Cardigan.

> I hear the Commander in Chief is convinced the enemy's fleet will come out and I think it possible they may against us here if we do not keep too many ships, but they will never face the screws I am sure and small blame to them.

By mid-July Henry Seymour had the smallpox, but:

> Nobody could have had it in a lighter manner than I had except the first night when the blood rushed to my head, . . . never felt very ill or indeed ill at all except for sore throat and loss of appetite . . . I escaped without mark except for a small hole in the bridge of my nose and that has half a mind to fill up, so

altogether it is a good thing to have got through. We have had
no new case for ten days past. Sir Charles Napier came twice
under the stern to enquire after me when I was ill.

[He was taking up his father's suggestion of angular screens
for the bows of the landing boats.] I shall make them out of our
spare cooking boilers if I cannot find anything better.

They had taken on board loads of wood from a nearby islet to
make platforms for mounting heavy guns 'when the troops arrive and
begin operation, if ever they do begin'. However the wood was so full
of bugs that Henry believed

We might work the guns with them if they were properly
trained. We do not know what the troops are to do but it is the
general belief we shall land them at Aland Islands. The French
ships have 2,000 soldiers on board their ships now and find them
greatly in their way too. We do a great deal of Entente Cordiale.
My friend among them is a Captain Bosse of the *Breslau* who is
a very energetic young man and very agreeable. He was sent
away with me to look after this place while the rest of the Fleet
were outside and up at Kronstadt.

On 28 June Sulivan was back from his survey in *Lightning* and
having breakfast with Black Charlie on board the *Duke* and with 'a
long discussion with him on charts, crews, gunboats, bombarding
batteries etc.' After which Charlie had taken Sulivan to tell his tale to
the French Admiral, and Sulivan noted that the cholera was increasing – in some of the large ships 'they have lost several men within a
few days'. He longed for 'open water, north of Gothland, a much
more healthy part, and we could blockade quite as well there'. But
the admiral was bent on a proper look at Kronstadt with a view to
possible operations there next year with a better-equipped fleet, and
he led him in in the little *Driver* next day.

'He made me point out everything to him'; but the Russians, after
Lightning's incursion on the previous day, were practising their long-
range guns. Sulivan noted that Black Charlie had lost none of his
lion-like personal courage but was too anxious about his ships and
worried about 'infernal machines', as floating mines were then called.
Sulivan anchored in the dusk off the lighthouse that he had explored
on a previous visit, 'and after all had dined with me, we spent some
time in the beautiful evening on the top, returning to the fleet before

dark.' The brief lovely northen Russian summer enchanted all but the cholera or smallpox sufferers, who horrified Charlie by their increasing numbers. Much the least frightening thing about the whole situation was the Russian fleet.

'I took a Russian prize, mounting ten guns,' Sulivan teasingly told his wife, 'but they are wooden ones mounted on an ugly little brig about a foot long.' He had found the toy in the deserted lighthouse, 'and thought I might fairly take it'. In spite of Black Charlie's Tom Tiddler's ground tactics, it seemed to be the only war vessel out of Russia that they were likely to capture; and by 3 July the ships were down at Seskar. Before this, Sulivan had had more activity: on the 1st he had been ordered by Charlie to take all the captains and commanders up to Kronstadt in the *Lightning* to have a good look for themselves, and on the 2nd the Admiral had sent him through Biorko Sound

> to see if there was a passage right through to the northward. He gave me *Magicienne, Bulldog* and *Desperate* and sent Watson with *Arrogant* and *Impérieuse* to anchor and forward his signals. The Admiral gave me positive instructions to have no fighting, saying he trusted entirely to my judgment to prevent it.

The temptation arose. On the point at Koivosto, Sulivan saw

> about 150 soldiers and a telegraph station, behind were thick trees that would shelter riflemen. I was therefore in a puzzle. [Not only had he been ordered to avoid fighting, but also] there might be sore feeling about no French ship being with us, if we had a brush, for the French Admiral says that if our fleet had an action, and he and his ships were out of the way, all the paving stones in Paris would not be enough to throw at his head!

So they came back to survey next morning with the French *Impérieuse*, making a plan of attack if fired upon – 'a very good plan, only it wanted one thing, and that was an enemy'. But the Russian soldiers 'had the prudence not to fire musketry, so we did not fire at them, though we could have destroyed them'. Sulivan thought he had been right to take precautions, as there was 'a kind of Cornish bank that might have concealed guns, and nothing is so foolish as holding an enemy cheap'.

> Perhaps I ought strictly to have fired at the soldiers, but it would

have been an almost barbarous cruelty to have poured in all kind of destructive missiles amongst men who had no means of retaliating. We might perhaps have killed or mangled a hundred poor wretches or more, as I could see them crouching thickly among the trees, but it would have done no good. . .

We all laugh now at our peaceable fight, after all the preparations we made. . . We are too apt to think of the glory, honour, etc., of a successful despatch. . . I do trust I may be able to set such ideas on one side, and to feel that the satisfaction of preventing unnecessary bloodshed is far more desirable. I am afraid some of my colleagues deem me too merciful.

He carried on the good work to the master of a Finnish coaster which they had stopped to question for information:

to their perfect astonishment I gave them a bottle of rum and a good lot of biscuit, two things they are fond of, and sent them back to their ship. They had been sure they would be sent to England and put in prison. . . The Chief was much pleased with what I did.

Opinions in the ships about Sulivan's non-action at Koivosto were decidedly mixed, but 'what good would it have done to our cause?' he demanded, 'or what credit to our navy, for five ships to pour their broadsides on two hundred defenceless men? I could not do it.' Sulivan was one of that not inconsiderable section of mankind that finds it almost impossible to kill an enemy until that enemy has first killed some of his friends. He thought that the cholera in the fleet was worse, and Admiral Corry's squadron was riddled with smallpox.

By the 7th the cholera did seem to be abating, and 'tonight our men went to an island to bathe, and brought off a few most delicious alpine strawberries'. Things really seemed to be on the move towards the Aland Islands, and on 9 July the *Lightning* coaled all night. 'I worked all night, watch and watch, having hot tea brewed for the men, thinking that for health the night would be better for working in than the hot day.' Sulivan was rewarded next day by 'something like a Sabbath'. He read 'a nice sermon' and 'said prayers for the time of pestilence'. Black Charlie had been against the use of this prayer, thinking it would imply a danger that would 'depress the men'. Sulivan, who had a soul above depression, thought this a sad viewpoint.

He found that the news that French troops were coming out had been a well-kept secret, and wondered at it:

> The fact is that so many letters of officers get published that it is not safe to let anything be known, and some of them contain most arrant nonsense, that must make the writers ashamed when they see it in print.

Some of them were pleased and proud, rather than ashamed. Complaints from the fleet had gathered volume and won wide publicity at home, particularly from those units of the fleet that were still boringly blockading the Baltic and had not experienced the foray up the Gulf of Finland and had no occasion to observe what any attacker of Kronstadt or Sveaborg was up against.

Charlie had added his comments to Admiral Chads's very full report sent to the Admiralty on 14 June, and enclosed the 'very correct drawings made by Lieutenants Nugent and Cowell', who had accompanied him in his close survey with Sulivan on board *Driver*. 'You will see by them that any attack on Kronstadt by ships is entirely impracticable.' Any approaching ship would be sunk by formidable batteries long before coming to grips with her Russian counterpart. He thought the best hope of taking Kronstadt was by an attack by land on St Petersburg. 'You might land an army either to the north or south and march on it.' This would need a very large army, or it would be the tale of Buonaparte all over again. 'You must expect the Russians will always out-number you, and if you fail, your army would be lost, whilst, if you succeed, it would probably be starved during the long winter.'

But, given heavy guns, and shallow-draughted ships, Kronstadt could well be bombarded. Fifty gunboats, he considered, would be needed, plus rockets, and much ammunition.

In reply, Graham accepted Charlie's evidence. The Board of Admiralty had 'full confidence in his judgement and placed complete reliance on his report'. They must now turn to what *was* feasible. 'Bomarsund will clearly be within your reach,' Graham opined. 'Sveaborg, if it were possible, would be a noble prize, but on no account be led into any desperate attempt. . . With 50,000 Swedes and 200 gunboats you might do something great and decisive before the end of September', he added wistfully on 11 July, still believing, in the teeth of the evidence, that the Swedes might change their minds.

Admiral Berkeley wrote warmly to Charlie on the same date:

Your survey of Kronstadt, and your judgment and *discretion* – I don't mean to play on that word – are highly approved. You have a difficult part to play, every tomfool expecting you to eat Kronstadt and the Emperor to boot. I believe the Government are perfectly satisfied with your proceedings, and . . . you deserve every credit for the manner in which you have handled your fleet in such waters. The world – the public – don't know what it is to command an inexperienced fleet – officers and men – in such a service, in such a sea, much more trying to the nerves than any general action.

As the fleet lay preparing at Baro Sound, sympathetic letters continued to arrive on board the *Duke of Wellington*. 'The entrance and forts of Kronstadt are evidently too strong for you to make any attempt,' wrote Captain Milne. 'It is rather disheartening to go away from before the enemy's fort, but it is sound discretion to do so.' Lord Bloomfield, now ambassador in Berlin, told Charlie 'I have always thought Kronstadt impregnable.' No hint of the coming storm reached the old admiral.

What really disheartened Black Charlie was the fact that a hundred men in the fleet had already died of cholera. For this the only known cure was to return to open sea, followed by taking every chance to go ashore for exercise. The fleet still lay at Baro Sound to await definite orders for the attack on Bomarsund. On the way to Baro a certain number of rude noises had been bitten back by the Royal Navy when the French *Du Guesclin,* despite her noble name, had gone ashore; it had taken the British ships eighteen hours to haul her off again. Charlie exercised the fleet in evolutions, sent away armed and manned boats, and directed marines ashore with scaling ladders to practise upon Renskar lighthouse, until in mid-July the needful orders arrived.

'With 10,000 men Bomarsund and the Aland Islands may be taken,' Sir James Graham announced; and the Cabinet 'being of the opinion that the presence of the Allied Fleet in the Baltic must be marked by some result', had accordingly persuaded the French Emperor, Napoleon III, to send a further '6,000 French troops, with ten guns, fifty horses, and caissons, to be embarked on board British ships of war and transports'. These were to leave on 16 July.

Bomarsund was to be 'the first hard blow in the battle . . . while Sweden is hesitating' England and France would have gained the islands. 'Sweden must become our suitor when we hold Aland,' the

ever-hopeful Sir James concluded, 'and we shall be enabled to command her future assistance on our own terms.'

In the event, the terrified Swedes were to decline to accept their
own islands even as a present. Long past were the days when
Gustavus Adolphus had led his men triumphantly deep into Russian
heartlands; his countrymen now dreaded to tangle in any way with
the might of Russia. The British and French might conquer and then
would sail away in their fleets; what then?

The said fleets, frustrated in the Gulf of Finland, were by now
desperate to have a go.

18

Bomarsund

The Aland Islands were a group of nearly three hundred isles and islets some sixteen miles off the coast of Sweden, and in part barring off the Baltic from the wide and chilly reaches of the Gulf of Bothnia. They were inhabited by Swedish Lutherans in neat log cabins with climbing roses round their doors and bibles on the kitchen dresser, who could be expected to greet the British in a friendly way. In winter when their cold green waters froze to a depth, packs of wolves would lope over the ice from Finland to seek what they could find. Another seeker had been Czar Nicholas I who had taken the islands from Sweden thirty-six years earlier and set up an Orthodox church and a formidable fortress named Bomarsund. To Captain Sulivan it looked more like 'a new terrace in a fashionable watering place', but was to prove somewhat tougher. It mounted ninety heavy guns and held a garrison of 2,500 men.

The activities of Admiral Plumridge and his ships had prevented these from being reinforced, but the way to Bomarsund lay up a narrow and intricate waterway. On 16 August this was carefully reconnoitred by the Master of the Fleet in a small ship. His report made it clear that the main thrust of the attack would have to be made by soldiers.

On 18 July the combined squadron weighed anchor, leaving only the *Impérieuse* and *Dragon* in Baro Sound, off Finland's south west corner. They were to rendezvous at Ledsund, from which Sulivan in *Lightning* had found a practicable passage into the Alands. Admiral Corry having returned home ill, Commodore Martin of the *Nile* was left in command of the squadron blockading Sveaborg and the Gulf of Finland, with *Royal George, Caesar, Cressy, St George, Prince Regent* and the French *Austerlitz*. A Russian force of around 10,000 men had been sent to Abo, but Admiral Plumridge with his steam squadron *Leopard, Valorous, Locust, Cuckoo* and *Hecla*, finding a passage to the north of Bomarsund, effectively cut off the fortress from any succour from this direction.

Edinburgh, Hogue, Blenheim, Ajax and *Lightning*, with *Amphion* and *Alban,* were ordered to Bomarsund to begin the attack, Black Charlie transferring to the little *Bulldog.* In this, with her consort *Stromboli,* he was to proceed up the waterway with the soldiers for their landing.

By 22 July the French squadron had caught up with the fleet at Ledsund, where their *Duperre* at once ran aground; this time the launches and barges of both fleets were rather brisker in getting her afloat. The French general, Baraguay d'Hilliers, in their Imperial Yacht *Reine Hortense,* had been to Stockholm in another attempt to enlist the Swedes as allies, but King Oscar I remained unpersuaded. On his visit to the flagship, the *Duke of Wellington* manned yards and saluted d'Hilliers with fifteen guns. All that could be done to assuage French self-esteem would certainly be done by Charlie.

There was still no sign of the wayward transports upon whom the attack depended. Rumour had it they had paused and were living it up in Copenhagen. Black Charlie wrote worriedly:

> The season is far advanced, and we must be quick; and as for ulterior operations, that is out of the question. . . Sveaborg is not to be taken with a handful of men, were we to begin in June instead of August; and about the middle of September we must be pointing south. These seas cannot be played with with fleets of large ships.

On 1 August Admiral Parseval and General d'Hilliers in *Reine Hortense,* with Charlie and Brigadier-General Jones in the *Lightning,* reconnoitred Bomarsund. As it grew shallower, wrote Sulivan, 'they all, great and small, went on board *Lightning,* and what with colonels, naval captains, captains and lieutenants on the staff they crowded our deck under the awning from the mainmast to the wheel. I gave them a good look at everything.' They were fired at by the Russians, some shots falling alarmingly close, but *Lightning* came off unscathed. 'If I was not pretty well proof against flattery I should have had my head turned,' reported Sulivan next day. 'The channels to the northward are particularly intricate, but we went at full speed in *Lightning* the whole way.' Charlie had been most impressed, and had been kept busy translating French compliments for Sulivan's benefit. Admiral Parseval had maintained, inelegantly, that Sulivan had a nose for hidden rocks like a pig had for discovering buried truffles in a forest. On the previous day Sulivan had led in the big ships to a lower part of the channel – 'we went on swimmingly through channels so narrow that the line-of-battle ships seemed like giants looking down on the small islands' – as *Lightning* was followed by *Edinburgh, Hogue, Blenheim and Ajax, Amphion* and *Alban* following.

Sulivan was ashore the next day, taking off a Russian officer of whose bullying the locals had earlier complained to him; after which they had brought him 'several sheep and nice lambs at three shillings and sixpence each, milk and cream'. Sulivan invited six local ladies to come on board where he regaled them with wine, biscuits and figs; one young mother was given a Swedish bible for her little girl. Later the crew of *Lightning* were rewarded with fresh peas, eggs and raspberries, to which they replied with coffee, sugar and wine; and there was jollity all round.

3 August came and went, and still no French troops had appeared. 'The summer is passing,' Black Charlie mourned to Graham, 'and every hour is precious.' Time would be needed to subdue the fortress with its granite walls: how much time no one knew. 'If the Russians can hold out till the weather gets bad, we shall be in a mess. All that can be done I will do, but this delay kills me.' The transports had been heard of at Kiel, and were thought to be still there. 'They appear to have forgotten that this is August and we are in latitude 60.10,' Charlie grumbled. General Baraguay d'Hilliers was to command the landing; without his reinforcements he would not proceed.

4 August dawned calm, warm and inviting; still no transports. Next day was the same, but by the evening the first of the transports was at anchor. 'It was a curious sight,' thought Sulivan, 'seeing a thousand French soldiers paraded on the deck of an English ninety gun ship. They have got on capitally,' he recorded delightedly, 'all pleasant and mutually pleased.' Others in the fleet felt the same; having fought the French almost continually for the last 800 years it felt extremely rum to have them as allies. Commodore Michael Seymour in particular had first encountered the French as enemies before he was in long trousers; his father, captain of the frigate *Amethyst,* having taken him to sea at the age of eight to confirm or eradicate an obsession with all things naval, where they had exchanged shots with the French off Brest. How would they all now work together?

The days, still almost nightless, made an early start feasible. On 8 August marines, sappers and miners, under the command of

Brigadier-General Jones, landed unopposed at two points to the south of Bomarsund; a seven-gun battery on Transwig Point had been silenced in a forty-minute bombardment from the steamers *Amphion* and the French *Phlégéthon*. A spirited party of marines and seamen filled 5,000 sandbags in the course of twenty-four hours and then toted them up a steep hill to surround the marine batteries, carrying on with the work under sustained fire and through the night.

At five in the morning of the 10th, Rear-Admiral Chads brought ashore his heavy guns, to be dragged 'over execrable ground and steep rocky hills' by parties of 150 sailors each from HM Ships *Edinburgh*, *Blenheim*, *Hogue* and *Ajax*, on sledges devised for the purpose by Captain Ramsay of the *Hogue*. The sailors were still barefoot; in response to an earlier batch of shoes sent back as all too small, *Edinburgh* had been supplied by the Admiralty with ninety-eight pairs, of which all but thirteen turned out also to be too small.

The French, once ashore, fought with their customary dash and skill, loudly cheering the sweating bluejackets and even lending a hand as they dragged their sledges upwards to where the big guns they hauled could command the main fortress. The exhausted men had hardly sat down and had time to prepare a meal before they were summoned back to their boats; the *Penelope* had gone aground. Amazingly, marines and sailors gave a loud cheer, abandoned their dinners, and 'took a short cut within range of the fire of the fortress', tearing down hill to reach their boats in forty minutes. *Penelope* lost two men and a French officer, and was obliged to jettison her guns before being floated off.

Next day the overland drag of the guns became merrier. There were now 200 sailors to each gun and the parties were accompanied and cheered along by their ships' bands. Charlie, who had seen sailors manhandling guns all over the globe, had never seen anything like it – 'the cheerfulness and exertions of the men were wonderful'. The French, always so much better equipped for this sort of thing, had brought siege artillery, 80 horses and some 500 engineers. 'The French', Charlie's namesake and cousin had declared during the Peninsular War, 'are our masters in war, in everything except courage and bodily strength'; and here in the Baltic their general organization seemed fine. Nobody sent them out barefoot and then supplied them with shoes too small.

The Russians now burned everything inflammable in the neighbourhood of the forts, and seemed prepared for a long and stiff defence. Some Polish Jews, delightedly deserting from the Russian army in this bleak northern outpost, brought the disquieting news that fifty Russian gunboats were expected.

At 4 a.m. on the 13th the French battery and mortars opened up on the western tower of the fortress, known as Fort Tzee. Their Chasseurs kept up a galling fire from behind every rock and tree, but the Russian garrison fought back steadily and effectively. It would be the mortars that really decided the matter, crashing down inside the walls with enormous force. Fort Tzee surrendered in the morning with fifty Russians dead and many more wounded. No sooner was the tricolor run up from its summit than the Russian main fortress turned their guns upon it and set it on fire. The French sensibly withdrew, which was as well, as the fire presently reached the magazine which exploded, killing a large number of Russian wounded and their doctor with them.

Great damage was meanwhile being done with the heavy guns, so manfully dragged overland, with which the British were attacking the eastern tower, Fort Nottich. After two or three hours of hot fire, two of the four Russian guns that had been brought to bear on the British battery were knocked out; and the large breach effected soon made possible the extinction of a third.

The Russian gunners of the fourth continued to fire with stubborn courage but, by half past five, the wall had fallen upon their gun, and further resistance was impossible. In all these hours there had been but one British casualty, Lieutenant the Hon. Cameron Wriothesley, of the Royal Engineers, wounded by a splinter from a gun carriage knocked off by a round shot, and dying soon after they got him on board *Belleisle*, the hospital ship. A hundred and twenty Russians survived to be made prisoners and given a good time on board the British warships for having fought so bravely.

Meanwhile General Baraguay d'Hilliers had set up his breaching batteries against the main fortress, diversions being created at the same time by shell fire from *Bulldog*, *Trident*, *Duperre*, *Edinburgh* and *Ajax*. On the further side Captain the Hon. F. T. Pelham of the *Blenheim* had landed a 10-pivot gun from his ship and set it upon the captured fort at Transvig Point, from which exposed position he contributed a good quota of shell fire. 'The little space in the anchorage before Bomarsund, and the intricacy of the navigation will prevent the ships approaching the main fortress as near as could be wished,' Charlie reported that night; but all the same, he did not expect the fortress to hold out much longer. Nor did it. *Arrogant, Amphion, Valorous, Sphinx* and *Driver* had now in turn joined the bombardment, and on 16 August the white flag was seen flying from Bomarsund's battlememts. The garrison marched out, and 2,255 Russian prisoners were embarked for Britain.

On 6 August, the day after the French troops had arrived and the *entente* was proving less *cordiale* than had been hoped, Sulivan had mourned:

This day has been like anything but Sunday. The difficulty of planning and arranging everything with the French chiefs is very great. The want of *one head* is very evident, and we have not very good managers to assist our chief. . . There is too much desire on the part of certain persons to have all to do.

The 13th was still less like Sunday. The guns were roaring and belching, and Sulivan, too close to Fort Tzee, narrowly escaped death when it suddenly blew up. He was cheered by having Commodore Michael Seymour on board (no relation to Henry Seymour of the *Cumberland*, except in the limited sense that they were both descended from Protector Somerset, uncle of the boy King Edward VI. 'He is such a good estimable man that it is a pleasure having him with me.'

The cholera on the other hand was truly saddening. 'The French have already buried some seven hundred out of ten thousand men, and 24 died yesterday,' Sulivan was to write in early September. He had been worried to see the Russian prisoners setting off for England on board *Hannibal* on 19 August, when the weather was still warm. 'The cholera still lingers in some ships. It commenced severely in *Hannibal* directly she arrived, and with nearly two thousand men on board it was no wonder.' How many of these Russian prisoners would arrive healthy at Portsmouth?

Sulivan had another source of anxiety: he reported

. . . parties interested in getting up a feeling against the old admiral. A man introduced himself yesterday as the brother of ***. I thought him only a travelling gentleman, but he tried to pump out of me opinions (which I do not hold) that would convey censure on the Chief, whom he evidently wanted to find complaints against. I was obliged to be rude to him to get rid of him, but before he went over the side he avowed himself the correspondent of the *Morning Herald*.

Then I gave him my opinion on the subject of newspapers and
their correspondents, and the falsehoods they publish, and the
system for puffing up some parties that was springing up, in a
way that will get me anything but favourably mentioned, particularly as I bowed him over the side in anything but a civil way
afterwards.

What was the enmity all about? 'It is too late for Sveaborg, even if we
had force enough to attack it, which we have not.' Black Charlie
meanwhile was writing a glowing report on Sulivan, his ship master,
Mr Evans, and Commander Otter of the *Alban* – 'Owing to their
exertions this fleet have found their way into creeks and corners
never intended for ships of the line; day and night they have worked,
and worked successfully.'

Others felt very differently about the whole affair. Henry Seymour
felt bitterly that no possible chance of distinction had come his way.
Things had started off well – at Hango:

I was agreeably surprised at being ordered to weigh with the
Comr. in Chief and the greater part of the screw fleet; the
Penelope was ordered to tow me as the wind was light. . . We
arrived at this very good anchorage [Led Sound] the same
evening.

Early next morning Henry had been excited to hear firing from' the
forts at the ships being led up by the *Lightning*.

We are rather anxious to be with them but I fear our share will
be chiefly to assist with boats, Marines etc. The French not
liking Ad. Chads to be without any French ships up there sent a
liner in tow of a screw steamer to join them but she took the
ground almost immediately. . .
  [He was pleased to be] made repeating ship and we are the
only English sailing ship among these magnificent screws. I
believe we are supposed to have a light draught of water which
delusion I encouraged till pressed upon the point.

Sir Charles, he had heard, had been put out by the non-arrival of
the French troops and the French refusal to start anything until they
arrived. Why? Henry wondered,

as we have plenty of troops with us to take possession of these

islands and I suppose the French troops can only be intended to
garrison them this winter and commence operations early in the
spring.

Nothing but frustration followed.

Adl. Chads sent down word that he did not want more ships
and Comr. in Chief is very anxious to send more. He thinks it
possible that the Kronstadt fleet might put to sea if too many of
us get huddled up at Bomarsund... I asked and got a sort of
permission to go with him and so did Keppel and Clarence Paget
and I expect to have a look tomorrow at what is going on.

A look had been about all Henry did get. 'The channels are very
narrow and abound with rocks under water.' His marines had been
ordered to be in readiness at a moment's notice, but that was it.
Cumberland lay at anchor in Led Sound with 'the *Duke, Acre, Princess Royal and James Watt,* and half a dozen steamers going and
coming all day. The French squadron are also here' – far from the
scene of action. And when the French main body of troops did arrive
in Led Sound, in *Royal William, St Vincent, Hannibal, Algiers* and a
couple of troopships, he thought that 'General Baraguay d'Hilliers
would have a good laugh when he sees the place that this fleet with
the 2,000 French troops that have been on board the French fleet all
along, over and above their complement, have waited for his assistance to take'.

'We all feel much humbled and disgusted, at all events I will
answer for myself, for I am firmly convinced 1,000 marines and
soldiers and 3 or 4 blockships would have been as effective as the
entire force now at our disposal.' Of course there would be 'reason
for congratulation' if the place surrendered without loss of life; but as
for *Cumberland,* landing the French would probably be all their
share of the work. 'I cannot help this grumbling as it has lost us all
here our only chance of distinction and I think the Country will be
justified in holding us cheap on our return.'

Furthermore, the cholera was back; seven men had died in the *St
Jean d'Acre,* and the *Princess Royal* also had it. 'We thank God, are
yet quite clear of it ... we use every precaution to keep the bilges
clean and dry etc.'

The British marines on the hill had built themselves shelters of fir
branches which, 'thanks to the fineness of the weather', were not

inadequate. 'The French were fully provided with tents and were perfectly settled in them within half an hour after halting.'

He noted with disgust that the *Penelope* 'had to throw her guns overboard and was towed off stern foremost. This has been the naval share of the work.' And the French!

> General Baraguay d'Hilliers said he would just place his field guns in advance and knock the wooden top off the upper tower and keep the fire of the Mini rifles down, but the old villain took 4 mortars and 4 largish 18 pdr brass field guns and placed them in position and commenced firing on Sunday morning at 4 o'clock . . . the French are burning to pay off the Moscow failure. . . Thus were General Jones and his marine battalion shoved out of all participation in the capture of this first tower which commanded the other two forts and will ensure their fall. . . This place could not have stood against two line-of-battleships but our chance was allowed to pass by.

Henry Seymour had had himself rowed up in his gig to see some of the fun, 'and Keppel and I pitched our tent near the Marine camp, and Wilfred joined us from the *Sphynx*. All too soon they were told to go back to their ships. The comdr. in Chief does nothing but express his fear that the Russian fleet will come out and that this fleet will be caught in the ice.' The French general had added insult to injury by signalling from a post he had established on a windmill – 'Generals do not require further assistance from the Fleet', and Henry thought that Black Charlie 'cannot have relished the signal made to him'. And although Cochrane of the *Driver*, who was attached to the French (to ease communications by his good French), had reported 'the best understanding', Henry thought that 'General Jones must have been a little sore at finding the French had stolen a march upon him.'

'We had nothing to do and we did it,' Harry Keppel wrote flatly from the *St Jean d'Acre*.

Of these rumblings of distant thunder Black Charlie seemed unaware; he 'begged to congratulate their Lordships on the fall of this important fortress with so small a loss'. (That is, if you didn't count the cholera victims.) But the small loss served only to convince the public at home that there hadn't really been a battle at all. Possibly a more important one had been won. After 800 years of steady dinging and banging at each other, English and French combat had always seemed almost a way of life, a part of the natural order of things. Black Charlie wrote: 'I am happy to say that the greatest cordiality has subsisted between the French General and Admiral and myself, as well as between the soldiers and sailors of the two nations.'

19

An Absence of Magnificence

The Russian Empire was like some huge animal with a widely diffused life. It could take a great number of knocks and wounds on its body and limbs without serious trouble. Despite all the Westernizing efforts of Peter the Great, it did not share the ethic of the West. It had no exaggerated sensibility over threats to *amour propre*, like the French. It did not, like the English, play cricket. It was impervious to pinpricks; and the fact that the English sailors were able to swan ashore from their warships and pick wild strawberries almost within a stone's throw of its capital city disturbed it not at all. Russia's cloak of mysticism held within it a callous realism. If it could come in near enough, let the British fleet bombard Abo (only full of Finns after all) or Reval (only full of Esthonians), to its heart's content; killing any number of people, mostly civilians, without even faintly affecting the course of the war.

The Crimean War in fact ended only when the new Czar, the French (who had satisfied their desire to make their point by a really smashing win over the Russians in storming the Malakoff fort at Sebastopol) and the British had simultaneously had enough; although the British, in spite of having lost 25,000 men and spent £50,000,000, were extremely reluctant to stop – the Czar was still the tyrant who dominated the Poles, and the cruel invader of Hungary. Everyone was to give back their conquests, the Aland Islands were to be fortified no more, all ships of war were to be excluded from the Black Sea, and the Allies gained their crucial point; which was that the future of Turkey was to be decided by Europe, and not by Russia alone.

All the same, as Colonel Anthony Sterling, writing from the Crimea, was to say of the Russians: 'It is a great nationality. I cannot believe that any amount of calamity will break up Russia. . . Some fine morning, when we are all republicans, a sudden pounce will place Russia at Stamboul. . .' The French, once they had made their point about reinstating their martial honour, badly bruised forty years back by the retreat from Moscow, were anxious to keep Russia on her feet as a

counterbalance to Austria and Prussia. The English were more concerned with Russia's long-term menace.

In England, home interest was centred on the Black Sea: this was,
after all, the Crimean War. And so much more of the action was to be
seen there, so much thrust, so much courage. 'Ninety-third, ninety-
third, damn all that eagerness!' their Colonel, Colin Campbell, had had
to reprove his double line of Highlanders, defending the British base at
Balaclava, and showing a mind to rush forward at the force of 400
Russian cavalry who were charging them. Russian soldiers on their
march south had been encouraged to take the English lightly. Captain
Hodasevich of the Tarantine regiment heard a fellow officer telling his
men:

> The English come and go on the sea, but there is no chance of
> their reaching Sevastopol; they would be afraid to. Let them try
> and fight us on land and we would soon send them packing. The
> French, we know, can fight, but the English! They are only used
> to fighting savages in a far off country. I can't think of the name
> of it.
> 'India?' suggested one of his audience.
> 'Yes, that's it.'

After this conversation on Easter Sunday of 1854 at Simpheropol,
the Russian encounter with the English came as a horrid shock.
After Alma, Captain Hodasevich recorded that he could not believe
men could be so brave, advancing in only a double line towards a
Russian column. General Liprandi, the chivalrous Russian general
in command in the Crimea, asked the British prisoners taken at
Inkerman, 'What did they give you to drink? Did they prime you up
with spirits to make you charge us in such a mad way?' William
Kirk of the 17th Lancers, an unwounded prisoner who had lost his
horse, answered, 'You think we were drunk? By God, I tell you
that if we had as much as smelt the barrel, we would have taken
half Russia by this time!' He was instantly slammed down for his
impertinence by Sergeant-Major Fowler of the 4th Dragoons, who,
however, corroborated his facts. Fowler, who had had a Cossack
lance through his back, stood up stiffly, saluted Liprandi, and told
him:

> On my honour, Sir, except for the vodka your men have given
> some of us, there is not a man who has tasted food or drink

this day. [The fight had started at dawn.] Our daily issue of a mouthful of rum is made in the afternoon, and believe me, Sir, we don't hoard it. I wish all the men who have gone to their account this day were as free of sin as they were of drink.'

Liprandi called them noble fellows and treated them with kindness, as did all except the Cossacks who had captured them. Even the food got better as the British prisoners marched north, and though many of them died of diseases picked up in the filthy hovels in the Russian villages where they spent the nights, the rest of the time they marched along singing and laughing, prisoners and guards arm in arm. Private J.W. Wightman, of the 7th Lancers, noted and admired the affection and cohesion between Russian officers and men.

The French went on record as thinking the British soldiers the finest in the world; both admired the Russian courage. Later all were to express admiration of the the way the French had fought at the Redan. It seemed to them amazing that Napoleon, with such soldiers, could have lost a war. Mrs Duberly, who, rather like Lord Lichfield in his yacht in the Gulf of Finland, had come for the interest of the thing, thought that 'the French can beat us in their commissariat and general management, but the Englishman retains his wonderous power of fighting that nothing can rob him of but death'. She watched amazed as the soldiers organized race meetings the moment the weather made it possible – 'men who had been starved with cold and hunger, drowned in rain and mud, wounded in action, torn with sickness' all the long winter, and had been fed, according to Temple Godman, a captain in the 5th Dragoon Guards, 'with gobbets of meat out of buckets like our keeper collects for the dogs at home'. Colonel Anthony Sterling agreed in marvelling at the astonishing high spirits of the troops, 'ready to knock their heads against any wall behind which they can find Russians. They are the true England, stars whose brilliance will be historical. . . I believe they would fight and die to the last man in this wild Tauris, rather than give in and give up.'

'Not much generalship on our side, though the usual determined English courage,' Captain George Maude summed up the fighting on the Alma. Russell, the *Times* correspondent, put the astonishingly high morale down to the way the officers shared the hardships of the men – the nights in the open, ragged clothes, short commons;

all that the officers had more of, he noted, was work and responsibility. Hadley Vicars of the 97th, a twenty-two-year-old who was
to be killed leading an attack, wrote home that there was no insubordination 'where officers treat the men with the same feelings as
their own and take an interest in their welfare'.

Lord Raglan, in command, was, like Black Charlie, in his late
sixties. It seems odd, in an age where life expectancy for the well-
to-do was thirty-five years, and nineteen years for the poor, that
supreme command was given to men of such an age, when initiative after a long life of hardship and fevers seemed to fade, and
the decisive will to falter. Lord George Paget of the Light Cavalry
Brigade, who thought the French most efficient but some of their
troops revolutionary and ill-disciplined, noticed with surprise that
the British troops continued to cheer Raglan to the echo when he
rode through their ranks, in spite of their sufferings; so much so
that, being a shy man, he took to skirting the camp.

At home, it was the glorious failures that captured the imagina-
tion. Tennyson showed no wish to burst into verse after the successful efforts of Campbell and his Highlanders to defend Balaclava,
nor to celebrate Ainslie's heroic action in fending off another Russian cavalry charge with 550 Highlanders in a supreme test of nerves
below the Fedroukine heights. Though the poet himself did thrill to
the sixty-one-year-old General Scarlett's brilliantly successful attack
with the Heavy Brigade:

> They rode like Victors and Lords
> Through the forest of lances and swords
> In the heart of the Russian hordes,

'The Charge of the Heavy Brigade' is not a poem of which anyone
except Tennysonian scholars has ever heard. Temple Godman
wrote:

> At length the Russians turned, as well they might, and the whole
> raced as hard as they could pelt up the hill, our men after them...
> I hope we may get a real good charge at their cavalry again but I
> think they will funk to cross swords with us after their licking.
> They have never licked the English yet... The Russians seem
> to fight well and be well led, they are most determined-looking
> fellows ... certainly more noble and braver than a Turk. [God-
> man was less sure about the Russian nobility after Inkerman.]

The Russian soldiers say their generals tell them never to spare the wounded, so they bayonet all they come across. Just fancy, one of their *Majors* was caught killing all the wounded. They are perfect savages. . . I wish they could see our men giving their wounded water, and their own rations of rum and biscuits. [He thought the Russians] mostly fine stout men but their faces are broad and flat and betoken great ignorance.

The British fleet, however, bucketing along off the Finnish coast, seemed to fight nothing but fog and gale and cholera (though this, Henry Seymour noted by the end of August, was confined to the *Hannibal,* where nine men had died). For the Navy there was no chance of deciding whether the Russians were flat-faced or noble, gallant or cruel; few had come near enough to see them.

The magnificence of Florence Nightingale had not yet blazed forth, and the mood of the country at home seemed to cry out for lost causes. George Maude wrote after Balaclava:

Nothing could have exceeded the courage of the regiments who, quite unsupported but trusting in support, repeatedly flung themselves upon immense bodies of Russians, with ultimate success.

But as far as publicity was concerned, and indeed, posterity, they flung themselves in vain; all that anyone could remember was the failed charge of the Light Brigade. 'C'est magnifique,' a French general had memorably declared, watching from the heights above the Valley of Death, 'mais ce n'est pas la guerre.' Lord Cardigan retired to a bath and a good dinner on board his yacht moored offshore; but to Temple Godman it had been 'a terrible sight to see them walking back one by one and the valley strewn with them. The Greys alone lost forty killed and wounded, all for nothing.' But it was magnificence that the home front was requiring from the Baltic fleet, and magnificence was just what they were not getting.

The officers of the Navy were probably divided into those who simply wanted to win the war, and those who were perfectly certain of winning the war anyway and wanted as much magnificence as possible while doing so. There was something to be said for Henry Seymour's proposition on the taking of Bomarsund – 'a very pretty affair if it had been done by 800 men ashore and 2 or 3 line-of-battle ships . . . abundantly sufficient in my opinion.' Taken the fort had been, but far from magnificently.

Black Charlie had felt that the Government opinion had been so far so good. It soon became clear that so far was now not considered far enough. 'I shall be anxious to hear what is your next move,' Graham wrote on 2 August when congratulating Charlie. 'Surely either Abo or Reval is open to attack.' Abo, now called Turku, is on the west coast of Finland, up innumerable creeks and inlets, all rock-strewn and uncharted, and so far inland that an attempt to take it, besides serving no purpose so late in the year, would have been rather like trying to capture Manchester by advancing up the ship canal with a fleet unsupported from on shore. Things were not going well in the Crimea, and the Administration needed a thumping victory. If a naval fight were not available, then the public demanded a proper set-to ashore, on Russian soil, with heavy losses on both sides.

The Swedes had hastily disclaimed all wish to repossess Bomarsund. In that case, said the practical French, the fort were best destroyed forthwith. Knowing the fond hope of Swedish cooperation to which Graham still held, Black Charlie felt obliged to wait for orders on this score.

But by now even Sir James Graham had lost hope in King Oscar I. Bomarsund was to be destroyed. 'I hope you will take care that the destruction is complete, and that not one stone is left upon another,' Graham concluded with Old Testament severity. 'I am more than satsfied with your proceedings,' he had told Charlie earlier in this letter of 25 August. 'I am delighted with the prudence and sound judgement you have displayed.' The *Edinburgh* was instructed to demolish the fortress with her guns. The first Lancaster had now arrived, but the destruction of Bomarsund's granite walls took ten days of unopposed bombardment.

Though the Admiralty had sent the message 'Satisfaction . . . cordial approbation' to Black Charlie and his officers and men over Bomarsund, a certain amount of needling from the home front had already set in, and Berkeley, while congratulating him, told Black Charlie that

some of the newspapers are not satisfied, because you have not had a sufficient number of killed and wounded. And, whilst the whole Government are pleased beyond measure at your trifling loss. . . John Bull, never content, expects more than is possible. I trust you will not be goaded on, or beaten out of your own determinations. I have every confidence that you will attempt all that is feasible, and that you will succeed in all you attempt.

Rather as if the Baltic expedition existed to sell newspapers, John Delane, editor of *The Times,* told Charlie:

We want some exploits. The public, though very patient, look to you and your fleet for greater results than I fear it is possible to give them. If we can't have Sveaborg or Kronstadt, however, we will take Bomarsund as an instalment. . . I hope that you will be able to use the French troops to harass the Russian army a good deal. . . The more men you can occupy in this way, the fewer she will have to send out against us elsewhere.

The thirty-seven-year-old Delane seemed unafraid of teaching his grandmother to suck eggs. 'The army in the east has hitherto been even more inactive than you in the Baltic', but they at least were about to attack Sebastopol. The thought that his friend Charlie was lagging seemed uppermost in his mind. 'I hear you have lovely weather, smooth water and hot sun, but it won't last long, and if you wait till October, you will not bring all your fleet home.'

This epistle arrived on 14 August, and a nettled Charlie replied next day:

I am sorry I have not been able to give the public a good butcher's bill, but had I attacked either Kronstadt or Sveaborg with my fleet, they would have had a bill *with* the loss of the fleet, or had we succeeded in withdrawing disabled, we should have fallen an easy prey to the Russian fleet, which would have been worse. One would suppose it was only necessary to look at the bird's eye view of Kronstadt or Sveaborg to convince the veriest dolt that to attack either with a fleet alone was impossible. You say there is grumbling in the fleet sent home, that probably comes from some poltroon who wants to get a name, full well knowing that he can talk big without having an opportunity for his courage to be put to the test.

I have the most absurd plans sent to me from people who ought to know better [and he outlined a couple of the silliest]. I have no patience with the nonsense that is sent to me every day.

The captain of the *Cumberland* had not much patience either. In a

letter sympathizing with him in his renewed illness, Henry Seymour
told his father:

> There are too many authorities here, what with British Admirals
> and Generals and French Generals and Admirals. They do not
> hit it off very well together but French General and French Ad-
> miral hit it off worse together than any . . . too many cats sent to
> catch the mice.

He thought the destruction of the Bomarsund fortress 'rather cutting
a caper over a dead donkey'. The granite only turned out to be two or
three feet thick, the rest of the walls were of brick.

> If the forts at Helsingfors and Kronstadt are built on the same
> pattern it is certain they could not stand against our shot but at
> those places the number of guns *en barbette* are almost too
> formidable to approach, and there is no doubt the Russians
> know the use of their guns.

The number of Russian casualties sustained were hard to come by

> as they make a mystery of it, but we found no dead, though a
> great many wounded. The French, as they had the misfortune
> to fire into one another, do not like either to mention their
> casualties; [and they had lost 240 men from cholera]. I feel sorry
> for the loss of Wriothesley, the engineer, such a nice young fel-
> low . . . [and for that of a marine] killed while asleep in camp by
> a random shot. . . Everyone agrees that whatever was ordered
> to be done was well done and more cannot be expected from
> junior officers.
>   There is an abundance of time left to take Hango, even a few
> ships could not take long about that, but I doubt if it will be done.
> Everything is now at a standstill waiting for orders from home as
> whether the place is to be destroyed completely or not. Ramsay
> declines changing *Euryalus* with me. [At least the ships were now
> well provided for] with stores of all sorts and provisions both
> fresh and salt. . .
>   Keppel has been unwell lately with a bad cough, he fretted
> himself into downright illness by being kept in the background
> while work was going on so near. Commodore Seymour [the
> second Sir Michael] is in command down here [at Led Sound] at
> present and everybody is loud in his praise and no wonder for he

does manage all his work in the most agreeable as well as fair manner among all the ships, and we are aware that he has done his best to get Sir Charles to go ahead somewhere.

Henry remained convinced that Bomarsund would need but half an hour to demolish under broadside; his comments on the eight days it actually took are not on record.

Sulivan was sad to see the Bomarsund forts go, well constructed as they were – 'the Emperor must have put a very great value on the place', he thought, 'to add so enormously to the fortifications. The work is beautiful.' Sulivan believed that the Czar must have meant Bomarsund for his most ice-free port, advanced towards Sweden and the Atlantic – 'by far the finest port in the Baltic, with anchorages for the largest ships'.

By 2 September it was already getting cold. The French army left for home on the 5th, in the midst of 'a terrific gale from the northwest', while young naval officers, unaware of the impediments, fretted at the lack of action. Midshipman Cornwallis Wykeham-Martin wrote to his aunt from HMS *Neptune* on 7 September:

> As for myself and the Baltic Fleet I quite blush. If I had my way both Helsingfors and Kronstadt would have fallen long ago. . . I am quite sure if we were to go into Helsingfors tomorrow we would destroy the forts and burn the fleet and the same thing would happen if we attacked Kronstadt. I wish they would let us try. . . There is one consolation, not a single Russian dares to show his nose outside. [From Alice Pollock, *A Portrait of My Victorian Youth*, London, 1971.]

Henry Seymour reported on the 4th that the Czar had destroyed the forts at Hango 'to forestall the allied fleet'; 'but he did not know his man and might have left them this winter at least,' Henry commented bitterly. 'It is now getting too late for any operations to be commenced.' The French troops had gone or were going, 'they have lost 6 or 700 men by cholera since the surrender. . . I shall not be sorry to get our head towards home as nothing further will take place I conceive. . . It is blowing a whole gale from the NW' and he doubted whether any letters could be got off.

On the 9th Sulivan wrote:

> The worst weather we have ever had in the Baltic, heavy gales from the NW to NNE every day, and here in a snug harbour we

had French ships driving, and all the fleet with 2 anchors down and topmasts struck.

He heard from Black Charlie that he had decided to send the sailing ships home early 'and I was glad to find it'. The *Daily News,* he told his family

> has by far the most truthful accounts of the proceedings of our fleet without exaggerations or puffing. Let them give full particulars and criticize as much as they like, but not publish anything that could give the enemy a useful hint ... [Sulivan had been told at first] that the old chief was too obstinate to take advice, but I never met any senior officer who was more open to reason.

The summer heat and calm of the Baltic seemed now to be finally broken up by gales; the return home was inevitable. 'You should begin by sending home, without much delay, the sailing three-deckers, the least weatherly of the line-of-battle ships, and the slowest and worst of the blockships,' Graham told Charlie on 29 August; and he should concert measures with the French 'for the gradual withdrawal of the fleet from the Baltic'. The party appeared to be over, with muted enthusiasm from the homeland.

The French, however, took an entirely different view of the goings on at Bomarsund, and the next ship out from France bore with her a field marshal's baton for General Baraguay d'Hilliers, straight from the hand of the Emperor Napoleon III himself. If anyone amongst the British forces enjoyed a hearty laugh at this event, he laughed within himself. The French had always been dab hands at magnificence. Failing the reality they could always invent some.

20

Who's to Hang?

On 30 August the French Ministry of Marine sent a firm message to Admiral Parseval telling him that operations in the Baltic were finished for this season. Black Charlie had meanwhile sent Captain Scott, with the *Odin, Alban, Gorgon* and *Driver* to have a look at Abo; and Scott on his return reported not unfavourably on the prospects for its capture. Baraguay d'Hilliers, whose troops were already depleted by cholera, thought it unwise to risk an attack in the foul weather which appeared to have settled in. Allied admirals and generals alike informed their governments that no more could be done this season against Sveaborg, owing to the want of gunboats and mortar boats. They were all now concentrating on the possibilities of the next season. The French troops were ordered home to Cherbourg and sailed a week later.

But General d'Hilliers had sensibly decided that he was not to leave the Baltic without a look at Sveaborg, and accordingly Sulivan, who knew the channels, was deputed to take him and his engineer, General Niel, for a view from the decks of the *Lightning*. In an ill day for Black Charlie, they also took Brigadier-General Jones.

Baraguay d'Hilliers was emphatic in his report. Sveaborg *could* be taken, but at this late season and with no gunboats and only four mortars, it was out of the question. Admiral Parseval concurred. But to Brigadier-General Jones, theirs seemed 'a very erroneous impres- sion of Sveaborg's fortifications'. He thought that 'a heavy bombardment from a combined operation by land and sea' could do the job, combined with 'throwing ashore 5,000 men on the Island of Bak Holmen'. He thought the operation would only take seven or eight days.

As the necessary French troops had departed and even one fine day, let alone a sequence of them, could not now be hoped for, Black Charlie thought the plan, as far as this year was concerned, was a nonsense, but was obliged to the French command and to the Admiralty. The French demolished it swiftly. Parseval and d'Hilliers thought it 'impossible'. General Niel, the engineer, was equally crisp.

'If the attack by the fleet should be made at a great distance, its effect would be absolutely nothing, and an attack by land would be insufficient.' Niel would not put aside the possibility that the ships *might* do it, but added that it did not come within his province to advise an attack by sea. An attack by land would be 'useless, insufficient and dangerous'.

Charlie, sending home his report, gave his opinion that with long preparation and a large force of gunboats, an attack on Sveaborg early in the season might succeed. But 'if you land at all, you must land a force superior to any they can bring against you; and I do not think the Emperor of Russia would leave such an important fortress with a weak garrison.' He was later to be dumbfounded by the interpretation put on this letter.

The verdicts of all the admirals and generals were united against the verdict of one brigadier-general, the hopeful Jones. But by the time Jones's report reached home, the Administration was in need of any straw at which to clutch.

On the 5th Admiral Parseval had received the order to take his ships home. On the 7th the French ship of the line *Tilsit* departed through heavy weather, accompanied by two frigates. That night the wind increased, *Majestic* parted her chain cable, and the storeship, *Nimrod*, was driven aground. Five days later Black Charlie received the first blast of the storm that was to blow his cherished fame to perdition.

In late July the last cheering letter that Charlie was to receive in the Baltic had been despatched to him from Regent's Park. The aged but still dashing Cochrane, who had fought for Greek independence and assisted several South American countries to throw off their Spanish or Portuguese yoke, was in accord with him:

My dear Sir Charles, Those only who are acquainted with the difficulties you have to surmount and the nature of the obstacles assigned to you to encounter, can appreciate the perseverance and moral courage requisite to overcome the one and ensure the other. My anxiety lest your zeal should induce you to yield your judgement to the notions of the uninitiated is now quite relieved, and the noble fleet you command is safe from the consequences of red-hot incendiary missiles, propelled from granite fortresses situated out of point blank range of combustible ships. Believe me that I sympathize with you.

The trouble with the uninitiated is that they tend to think that they can initiate themselves by a twenty-minute chat with a professional who may or may not be conversant with the actual case under discussion. Charlie was to suffer from a great many of these.

Like others in office, Admiral Berkeley was not above attributing his own feeling to the emotions of his fellow countrymen.

> John Bull is getting uproarious, because nobody is killed or wounded; meetings are being called to condemn the Government, because Kronstadt and Sebastopol have not been captured, and the return of the French troops, or rather the reported return, excited derision. . . [Berkeley seemed unaware that Graham had instructed the Admiral to send most of them home.]
>
> I do not know what to do about recalling some of your fleet. We must first know decidedly whether or not any further operations are to be undertaken. I perceive that General Jones thinks that Sveaborg might be destroyed. I certainly hope that there will be unanimity in your councils.

This Admiralty hope at least was to be fulfilled. On the 4th the Admiralty had told Charlie to consult with his French colleagues and the admirals as to what operations remained to be undertaken this year; bearing in mind that 'any object to be gained must be worth the attempt, and that useless expenditure of life, with destruction of ships, should not be hazarded for any object unworthy of the risk and the cause' in which he was engaged. The French generals, having already sailed south, could take no part. Gathered together on board *Duke of Wellington*, Charlie's own admirals and the French admirals Parseval and Penaud were of one mind.

> In consequence of the advanced season of the year, nothing could be undertaken against Sveaborg, or any other fortified place on the coast of Russia, with a chance of success, and we are also of the opinion (with the resources at present at our disposition) without the loss of a great many men and seriously compromising the ships.

Black Charlie accompanied this forthright decision with an equally forthright letter, which was to cause great offence:

> I daresay there is a great deal of dissatisfaction in England that

more was not done by so large an army; but the fact is they came too late in the season to carry on any ulterior operations, whilst their departure has been hurried. I wished them to go to Abo, which was a purely military operation, but no one seemed to like it, and as a heavy gale of wind came on the night they left Ledsund, there is no knowing what might have happened had we gone there. The French Rear-Admiral's ship drove into our hawse, our dolphin striker thumping against her stern, and our cable out to the clinch. Had she fallen on board us, and had we both gone ashore, and taken another line-of-battle ship with us, the people of England would perhaps have come to their senses and seen that operations in these seas are not easy at this season of the year.

Their lordships will observe that General Jones proposed landing 5,000 men at Sveaborg, and placing batteries against it, and he thought this a good season to do so. Had the French General been unwise enough to follow this advice, or had the Admirals been indiscreet enough to have countenanced an operation that by his own account required seven or eight days to have brought it to a successful termination, the troops would have been made prisoners, and probably half a dozen of the ships lost. This would have been a rather bad finish to the first campaign in the Baltic.

If their lordships will read with attention Admiral Chads's report, my own, and General Jones (with the exception of what I have stated) they would find us all pretty well agreed as to the proper mode of attack on Sveaborg and Kronstadt; and that *either ought to be attacked in the proper manner, or not at all.* I have received many propositions for attacking both Sveaborg and Kronstadt but I never will lend myself to any absurd project, or be driven to attempt what is not practicable, by newspaper writers, who, I am sorry to say, I have reason to believe, are in correspondence with officers of the fleet, who ought to know better.

The Admiralty had not waited for this joint report by all the responsible authorities on the spot. On the 9th they wrote to tell Charlie to lay Brigadier-General Jones's report before the French General-in-Chief and admirals, and if it changed their minds, to proceed upon it. On 5 September, four days before this letter was written, the French Minister of Marine had written to the Admiralty asking for steamers to tow the French transports home, and by the 16th, when their letter of the 9th was delivered on board *Duke of Wellington,* the French transports had long since sailed homeward.

Next day, though Graham was aware that the transports must have sailed, Charlie was told by a letter dated the 12th, to call another council of war:

> ... the French fleet is still with you, and you must lose no time in conferring with Admiral Parseval and in ascertaining whether he is willing to join in a naval attack on Sveaborg, such as General Niel regards as certain to lead to success. It must be remembered that the destruction of Sveaborg has always been regarded as an object of great importance from the commencement of the war.

Graham brushed aside the fact that he had often told Charlie that blockade was the primary object, and as often cautioned him against running his ships against stone walls. In a private letter to Charlie, Graham wrote:

> General Niel speaks of eight or ten sail of the line as sufficient for the purpose. If the *French be disposed to risk one half of this number,* I do not suppose that volunteers to an equal amount would be wanting in the British fleet. [There was, all the same, a let out.] If, unhappily, nothing more can be done, it is wisest to send home at once the smallest and least effective of the steamers, and the least weatherly of the large ships.

Wearily, Charlie again summoned his admirals. Once more, the seamen rowed them on board the *Duke,* through the drenching seas.

> We, the undersigned, have examined the report of General Niel that Sveaborg can be successfully attacked by ships alone.
>
> We have given our unanimous opinion that neither the season nor our resources permit such an attack without the loss of a great many men, and seriously compromising the ships, and Rear-Admiral Martin, having maturely considered our report, adopts the same opinion.
>
> After having read General Niel's report, we see no reason to change the opinion we have already expressed.
>
> The French Admiral, having already given his opinion and signed it, declined the conference.

Given under our hands on board the *Duke of Wellington* at Ledsund, the 18th day of September, 1854.

CHARLES NAPIER   H.D. CHADS

MICHAEL SEYMOUR   H.B. MARTIN

Though lacking in the required magnificence, this reply was definite enough. Unluckily, Charlie was unable to resist ramming the point home. What reliance, he asked, could

> be placed on the opinion of two military engineers on naval subjects, when one decided that Sveaborg could be destroyed by 5,000 men, guns, mortars and rockets from the island of Bak Holmen, combined with an attack by the Allied Fleet, in seven or eight days; whilst the other decides that it can be laid in ruins in two hours by the fleet alone?

Fatally, Charlie went on to rub salt in the wound by sending Graham a copy of the report on Sveaborg that he had made on 18 July, which that official seemed to have neglected to read.

The fortress of Sveaborg, he had written, was assailable with a reasonable chance of success

> by fitting out a great number of gunboats, carrying one gun with a long range, and placing them west of Sveaborg and south of Helsingfors... The islands within range may be all put in requisition for 13 inch mortars... Back these by the fleet, to relieve the men, and in the course of the summer Sveaborg could be reduced to ashes.

In reaching this opinion he had been

> assisted by Admiral Chads, who is a practical man, and knows more about gunnery than any man in the service. [If they would study the plans of Sveaborg at the Admiralty] and would lay them before the engineer and artillery officers, I would be bound for it they will agree with me that this is the only way to destroy Sveaborg, without an army superior to the Emperor of Russia's, which we are not likely to bring into the field.

Already, writing in mid-July, Charlie had said 'It is too late this year, but be prepared next, now we know the anchorage, and begin early.' Now it was late September – what did they expect? A justifiably plaintive note crept into the old admiral's voice; and did him no good.

> It is all very well for people to talk big, and say what they will do; but put a fleet of twenty sail of the line into their hands, and let the fleet be conducted amongst unknown rocks and shoals not yet surveyed – and at this season of the year, when you cannot depend on the weather for two hours – and when it would require two days to buoy it off; and then suppose a gale of wind to come on, and suddenly, when you are at anchor, as we have already seen, what would become of your ships? Add to that a fleet, superior to your own, and ready to pounce upon you should you be disabled.

It was a screed lamentably lacking in magnificence; and was also the kind of plain speaking for which Graham by no means cared.

To Admiral Berkeley Black Charlie protested with equal frankness, 'I do not require a council of war to make me do my duty, nor, after all the praises that have been heaped upon me, and after the warnings which I had received, to be goaded into rashness.'

'Of course it was settled that the sooner they could get the ships home the better,' Henry Seymour reported dejectedly as the council of war dispersed to their several ships,' He was writing home on the 20th; and his ship's return sounded equally melancholy. 'Mr Rowe died yesterday I grieve to say of the effects of one of his debaucheries'; and on 2 October *Cumberland* was 'full of disaster'. They were not half way home – 'we have had the most provoking baffling foul winds ever since we started . . . and last night just when we got our head the right way, a bungling French steamer managed to get right athwart our hawse and damaged us considerably.' It was altogether a dispirited and frustrated party that straggled back to its home port with a sense of little accomplished.

Sulivan, still in the Gulf of Finland, felt differently, writing on 25 September:

> With all the old chief's failings it is lucky we had a man with moral courage enough to stand firm against the whines of the Press, as well as against the wishes of some men out here, who, caring only for chances of personal distinction, would have wanted him to run their heads against any stone walls that offered.

There had been talk of a medal for Sulivan's outstanding skill in navigation, but, he thought, 'the way the admiral treats me is sufficient reward for all I have done'.

On 17 September Admiral Parseval had sent home his second in command, Admiral Penaud, with five of his ships. (Penaud, in the opinion of Henry Seymour, was the better seaman of the two.) On the 19th Parseval himself sailed for France with the rest of his squadron, leaving four steamers to assist in the blockade. Always friendly, he had taken his part, and stood by Charlie firmly throughout; staying in the Baltic for a month longer than he had originally promised. He was no fool, and had no intention of risking his ships any longer as a cat's-paw for the Whig Administration of Britain. Arrived back in France, he and his fleet were warmly congratulated, receiving their decorations from Napoleon III in person, plus the statutory kiss on either cheek.

A very different fate awaited Charlie. 'We shall have blue-books and parliamentary papers without end,' Admiral Berkeley warned Charlie on 24 September; and he summed up the situation with considerable frankness. 'The attack failing against you will be levelled at the Board, or, failing against the Board, will be levelled against you.'

On 18 September a single and not fully efficient gunboat had arrived to join the fleet at Ledsund. Whoever was to blame for this dilatory and inadequate reinforcement, it was now pretty clear who was to hang.

21

A Clap of Thunder

The last of the French three-deckers had dwindled away to the south, their white sails dimming swiftly under the relentless rain and winds. Black Charlie raised anchor at Ledsund and took his remaining ships to Nargen, once more within the Gulf of Finland. With sixteen three-deckers of his own and auxiliaries, he reckoned he could still take on anything the Russians dared to send out. 'That infernal gulf,' Berkeley had called it. 'How long do you think it will be right to permit the big ships to remain? Autumn is getting on fast,' he had pointed out on 15 August. But now political pressure against the Government was mounting, urging the Admiralty to postpone autumn, preferably for another three months.

On 13 September Delane's leading article in *The Times* had expressed the opinion that the return of the British fleet would be 'unnecessary, ill-timed, and calculated to damage the cause of the Allies and serve that of Russia.' Judging by what had happened at Bomarsund, thought Delane, the fleet's guns would have no difficulty in demolishing the defences of other Russian fortresses. 'Sveaborg and Kronstadt, and not Spithead, should now be the destination of Sir Charles Napier.'

Charlie's feeling towards *The Times* was one of gratitude; the paper had often backed him in his shouts for reform. He replied with mildness:

> I can assure you, were you in my position now, riding out a gale of wind blowing directly into Reval, which gale has been blowing sometimes from the south west and sometimes from the north east for this last month, you would think it high time for the fleet to move out of the Gulf of Finland further south. . .
>
> I have had a squadron of frigates looking out off Sveaborg since April, and no words of mine can express my admiration of Captain Watson and his squadron for the blockade they have kept up in the worst of weather during this month; and in doing

so there is not a ship that has not lost an anchor and some two; he has had only seven miles of clear sea to work in, the rest being rocks. One of his ships has been on shore, and a wonder to me is that half of them have not been lost. . . Sveaborg is not so easily taken as people think, and if attacked at this season of the year, the probability is, instead of bringing away the Russian squadron you would leave your own on the rocks; and Kronstadt is still more dangerous, and still stronger. . .

I am quite sure, if you knew our difficulties, you would give us praise instead of censure.

On 22 September Charlie made a reconnaissance of Reval, deciding that its defences made it too dangerous for an attack in foul weather. Next day, the first fine one for a month, he took a fresh look at Sveaborg, Captain Sulivan in the *Driver* piloting him up its intricate passage, hardly 400 yards wide and scattered with rocks; they anchored abreast of Grohara Island. Two days later Charlie sent two detailed plans of how Sveaborg might be successfully attacked next year, when he hoped that the necessary Lancaster guns, gunboats and 13-inch mortars would be ready. He said the attack must be made in the fine summer weather; a naval attack might succeed though 'we must calculate on ships being set on fire by red-hot shot and shells, of which the Russians would have abundance. Whether successful or not, such ships would be in no condition to meet the Russian fleet afterwards.' So long as the mortars were there, he did not think it really mattered whether they were mounted on islands or on gunboats, but 'the latter have the advantage, for when the shells begin to tell and our blood begins to warm, the ships would move up to the batteries, and close quarters would finish what the mortar-boats began.' If the attack were to be made in the bad weather of autumn, the loss of ships was impossible to calculate. With troops, it would be an easier matter. 'I beg their lordships will not suppose for a moment that Sveaborg cannot be attacked. I think it can; but it must be with caution and judgement.'

For political reasons, soon to be greatly reinforced by false news from the Crimea, the Admiralty interpreted this plan for a future year into a promise to attack Sveaborg at once.

Sealing up his report, Black Charlie told Admiral Plumridge to take his ships to Kiel, but the gale was so strong that not until the

27th could Plumridge set sail with *Neptune, St George, Monarch* and *Regent*, the *Hecla* and *Driver* steamers, plus two French steamers, *La Place and Phlégéthon*. 'The weather has been so bad the last month, that, even had the French fleet and army been here, no operation was practicable,' Black Charlie told Palmerston; and writing to Newcastle, Secretary of State for War, Charlie told him:

> I have ordered the sailing ships to Kiel, as I do not think them safe here, and I shall proceed there shortly myself, leaving a strong squadron of steamers at the entrance of the Gulf, the blockade of Sveaborg being impossible any longer. The officers who have been there have not had their clothes off for weeks, and deserve the greatest credit.

His own was running short. On 3 October Charlie received a letter from the Admiralty telling him that lessening the strength of his fleet had been

> inexpedient; and the sailing ships and even the three-deckers must be detained till the last moment consistent with their safety. An autumn cruise for the Russian fleet in the Baltic, when the British fleet had abandoned it, would bring dishonour to our arms. At all hazards, so great an evil must be averted; and you will remember that in former wars, when the power of steam was unknown, a squadron of British line-of-battle ships maintained the blockade in the Baltic till the end of November.

In these ideas the over-influential Delane had had a hand.

> If our fleet retires from the Baltic before the season is actually closed, and an opportunity still remains for action [a *Times* leader had thundered], the Russians will instantly sally forth into the seas thus conveniently vacated, will re-occupy the Aland Islands, hoist their flag again on the ruins of Bomarsund, parade their vessels along the coasts of Sweden and Denmark, and then issue a swaggering manifesto to the world, setting forth the ignominious retreat of the Allied squadrons with nothing accomplished. . .

It all had a magnificent ring, and many felt convinced of its correctness.

In reply to the Admiralty letter, Charlie was firm. No Russian would come out at this season; 'but I will watch the enemy as long as it can be done with safety to the fleet, and shall take care that no Russian ships get into the North Sea.'

As for blockade in former wars:

there is a great difference between the Baltic and the Gulf of Finland. The journals of Sir James Saumarez are now before me. No ships remained in the Gulf after the 1st of October, and the Baltic was blockaded from the Swedish port of Carlscrona which is interdicted to us – and from the Belt.

Patiently, he tried to make plain to his chiefs that the North Baltic at this season is swept by incessant gales. (The fact that on the map it had land all round it seemed to have persuaded the Admiralty that the wind could not seriously blow upon this sea.) Gales had now blown hard from the SSE to NNW for twelve days.

How we should have fared had the wind been from N to NE I don't know, but it is certainly far from agreeable to have Reval right astern in a heavy gale of wind, depending on our chains; for should the wind be heavy on a dark night, we could not depend on our screws taking us to sea; and in the event of our parting the cables, we must go on shore. [Which would have meant ignominious capture by the Russians.] That is the opinion of many here. [At the same time, he would of course obey orders] short of hazarding the fleet. [He told Sir James Graham,] If I have done wrong in sending the sailing ships to Kiel, I have been led into it by your letter of the 29th August.

Charlie went on bluntly:

I have not the least idea that the Russians will move from their ports at this season of the year. They are much too wise to do anything of that sort; and as to their finding their way into the North Sea, I look upon that as impossible. [If they did try,] a squadron in the Belt and one at Elsinore would watch them much better than the Gulf of Finland, which is very dangerous. [And though the Admiralty could depend on his not leaving the Baltic,] as to the Gulf of Finland, I must use my own discretion.

Determinedly, he closed his letter and sent it off on its perilous passage by ship's boat to the waiting steamer. His discretion was about to receive its sternest test.

On 2 October Charlie's plan for next year's assault on Sveaborg reached the Admiralty. On the same day news arrived in London of the successful storming of Sebastopol in the Crimea.

By the 4th, detailed reports of this triumph had come to hand. Delane found the news intoxicating; Printing House Square vibrated with patriotic emotion. This was, *The Times* declared, 'the most splendid achievement of modern warfare – an exploit alike unequalled in magnitude, in rapidity, and in its results.' Delane went on to declare that the British public demanded that this 'glorious success' must be followed by one of equal éclat in the Baltic.

He granted Charlie and his fleet something: they *had* had the expected results:

> The ships of the Czar have been blockaded with ignominy in their own harbours and vainly defied to combat day after day. The maritime commerce of Russia has been destroyed, its ports have been invaded, and its coast towns shown to be at our mercy. Above all, the vessels of war have been rigorously confined to their moorings, so that the Russian flag has been swept from the seas and a perfect safety assured for the commerce of the Allied powers.

But the public, *The Times* went on, demanded more. If the Russians, 'skulking behind stone batteries', refused to fight, 'combat should be forced upon them . . . the prestige of such fortifications had been demolished at Bomarsund. . .'

'The operations in the Baltic, as far as they have gone, have been conducted with great skill and with the best of results – a bloodless success. . .' (There was the rub; for there is no doubt that a great many people receive an unacknowledged thrill out of the effusion of someone else's blood, and newspapers would hardly sell unless they did.)

'All this is excellent in its way,' Delane conceded, 'but after granite has been proved so weak and ships' guns so strong, are we to renounce the hope of doing something more?' Were the Baltic fortresses 'more impregnable than Sebastopol? Can even Kronstadt and Sveaborg be really beyond the reach of those powers who in a ten day campaign have conquered the Crimea and its garrison?' It was 'highly desirable' for the Baltic fleet to do more. 'At present we can only say that, after having triumphed in the Black Sea, we are not likely to be content with merely holding our own in the Baltic.'

On the day that this appeared Delane directed a more vehement reproach to Charlie, thirty years his senior, rolling on board the *Duke of Wellington* in the continuous gales off Reval. This, and simultaneous letters from Graham and Berkeley, struck Black Charlie 'like a thunderclap'.

Delane wrote:

My dear Sir Charles, As a friend, I am bound to tell you what perhaps no one else will have the frankness to write, that your conduct in the Baltic has caused extreme dissatisfaction to the Government and to the public, and has already gone far, very far, to tarnish your well-earned reputation.

Delane expressed himself unwilling to believe that Charlie had done 'less than any other man could do', and at this point his emotions got the better of his grammar, *Times* editor or not:

I confess that your letters do not convince me that you should be unable to do nothing more than the reduction of a petty fortress and the enforcement of a strict blockade. Of course there are difficulties and great ones – of course the weather is not the most propitious; but the country, and especially your friends, have been taught to think that you were the man to overcome difficulties, and that such a steam fleet as you have was almost independent of wind and weather. Since you have gone out, too, everything has tended to demonstrate more than ever the hollowness of the Russian strength.

   Her best armies have been routed by a mob of Turks, and have recoiled before a paltry fort [Silistria]... Now too, their own great fortress of the Crimea, which it was thought would require a regular investment and a prolonged siege, has been taken by assault within ten days after the troops had landed, their fleet burnt, and their army captured or destroyed. Do you think that after this the public will be satisfied with an excess of 'discretion', which preserves your fleet indeed, from all injury, but which leaves the enemy the same impunity? I assure you they will not; and the Government will be supported by the country in removing you from your command, if nothing more is done than you have yet attempted. In the profession, and among the officers of your own fleet especially, your conduct is most severely condemned. They declare that Reval, Helsingfors, or Kronstadt itself, might have been long since destroyed – that you, thirty years ago, would have been the man to do it; but that now your nerve has failed you, and that you think of nothing but getting safe back to Portsmouth. I am sure there is no truth in this; but it is said everywhere; and the fact that, with so splendid a force, you alone find the Russians unassailable and invincible, when everyone, with much less means, defeats their armies and destroys their forts, is strong against you. For your own sake, then, and for that of your friends who have so long supported you and asserted your claims, do make an effort, cease to find difficulties – any old woman can find them. Strike a blow which shall be worthy of your once great reputation, and of the country, and eclipse, if you can, the glory of the capture of Sebastopol by the destruction of Kronstadt.

Unless you do something of the kind, you are a lost man. . .

This, I know, is not pleasant reading, but it is the truth, and even Admirals should hear the truth sometimes. Pray believe it, and act so that your friends will not have to blush for you, and to hear even Dundas extolled at your expense. You have to choose between glory and disgrace, for the failure to achieve one will ensure the other.

I give you the best proof of my friendship in writing this letter; and am, my dear Sir Charles, with sincere good wishes, very faithfully yours, JOHN T. DELANE.

This letter reached Charlie on 10 October and was accompanied by an official despatch from the Admiralty, and a private letter from Berkeley, both singing the same tune. The Board told him:

We are not prepared to sanction the withdrawal of the Fleet from the entrance of the Gulf of Finland until ice shall have closed it. Baro Sound is in most winds a safe anchorage, and your command of steam power . . . will enable you to keep your position.

Brushing aside Admiral Chads's report of 14 June, and Charlie's own plan for the attack of Sveaborg of 18 July, their lordships declared that his recently received plan for the attack of Sveaborg altered the picture. He had said that it could be attacked and destroyed, now, at that time. He had better make good his word, go ahead, and do it.

'What then are the obstacles to the immediate attempt?' Plumridge had been halted at Kiel, told to revictual and hold himself ready to rejoin him, the French fleet likewise had been turned around. The bad weather? Choose a fine day and attack Sveaborg, Sir James Graham suggested, from his cosy desk in Whitehall. 'Some risk must always attend every great operation.' (Even the optimistic Brigadier-General Jones had said the attempt would need seven or eight days.) Napier was not to worry about an attack from the Kronstadt fleet, soon to be iced in; and Sir James had it on good authority that Kronstadt was invariably ice-bound a fortnight earlier than was Sveaborg – so now was the chance. 'Recent events in the Black Sea will not encourage the Russians to attempt any enterprise of more than usual hazard and daring at this precise moment.'

It was true that 'the Lancaster guns and mortar vessels have not been sent into the Baltic'. (By seemingly not reading Charlie's July report) 'we were led to believe that Kronstadt or Sveaborg were unassailable by naval means alone.'

> Your second reconaissance of Sveaborg opens a new view, and the presence or absence of a few guns of an improved construction, or even of mortar vessels, cannot make the whole difference between a possible and an impossible attack.

And, come what might, the Admiralty was not going to accept the blame. 'This order is founded entirely on your own last report. The final decision must rest entirely on yourself.' Calculating 'the ordinary chances of war', and giving full consideration to the enemy's strength, 'it will be your duty, with the concurrence of the French Admiral' (who was by now, sensibly enough, in Paris) 'not to omit the opportunity.'

The letter from Berkeley, his fellow admiral and friend, came as the unkindest cut of all. He too had misinterpreted Charlie's plan for next year's attack on Sveaborg (or was pretending to do so), and had taken it as an offer to assault it at once. He wrote:

> Your letter would make all who have read it believe that the responsibility was too heavy for your shoulders, and that you would willingly transfer it to the Board. This must not be. . . Through good and evil report you must act with firmness and according to your own judgement. The public will do you justice in the long run; as I firmly believe that you will do all that can be done or attempted with propriety.

Five days later, on 9 October, news arrived in London that

Sebastopol had not in fact fallen; it was to survive many a weary month of siege while the British soldiers famished and died on the bitter, shelterless heights above the fortress. What Delane's thoughts were on having made such a cake of himself we know not; but the Admiralty swiftly gave Black Charlie permission to move his storm-battered ships to Kiel.

22

Defiance

To some extent Black Charlie remained a simple fellow, expecting people to be honest, and amazed when they were not. Although the letters from Graham, Berkeley and Delane, arriving simultaneously, had struck him 'like a thunderclap', and deeply horrified him, it was some time before the penny dropped. The Admiralty and the Government it served did not seriously expect him to hurl his fleet up a narrow, blocked seaway in conditions of continuous storm against stone-walled fortresses that it was hardly possible to bring into range before becoming disabled. They were not going to order him to do it. They simply wanted him to save their face by *himself* deciding not to do it.

He was between the devil and the not deep enough blue sea. If he went ahead on this hopeless project and failed – he was to take full blame. If he did not, he was a coward and a failure – and also to blame. Judging from the straightforward letters he wrote at this point, arguing with the Administration as if they were all along acting in good faith and as rational beings, he had not yet fully realized the official perfidy; or, if he had, was not going to let himself believe it while there was still the smallest chance that they would come to their senses and stand by him.

The three letters that had reached Charlie on the 4th at Baro Sound had indeed struck him 'like a thunderclap', as he later described it; those about him reported that 'he seemed for a while utterly prostrated'. His beloved honour was impugned; he had been called an old woman, ordered to engage on an impossible assault, and told by a friend not to shift off his responsibilities. By putting an imaginary construction on his plan for next year's assault on Sveaborg, the Administration had convincingly managed to shift all blame onto him. Time and evidence might clear him, but the slur of cowardice would remain.

Of one thing he was certain. Coward and old woman he might be, but he was not going to sacrifice his ships in a suicidal and profitless attack, impossible of success. It needed all Charlie's courage and confidence to rally his forces and reply rationally to the letters. Sensibly, he waited a week before rounding on Delane, though he might have done better to have waited forever.

> You have written me a very cutting letter, which I have no time to answer at present. . . I wish you had been here for the last five weeks and seen the weather we have had. [Charlie explained his movements briefly since coming into the Gulf] – and still the public think we ought to have gone in a gale of wind into unknown channels amongst sunken rocks and attacked Sveaborg and even gone up to Kronstadt.
>
> Had I done so I should have lost the fleet. The work here is not fair fighting of batteries, but it is fighting rocks and shoals, and if, instead of sitting in your office, you were here, you would find it no joke.

To the Admiralty Charlie was necessarily more detailed. He had already given them 'my reasons for withdrawing from this anchorage' and he enclosed a copy of his letter, lest it had gone astray. 'Notwithstanding their Lordships' letter of the 4th inst, I still think it my duty to persist in my intention. . . I thought I was following up Sir James's wishes (vide his letter of 29th August).'

> Neither this anchorage nor Baro Sound are fit for a fleet in the winter. . . Their lordships ask me, if I think Sveaborg can be laid in ruins, why I do not attack it? I reply that before the ships could go alongside the batteries, my plan was to have it first bombarded with 'mortars, shells and rockets', from the Island, and with 'gunboats, Lancaster guns' etc. for a day or two; and then when well bombarded, the ships would go alongside and finish the work.
>
> The want of means is one obstacle, the weather the next, why I do not attack it.
>
> Their Lordships tell me to choose my day. There has not been a day since I have been here (Nargen) that it was possible to attack Sveaborg. It requires many days. The channels are studded with sunken rocks. They must all be sounded and buoyed. If it came on to blow, the fleet would inevitably be lost, and I should be unworthy of the command I hold if I risked it. It would be a long operation. Their Lordships have not the

most distant idea of the dangers. Whether the Russian fleet in Kronstadt would venture out if we were disabled, I know not; but the Sveaborg fleet would.

I have never altered my opinion that Sveaborg must first be attacked by 'mortars, shells and gunboats'. But I never would have advised them to be sent here at this season.

My second reconaissance was never intended to open a new view. The view I first took and the last were the same.

Their Lordships say, the final decision must rest with me, and if the attack be desperate, must on no account be undertaken. I look upon it that no man in his senses would undertake to attack Sveaborg at this season of the year; and even in a fine season, I doubt much the success, without the means I have pointed out.

A telegraphic despatch has stopped the French Admiral – which I am glad of – his presence would be useless; and I have directed Admiral Plumridge not to come here for the same reason.

When a Council of War composed of five admirals, viz., Vice-Admiral Parseval and myself, Rear-Admirals Penaud, Chads and Seymour, and in whose opinions a sixth (Rear-Admiral Martin) concurred, had given their opinions that neither our resources nor the season would permit an attack upon Sveaborg, I should have thought that both their Lordships and the public would have been satisfied; and I beg further to tell their Lordships that there is not an Admiral in the British service who would have ventured to attack such a fortress at this season of the year ... judging from the altered tone of their letters, I have reason to believe I have lost the confidence of their Lordships. If that is the case I shall be perfectly ready to resign my command. But as long as I hold it, I will do what I think is for the good of Her Majesty's Service and for the safety of the fleet I command, which I think is greatly endangered by our present position, and we are risking our ships to no adequate purpose.

Mr Delane and Sir James Graham were, after all, landsmen who couldn't be expected to know; and it was to Berkeley, an admiral, who should, that Black Charlie directed his most indignant blast.

I never was more astonished in my life than on receiving your letter. I have read over my reports on Sveaborg, and where they

differ I am at a loss to know, unless that in my second report I
point out the preparations for attack are of more importance
than in the first, and that is after still closer reconnaissance, and
I most distinctly said that at this season of the year the thing was
quite impossible; we have nothing but heavy gales.

I was perfectly aware that any attack on Sveaborg would be
on my own responsibility, and I never wanted to throw it on the
Board, but I distinctly stated that nothing could be done at this
season of the year, and that was my opinion and the opinion of
the French Admirals and Chads also; and my reconnaissance
never changed that opinion and I do think it most unjust that
you should write to me in the way that you have done, and,
so far from thinking of attacking Sveaborg now, I look upon
the fleet as lying in a most dangerous position, and I never
attempted to get rid of my responsibility.

You tell me through good and evil report I must act with
firmness and according to my own judgement and it is just on
that account that, so far from thinking of attacking Sveaborg at
this season of the year, I am making preparations to withdraw
the squadron from the Gulf. It is too bad that both Graham and
you, who desired me to begin to withdraw my ships, should
now throw me overboard. You have no idea of the weather here
or the dangers of the coast, or you would not write to me as you
do.

I hear from a quarter that I know to be good authority that
you are all dissatisfied with me. I cannot help it; I could do no
more. I proposed the attack on Bomarsund, after returning from
Kronstadt; it was done, and after that the season was too late
and everybody opposed to it; but these engineers have set all this
going and ruined my reputation with the public. There is not a
man in England who would venture near Sveaborg at this time
of the year, the dangers and difficulties are so great. I wish to
God you were here to see them!

Do you never look at the charts, where one half the sunken
rocks are not shown, and ask yourself whether you would risk
your fleet amongst them? Not a man on earth would do it, and it
is hard that my reputation should be blasted by engineers, and
others who know nothing of the localities. When we reconnoitred it the other day, it was all we could do to keep clear of
the rocks in a small steamer.

Briefly chastened by the news that Sebastopol had not fallen, the Admiralty next told Charlie, 'You are now at liberty to exercise your discretion in withdrawing to the southward'; though he was of course to leave 'a light squadron of observation' at the entrance of the Gulf to watch the Russian fleet. Plumridge was told to 'take advantage of the weather' in bringing his ships the short, familiar journey from Kiel to the Downs; even so, the flagship *Neptune* went aground. The weather in the North Sea seemed somehow more real to the Admiralty than the weather in the Gulf of Finland.

Watson's squadron maintained their watch until late November, in intense cold, heavy gales and blinding snowstorms, in one of which *Euryalus* ran into *Impérieuse* with considerable damage to both. By sheer luck, and skill in repair, neither of them was lost. 'I have not words to express my approval of the persevering conduct of Captain Watson and all his squadron,' Charlie told the Admiralty. They had been on station from early March until late November with little intermission; 'and I do not believe, in the height of the last war [Napoleonic] a stricter or more dangerous blockade was ever kept up'. Whatever was thought of Charlie personally, he was determined that Watson should be given his due.

Captain Sulivan was equally determined that Charlie should be given *his* due. On 15 October he asked:

Is it not too bad that the chief of a fleet should be attacked for not committing an act of madness? . . . I suppose there will be an outcry at home about doing nothing here, but we might as well try to reach the moon.

Those who contend that a fleet can destroy the strongest fortresses should confine themselves to places where there is space and depth enough to admit of ships being fairly placed against the batteries.

It is extraordinary that the public expected only Napier and the Baltic Fleet to perform such wonders. Why have the Black Sea admirals not been equally blamed because they did not take Sebastopol with the fleet alone?

It is rather amusing to find ignorant persons talking and writing of what Nelson would have done, and to hear a line of block-ships and Copenhagen which he attacked compared to Kronstadt. . .

If Sir Robert Peel had studied the naval history of the French

war, he would have learned that Nelson never attacked a battery
with ships, except very slightly the first day at Tenerife, when,
thinking it impossible to succeed that way, he gave it up and
tried to carry the place by storm. . .

If Sir Charles Napier and Admiral Parseval are to be so
severely censured for not getting at the Russian fleet inside the
strongest fortress in the world (against an attack by ships), what
would have been said of them if they had found an inferior force
of the enemy in such a place as Port Baltic and had declined
attacking it? [Sir James Saumarez had done just this,] yet Sir
James Saumarez is one of our brightest examples.

It seemed that the Administration were gunning for Charles not so
much for anything he had done or not done but because they did not
care for his brusque and forthright way of addressing them. Admiral
Dundas, on the other hand, was a member of the Board, and in
addition, had the most courtly of manners.

However you looked at it, Charlie now knew that he had disappointed his country. The coming of steamships had been enormously
helpful to the seaman, but the general public had been left with the
idea that the coming of steam nullifies the effects of wind and tide,
fog, ice and rocks. Its expectations had been enormous. Steam there
might be, but there were still only wooden walls, though the enterprising French had three ironclads in the Black Sea.

Another week of watch and ward was to be held, before the
Admiralty orders for return arrived. Lying off Nargen in the Baro
Sound, Black Charlie's thoughts must have been melancholy, as the
early northern nights descended upon the racing seas and the low,
wooded islands with their surround of mourning waves, the timbers of the *Duke* groaning, her cable chains straining, her lanterns
monotonously swinging, and the wind howling above in the rigging. Such ships had been his home since childhood, with their
close quarters, amazing discomforts, dull food; with the cold, the
homesickness, the long watches. How much worse for the seamen on
duty, whose lot he had always tried to better, sent aloft on the icy
yards with every shift of the wind, for the frozen midshipmen
running the boats, for the officers of the watch, on deck through the
bitter hours of darkness.

Older men, Charlie included, could remember the long British
blockades off Brest, when, according to the American historian

Admiral Mahan, 'only those few storm-battered ships stood between Napoleon and the dominion of the world'. These blockades, however wearisome, at least had had a point – the French ships frequently came out; the Russians, seemingly, never did. And from Brest there was always the hope of the short run to Plymouth, to revictual or refit, and to enjoy the blessings of the land. Here, at Baro, they were on 60°, the same latitude as the Shetlands, as Cape Farewell on Greenland, as Canada's Hudson Straits or as Alaska, with an icy land mass hard by, to chill them to the bone.

Here were no friendly ports to which to run, and barely a hundred and fifty miles east, the Icy Muscovite, Czar Nicholas I who slept for preference (and was shortly to die in) a narrow camp bed with a straw mattress in a bare little room at the top of his surpassingly beautiful Winter Palace. Queen Victoria, visited by him, had thought his profile lovely but his mind uncivilized, and had been disturbed by the 'formidable gaze' of his cold, blue eyes. Terrified by the 1848 revolutions in Europe, the Czar had become ever more autocratic and reactionary, causing more and more of his subjects to be flogged to death or exiled to Siberia. In St Petersburg they were laying bets that the impetuous Charlie would attack Sveaborg or Kronstadt, and longing for him to commit suicide by doing just that.

Any port in a storm – but not St Petersburg with the Czar of all the Russias at the helm. His people had carried over from the Napoleonic Wars a reputation for beheading their prisoners of war; with some concentration the three-deckers off Nargen looked to their anchor chains. One of Admiral Dundas's Black Sea squadron, HMS *Tiger,* had been stranded off Odessa, the Russians capturing her guns, one of which still adorns the square outside the City Soviet of that town. This seemed in no way to affect the Black Sea admiral's reputation; perhaps it was all part of the magnificence of the Crimean failure.

A puff of political wind could blow away the fame of a lifetime, and history told that it often did. Black Charlie was faring no worse than many another. But he was never going to say die, and while he breathed, would breathe defiance.

Leaving the Gulf of Finland on 19 October and anchoring at Kiel on 22 October, Charlie and his ships were kept kicking their heels there until December, during which interval Charlie did not improve his prospects by engaging in a spirited but acrimonious correspondence with the home authorities. Writing from Hamburg where he was staying with an old soldier friend, he told his daughter:

I have had much annoyance, they seem to want to throw the blame upon me for not doing impossibilities, and Graham has behaved very ill.

I have written him a very sharp letter and to the Admiralty also, and told them that if they are not satisfied, they had better remove me; so I suppose they will.

This is a fine city... I have not heard a word from the Admiralty since my arrival, so cannot tell you what my movements are to be, but I hope home. I long to see you all after the long and wearisome blockade. God bless you, my dearest child...

A humbugging letter from the Admiralty next arrived, telling Charlie that they quite understood his not wanting to attack Sveaborg after the French had left – this had in fact had nothing to do with Charlie's decision – and insisting that they had only ordered the attack because everybody else had seemed to disagree with him, and he had himself said that Sveaborg could be attacked. In a further letter they added that they could not 'with confidence express satisfaction with the decision taken at Ledsund not to attack Sveaborg after the fall of Bomarsund'. Brigadier-General Jones's report made 'a great impression here'; and with all those soldiers present, the works at Sveaborg might have been destroyed, 'the month of September afforded ample time for the operation'. Graham went on:

> No doubt at the time of the Equinox there are heavy gales of wind in the Baltic; it is a narrow sea; and there is danger to large ships in maintaining this blockade even when at anchor. But war is not conducted without risks and dangers, and prudence consists in weighing them and firmness in overcoming them; and nothing great by sea or land can be achieved without considerable peril, as your own experience and example have demonstrated.

These truisms, with their hint at a lack of courage, exacerbated the old admiral still further. He would return to Parliament. Only there, perhaps, could he continue to fight to clear his name. He applied for permission to go home ahead, having been asked to stand for Marylebone; but this was refused. He told Graham:

> It is far from my wish to enter into a controversy with you, but I will not admit that I have brought it on myself; there is not a

word in either my public or private letters that justifies the construction that you and the Admiralty have thought proper to put on them. I have documents enough in my possession to justify my conduct. Enough has not been done to satisfy an 'impatient public', as you called them. Someone must be blamed, and I am the chosen one; but I will not allow myself to be crushed because I could not do impossibilities. All the stir has been caused by the opinion of two engineers, both of whom expressed reservations about their plans, in addition to the report of the capture of Sebastopol – not yet taken – though the fleet there is assisted by an army of 70,000 men; and I have been expected to take places much stronger, with a fleet alone.

The same people who warned me so often against unecessarily risking my fleet are now dissatisfied because I did not expose them to destruction. I presume you have seen Captain Sulivan by this time; he is capable of opening the eyes of the Government, if they are not hermetically sealed.

He told his stepson, Colonel Elers-Napier, on 15 November:

I have seen letters from Dundas's fleet; they are singing small. [The C in C operating in the Black Sea was generally known as Admiral Damned Ass.] Some of our wiseacres here are beginning to open their eyes. . . Depend upon it, this attack on me, fanned, I have no doubt, by some of the Ministers, will not end here. I have accused them of perverting my letters, and I got a letter yesterday from the Admiralty, saying they would not permit an officer to accuse them of deliberately perverting letters; but not a word more – there it rests. I wrote Graham such a tickler that he has not ventured to answer, and he ought to have superseded me, if he durst; however I shall wait quietly to see how the cat jumps. . . The ships were all surrounded by ice this morning; a couple more days of hard frost and we shall be frozen in.

At last came the order to sail for home. In December the *Duke of Wellington* passed the Island, and made Portsmouth harbour. Not a ship had been lost since the fleet sailed nine months earlier, in an epoch when ships were more often lost through the perils of the sea than by the action of the enemy. This negative achievement would not be enough.

Behind the harbour was the green hill of Portsdown, and beyond it Catherington and home. But Charlie was soon away up to London: 'I have seen Graham and given him my mind,' he told his wife. Some friends thought he had been 'shamefully treated', he was going to see Lord Ellenborough, 'and I think I shall be down on Friday. My leave is out, and I intend having no communications with them whatever. They want me to throw up my command, but Lord *** advises me to do nothing as yet; he says that is what they want.'

A letter from London reached Portsmouth before the Admiral did:

> The Baltic fleet being now dispersed in different harbours of Great Britain, and several of the ships which composed it being under orders for service in the Black Sea and Mediterranean, you are hereby required to strike your flag and come on shore.

No recognition, no thanks.

Wintry seas slapped along the Hard. The boatswain's whistle shrilled; for the last time the Admiral stumped ashore, a fourteen-stone scapegoat, stout, untidy; Black Charlie, no longer black-haired, his tired, defiant body seamed with the wounds of nearly sixty years' service. His stepson, meeting him, found him suddenly an old man.

Three score years and ten or no, he would show them. Not for him to creep away and die. His last letter to Graham had concluded, 'I have gone through the world with honour and credit to myself and just as I am about to leave it, unworthy attempts are made to ruin my reputation; but they will fail.'

23

End of Voyage

Politicians come in for a good deal of undeserved stick. They would not be in their thankless job unless they deeply believed that by taking it they could contribute to the betterment of their country and of the world. Unhappily, this purpose tends to harden into the conviction that these admirable ends can only be achieved by the maintenance of their own party in power. In practising the art of the possible, the idea of pure and abstract justice cannot but become a little obscured; and if an admiral or a general or two has been thrown to the wolves en route, so be it. If they can't stand the heat, they should have stayed out of the kitchen. There's always gardening for them, family life, sport, private good works.

But in Victorian times, and earlier, men placed a value upon their own untarnished honour that seems to their descendants somewhat exaggerated. 'Who steals my purse steals trash' etc. Such a conception was deeply embedded in men, and particularly in Scotsmen, and perhaps more particularly still in old aristocratic fighting families such as the Napiers. Charlie's courage and his honesty were being publicly impugned, and he was not going to rest until such slanderers had been made to eat their words. The maintenance of a dignified silence was no part of his character.

Christmas Day of 1854 was not allowed to be a season of goodwill alone. Though now surrounded by a family he adored, Charlie sat down to acknowledge the letter telling him to strike his flag – would the Board now tell him 'whether I am to consider my command is at an end'. And, whatever they thought of him, he much regretted that they had abstained from thanking the admirals, officers and seamen for their services. Grudgingly the Board now expressed to Charlie 'the sense their Lordships entertain of your exertions during the period of your service in command of the Baltic fleet'.

Good resolutions of a pacific kind, if taken in the New Year, petered out remarkably soon. On 2 January Black Charlie was pointing out that the French Emperor, in his speech to the Chambers, had paid a just tribute to his fleet and army in the Baltic, recording the success of their efforts; no reference to the Baltic had been recorded in the Queen's Speech here in Parliament. He ended by demanding a court martial to investigate his conduct.

> I have now again well weighed and considered this painful subject. I have consulted friends, and I am of opinion, and so are they, that my character has been attacked by the First Lord of the Admiralty, and by the Board, and, coupling that with my dismissal from the command, I have nothing left but to demand that my conduct be investigated before a court martial.

The court martial was refused. The Board's second refusal took the war into Charlie's camp. Unwilling as they were to 'pass censure upon any part of your conduct', they have not failed to observe that

> from the moment of your first quitting Wingo Sound without orders, and down to the present time, you have repeatedly thought fit to adopt a tone in correspondence with their Lordships which is not respectful to their authority, a course which if generally adopted by officers would be destructive to the discipline and injurious to the best interests of the service and is not calculated to inspire confidence in one entrusted with an important command... This decision is to be considered as final.

Dead end. Charlie now applied to Lord Aberdeen, who said he was just retiring; to Newcastle, who said it was a matter for the Admiralty; and finally to his erstwhile supporter, Palmerston; who didn't answer. Perhaps Charlie's exertions had only succeeded in exhausting his stock of Parliamentary goodwill. But in March, Mr Malins, QC, brought a petition for the investigation of Napier's case before the Commons, moving for a copy of all correspondence. Graham replied with his usual measured ability, the Government asserting that the production of the correspondence would be detrimental to the public service – motion withdrawn.

In July came a ray of light. Sir Charles Wood, who had succeeded Graham at the Admiralty, told Charlie that he had recommended a GCB for him to the Queen, and that she had agreed. Charlie must have longed to accept this highly coveted honour; a kind of sad pride stood in the way. Explaining the circumstances to the Prince Consort in a short letter, he ended: 'I do not think I can accept an honour until my character is cleared.' That was that and Black Charlie was never employed again.

He was denounced from many directions, and defended himself with great spirit and considerable acrimony; at one point referring to Sir James Graham's 'treachery', a term which however well justified does not win friends or influence people to take your side. Honour was indeed dearer than life to Victoria's men, and once it had been publicly impugned they were prepared to go on for ever, defending, counter-attacking, defending again, and becoming ever more furious. Duelling was forbidden, but letters to *The Times* were not; and for this form of sparring the zest of Victorian gentlemen never flagged. Enraged above all by accusations of hesitancy, Black Charlie continued to demand a court martial where all the relevant facts could emerge; and continued to be refused.

William Napier, now general and KCB, and clan champion in the field of invective, leapt to the defence of Black Charlie's honour.

> He caused the thirty sail composing the powerful Russian fleet to shrink like rats into their holes; he took Bomarsund, caused Hango to be blown up, interrupted the Russian commerce, and for six months kept in a state of inaction certainly 80,000 or 90,000 good troops.

Charlie might not have shaken the Icy Muscovite but he had certainly contained him. The naval historian C. C. Lloyd wrote:

> His instructions and the nature of his force prevented him from taking any effective action against the Russian bases either by direct attack or by blockade. When he arrived at the mouth of the Gulf of Finland he found that the Russians had locked up their ships in the impregnable fortress of Kronstadt at the head of the Gulf. Having captured Bomarsund in the Aland Islands, he had no alternative but to take his fleet home before the Baltic froze.

Controversy raged. Some thought that Black Charlie had been futile and ineffectual beyond words. Others declared that 'to have attacked the strongholds of Russia, and have lost Britain a fleet without taking a fortress, would have been the act of a selfish, fame-seeking madman – and not of a Napier'.

Bets had run high in St Petersburg, a Russian officer reported, that Black Charlie would fall into the trap. 'To our surprise, he did not,

and his fame with us stands higher than ever. Instead of blaming him
for not fighting our forts as we wished, the English nation ought to
thank him for not losing their fleet.'

Black Charlie's best justification was to come in the equal ineffec-
tiveness of the expedition sent to the Baltic in the summer of 1855 –
according to Lloyd, 'a far more serviceable force, consisting entirely
of auxiliary steamships, together with a number of mortar and bomb
vessels'.

In April 1855 this new fleet sailed for the Baltic, with Admiral R. S.
Dundas in command. A *Times* leading article pointed out:

> The Baltic fleet of this year is in all respects much stronger than
> the last. It has more steam power, more guns, a new class of
> gunboats and floating batteries, adapted for creeks and shoals,
> and – what more than anything marks a resolution to do some-
> thing – a new commander. . . Whatever his instructions, if any,
> no doubt he knows he has to do more than Admiral Napier. If
> he does not accomplish more, he will certainly find himself next
> November under orders to lower his flag, with small prospect of
> ever hoisting it again.

Thus adjured, joined again by Admiral Penaud, with a force
amounting to a 101 vessels and 2,500 guns, the fleet bombarded
Sveaborg on 9 and 10 August 1855, succeeding in setting fire to a
number of wooden buildings. Dundas himself admitted that the sea
defences were hardly dented. The big ships had not penetrated the
approach channels or succeeded in bringing the granite walls of
Sveaborg within range; the damage effected had all been done by the
shallow-draught gunboats and mortars for which Black Charlie had
asked in vain the year before. 'Kronstadt still being regarded as
impregnable, Sveaborg near Helsinki was bombarded with over a
thousand tons of projectiles, an operation without any strategic
significance whatever.' (C.C. Lloyd.) Dundas came no nearer to
taking either Kronstadt or Sveaborg than had Charlie, but on his
return was warmly thanked by the Admiralty, a pure example of the
advantages of tactfulness.

He had at least done Charlie some good; perhaps there *were* more
difficulties in a Baltic attack than had previously been admitted.
When the Parliamentary seat for Southwark fell vacant, Charlie was
offered it, all expenses defrayed by a committee, and topped the poll

exactly a year after he had left his stormy anchorage of Reval. His sunset was to be rosier than the bleak year that had intervened.

Now, at last, he could take up his own cause in the House. On 13 March 1856 he moved for the appointment of a Select Committee to inquire into the operations of the Baltic fleets. The subsequent debate must have made sad hearing – brave men who had grown grey in the service of their country insulting each other across the floor of the House. There had been those who had thought in the forties that active Charlie in the Lebanon had indeed ridden rough-shod over his gentle, dilatory commanding officer, Admiral Stop-ford; and when Graham and Berkeley raked up old gossip to this effect, it became clear that what Charlie called 'a second field day' would be necessary. The sympathy of the House had clearly been with him; and having thoroughly ventilated his case, he asked leave this day to withdraw his motion.

Graham, failing to justify himself over the Baltic, had come up with the allegation that Napier had advised Stopford not to attack Acre, which was all of a piece with his caution in the Baltic; while Berkeley insisted that Charlie had, as well, told Stopford that if he sent him into the position marked out for him, his ship would not swim for an hour. Perhaps Delane had relented a little towards his old friend, on discovering that the Russian fortresses were not such easy nuts to crack as he had supposed; in any case he printed Charlie's letter in *The Times* which categorically refuted both these allegations.

The day after the second debate in the House, on 5 April, Charlie wrote to his daughter:

> Well, my dearest Fanny, Sir James Graham attacked me last night, and brought such a host of evidence that he had selected by putting leading questions to people, that I looked upon myself as ruined. I had just to bring the House round to my side by plain statements, and then I produced Stopford's letters, which fortunately I had, or I should have been lost.

There had been an appalling moment when Charlie had failed to find the letters, turning his papers and ransacking his pockets in vain, his face going slowly crimson, while the members waited, rows of tall-hatted men in frock-coats and side-whiskers, English imperviousness confronting Scots passion, as Charlie ruffled through, increasingly perturbed, until the search ended.

The moment I read them I was cheered by the House, and both Graham and Berkeley were attacked by Lindsay, Roebuck and Malins, and they were completely floored; they had only Cowper to say a word for them; the Government even abandoned them. It was a most trying night and ended triumphantly.

The GCB had flown forever; but maybe that Charlie, in the relief of his vindication, could forget even this.

By the summer of 1856 the Crimean War had ended; and with the civilized Georgian and Victorian habit whereby the combatants tended to make friends again before the ink on their treaties was dry, Charlie breezed off to St Petersburg, with an introduction to the Grand Duke Constantine, where he was received with the utmost friendliness. This Russian admiral – described by Charlie as a frank, open-hearted sailor – behaved in a manner ludicrously unlike his recent Russian counterparts, facilitating in every way Charlie's inspection of the fortress of Kronstadt from within. Charlie found it one of the strongest fortresses in the world, and was happily able to confirm that any attack on it without troops or gunboats would have been madness. But his old enemies couldn't quite leave him alone. An ambitious young man at the Admiralty, Robert Peel, son of the statesman, sent on embassy with Granville for the coronation of the Czar Alexander II declared in a public speech on his return that everyone, from the Grand Duke Constantine down to the youngest midshipman, had declared that had the energy of the admiral equalled the pluck of the British Navy, Kronstadt would have been in the dust.

Duke Constantine, indignantly appealed to by Charlie about expressing such a very different opinion, replied that he had only spoken to Peel for five minutes, and that Kronstadt had never been mentioned. Palmerston, also appealed to, sensibly replied by asking what the fuss was about, 'as everybody knew that he had acted with sound judgement in not attacking Kronstadt with the means at his disposal'. Everybody knew this; but there remained a lingering doubt that possibly a younger man might have achieved a more active harrying of the Russian coast in other places; on balance the campaign of 1854 in the Baltic couldn't really be accounted a success – not as the Royal Navy counted success. The slender, fiery ghost of Nelson haunted them all. And indeed haunted the whole nation, still in love with its Navy, however grim the condition of her seamen was allowed to remain.

In the spring election of 1857 Charlie was again returned for Southwark, and promoted in the course of seniority from Vice-Admiral of the Red to Admiral of the Blue. At the end of 1857 his wife died, a faithful and loving companion ever since the day he had married her in the last year of the great war against France that had dominated his youth and early manhood. Even the four children he had taken on with her and adopted as his own had proved stalwart and affectionate supports. His own daughter, Fanny, and her children were also a joy to him, spending much time with him; but for the most part he had now to battle on alone.

There were gleams of recognition and reassurance. In 1859 Charlie was part of a Parliamentary delegation at the opening of the port of Cherbourg, and here Napoleon III sent for him. 'He shook hands with me very kindly,' Charlie told his daughter, 'and asked me to accompany him round the dockyard, which I did, for a considerable way.' The French, those old foes and new allies, at any rate knew about him and respected him.

The debate in the House had brought Charlie into the public eye again; and Sulivan wrote to an old shipmate, Captain Hammond of Fakenham in Norfolk, to say how glad he was that Lord Townshend, another Norfolk man, had defended Sir Charles Napier against the attack of Sir Robert Peel.

> For whatever may be said against Sir Charles on other points, it is most unjust to accuse him of want of courage in not attacking with a fleet a place which it is impossible to place ships so as fairly to try whether their broadsides or the batteries are the strongest.
>
> No one but a madman would have run his ships into a long narrow channel, with at most a foot of water to spare, out of which they could not pass; where the slightest yaw, in the smoke, must have put them on shore, where there was hardly room for two ships abreast; where they would have been under the raking and cross fire of hundreds of heavy guns, against which they would have been able only to bring a few bow-guns to bear. The attempt could only have ended in the total destruction of every ship that went in.
>
> Had Napier played the Russians' game for them, and the

result had been their destroying our fleet and getting command of the Baltic and the North Seas, those who have abused both him and the Government would have been the first to cry out against the *madman* who lost the fleet and the Admiralty that appointed him.

Sulivan went on to praise the old admiral's courage for his firmness in resisting the pressure put upon him to attack the fortresses with his ships, the very thing the Russians were hoping he would do. The Admiralty, he thought, had blamed Napier unnecessarily on many trivial matters. Sulivan's son, editing his father's letters and writing later, held that where Napier was to blame was in his delay in examining Bomarsund and Sveaborg:

> Had the latter been reconnoitred earlier, there would have been time to have sent home for mortars and for the bombardment to have taken place that first year. [Whilst Napier was] brave enough under fire or in personal danger [his advanced age made him] terribly nervous about the safety of his ships at sea etc. and when broken down in health (chiefly from the attacks made upon him by the Press), owing to this anxiety, he brought home the fleet earlier than he need have done.

The *Dictionary of National Biography* was to describe Charlie as 'a strange medley of naval skill and courage, eccentricity, slovenliness, shrewdness and imprudence', which adds up to a picture of someone burly but slightly mad. Clowes, the great naval historian, also damns him with faint praise, pointing out that of the Crimean naval officers, Napier was 68, Dundas 69, Lyons 64, Chads 66. 'From officers of such advanced age it was perhaps unreasonable to look for the energy, activity and mental suppleness that distinguish younger men. . . The Navy, all things considered, disappointed the expectations of the Country.' The ghost of Nelson haunted historians also.

Black Charlie never lost a kind of seagoing innocence, an ignorance of the subtle ways of the world. He kept a confident belief that men on the whole are reasonable beings, that if you explain to them they will understand, that if abuses are aired there are always enough men of goodwill to set them right. Once informed of wrong, men, or at any rate Englishmen, would act to set it right. No amount of neglect, no number of rebuffs or of unanswered letters made him stop pressing for reform; and in his eagerness he tended not to notice the numerous and sensitive toes upon which he trod. Most, though not all, of the causes for which he pleaded were won; most of the abuses were remedied before he died. How much of this was due to Black Charlie, and how much the forceful tactlessness of his demands harassed official dignity and impugned official honour, thus delaying the process, is impossible to tell.

'He was always fighting the Admiralty,' wrote a naval contemporary; and this was true, whether over the need to provide for seamen's wives whilst they were away for years at sea, or over the advantages of ironclads over wooden walls, of steam over sail for warships.

> They were too strong for him; yet he was always working them up to something, and it was his agitation that was the means of getting all the good that has been done for the last twenty years. He certainly might be justly styled the sailor's friend, advocate, defender, for he was always at his post when there was any move on the Board about them, and always looking out sharply after their interest.

Not Sveaborg, with its huge stone walls and its well-mined approaches, not fortress Kronstadt, with its bristling frieze of guns and the holy domes gleaming golden behind them, was Charlie's hill to climb, but the more tedious and slippery slope of official apathy at home. The battle he had won was against indifference in the face of inhuman wrongs like flogging and impressment, a fight less bloody, less famous and less dramatic than a sea fight might have been; and tirelessly (if tactlessly) he fought it.

Beginning to ail with age, Charlie went on advocating reform in the House; allotments of pay for seamen's wives, pensions and monthly payments and long leave for men whose ships were laid up in winter quarters; and pressing for an inquiry into the state of affairs at Greenwich Hospital, then the naval counterpart of the Royal Hospital at Chelsea.

At home he would stand by the gate of his house on the Portsmouth Road, talking to seamen and assisting whom he could. The lines around his mouth deepened, and maybe his temper did not improve, though for all his 'tautness' he loved life, and liked others to enjoy it too. He was a disciplinarian and had brought his ill-manned fleet in the Baltic to a fine state of efficiency, but he had hated the old degrading and hardening punishments and done his utmost to abolish them. He had loved his wife and children and had been loved by them. He had delighted to see 'all hands on deck to dance and skylark'. Bored by uniform, or perhaps not above guying himself, he was indeed considered a bit of a show-off by less flamboyant officers; wearing his three-cornered hat 'athwartships', corduroys on the quarterdeck, and even occasionally a yellow suit with red buttons which he had won in a bet at Port Mahon. 'I believe you might substitute a green or black coat for his uniform one without his being a bit the wiser,' Lieutenant Elliot of the *Powerful* had thought.

The shades of evening were closing in, but gleams of glory still enticed Black Charlie. In 1858, now Admiral of the Blue, he proposed to Garibaldi that he should take command of the Neapolitan fleet, 'to appear off the coast of Naples, with which I am well acquainted, and secure the capital by a short and sudden blow', with a view to dethroning Bomba, King of Naples. Might he end up as liberator of Italy from her age-old domination by the Hapsburg Empire? It was the kind of cause he loved. 'I am in correspondence with Garibaldi, whose aide de camp has been with me,' Charlie wrote on 28 August 1860. 'If he can procure two or three well-armed steamers, I will go out and do my best to take the Neapolitan squadron.' Visions of operating once again on the wine-dark and marvellously *deep* Mediterranean haunted him. But Black Charlie was no longer the sprightly lieutenant who had trailed his coat past Naples harbour in his ill-found but redoubtable *Thames* frigate. He was then, in fact, seventy-two, and, much to his regret, Garibaldi politely declined his offer. Coming down to earth, he had written, 'I cannot move till the harvest is over.' A few months later he was harvested himself, dying at Catherington on 6 November 1860.

In the summer of 1860 he had made his last speech in the House, on improvements necessary in the fortifications of the coast. A week before he died he had been dining with his old flag captain, Sir Michael Seymour. Seventy-two years old, he had been in the Navy for sixty-two years. He had commanded the last great sailing fleet of all those many that had put to sea from his country, but there had been no one to come out and challenge it; his predecessors had done their work too well. The famous victory of which he dreamed had eluded him; it is to be hoped that as he died he could feel that his less famous battle for seamen's rights had been won.

During his brief illness there was not a murmur from him. His daughter marvelled that one so impatient and strong-willed could be so patient and resigned. 'When a strong man is down he must be patient,' Charlie told her; and after this uncharacteristic utterance, hardly spoke more, except to make his peace with God.

Black Charlie died at dawn on a dark November morning.

Thus sank at its moorings in harbour the noble old vessel that had so often weathered the storm and encountered the enemies' broadsides during the long and eventful voyage of life.

So wrote his stepson, General Elers-Napier, perhaps not without a sigh of relief (as well as of sadness) that the journey was done before the faculties had failed.

'All the faults of his family,' Sir James Graham had said of Black Charlie when recommending him to Queen Victoria; and both Charles Napiers had certainly shared the same fault – a tendency to be outspoken, to point things out in direct language. 'The tone of his correspondence had become offensive,' Governor-General Dalhousie complained when virtually sacking the soldier Charles from his post as C in C, India, for pointing out that the newly conquered Sikhs of the Punjab were unlikely to settle peacefully under a Bengali code of laws. Graham told the sailor Charles that in his letters to the Board 'you have repeatedly thought fit to adopt a tone in correspondence which is not respectful to their authority'.

The fact, ungrasped by Graham or the Board of Trade-trained Dalhousie, is that if a Government employs Charles Napiers who are not afraid to take on and defeat 30,000 fanatical Baluchis with a mixed force of 2,700 men, or who single-handedly pursue three French line-of-battle ships for fifty-five hours in a lightly armed brig the size of a fishing boat, this Government must also put up with the fact that they are also not afraid of uttering home truths to ministers of said Government.

Of course the man on the spot is not to dictate to the elected ministers of a democratic Government, but he is at least to be listened to with care and attention. To oppose with reasoned argument makes more sense than to swoon under personal affront and spitefully discredit the offender.

Sailors carried Black Charlie to his grave at Catherington, whose churchyard then commanded a fine view over the Solent and Spithead, smiling in summer or wind-whipped under winter gales. Very many friends but no official representatives came to his funeral; he was still under an official cloud.

Sailors in thousands contributed to his memorial column at

Portsmouth. Retired seamen who had served with him called their pubs after him – the Napier Arms, or the Charley Napier; he became, briefly, a part of their mythology. Charlie Beresford, writing in 1914, thought him a fine seaman, and of all sailors the one most victimized by the politicians. He must have forgotten Byng, for Black Charlie was never actually hanged from his own yardarm, or shot on his own quarterdeck. He was immortalized in Thackeray's *Little Billee* –

> I see Jerusalem and Madagascar
> And North and South Amerikee,
> A British flagship a-riding at anchor,
> And Admiral Napier, KCB.

But many anthologies now substitute Nelson's name for his.

Admirals Napier and Dundas became a popular pair of Staffordshire china figures – a circumstance that would have surprised and amused Black Charlie very much. With bold cheek-bones and improbably pink cheeks, a high stomach and a confident stance, he trails a pink-lined boatcloak and stands by a pile of cannon balls, looking forth in glazed authority from many a cottage chimneypiece and many a suburban window-ledge, a monument to his vigorous and sturdy profession and to his robust epoch. Of late, his replicas have become quite precious and expensive, and to Black Charlie, who always considered his own life expendable, this development would seem the most rum of all.

Seven weeks after he died, HMS *Warrior,* Britain's first ironclad, was launched at Blackwall, followed by *Black Prince,* in Glasgow, two months later. It takes time; but it happens. Pray God it may not sometime happen too late.

Rockingham 1968, revised Collingbourne Ducis 1988.

Select Bibliography
Index

Select Bibliography

Bourchier, Jane, Lady, editor of her brother's letters, *Letters of Admiral Sir Henry Codrington*, London, 1880.

Dasent, A. I., *John Thaddeus Delane: His Life and Correspondence* (which omits his needling letter to Charlie).

Delane, John T., leading articles in *The Times* of 13 September 1854, 'Return from the Baltic, Disappointment of the Public', and of 4 October 1854, on the supposed fall of Sebastopol, letter to Charlie, 4 October 1854, omitted from his collected letters, but printed by H. Noel Williams from Mrs Jodrell's collection of her father's letters.

Dundonald, 10th Earl of, *Autobiography of a Seaman*.

Dundonald, 11th Earl of (with H. R. Fox Bourne), *Narration of Services in the Liberation of Chile, Peru and Brazil*, 2 vols.

Earp, G. B., *The Life and Exploits of Commodore Napier*.

Elers-Napier, Major-General Edward, *The Life and Correspondence of Admiral Sir Charles Napier, Reminiscences of Syria*.

James, W., *Naval History of Great Britain*.

Lloyd, C. C., *Captain Marryat and the Old Navy*.

McCarthy, Justin, *History of Our Own Times*.

Napier, Admiral Sir Charles, *Account of the War in Portugal*; *History of the War in Syria*; *Campaign in the Baltic*.

Napier, General Sir William Patrick Francis, *Life and Opinions of General Sir Charles Napier*, 4 vols.

Noel-Williams, H., *Life of Sir C. Napier*.

Pollock, Alice, *A Portrait of My Victorian Youth*.

Ziegler, Philip, *William IV*.

Index